The Postcolonial Millennium

This book comprises a collection of essays that address a significant gap in the study of Malaysian literature in English by exploring selected local and diasporic writings produced in the new postcolonial millennium, including works by established, emerging, and new writers.

The literary developments in this new millennium have been substantial and are reflected in the production of new voices, viewpoints, themes, trends, styles, and forms. By articulating these changing postcolonial perspectives and conditions, the chapters in this volume can inform and enrich the study of nation, society, and culture in a globalized and hyperreal age. Tapping into the difference, diversity, and hybridity of 21st-century historicized and glocalized multicultural Malaysia, the millennium writings explore the changing identities and relations and their social, cultural, and political dimensions through the intersections of race, gender, sexuality, and class. By examining new, different, or changing ideas, forms, themes, and representations, this book considers the vital ways the millennium voices and viewpoints can potentially help us critically rethink and resituate postcolonial studies on Malaysia as they spotlight challenges and new directions in the field.

This book will be of interest to researchers, academics, and scholars in the field of Malaysian writing in English, Southeast Asian literature, Asian literature, diaspora, and literary studies. The chapters in the book were originally published as a special issue in the *Journal of Postcolonial Writing.*

Mohammad A. Quayum is a full-time researcher and Professor in the College of Humanities, Arts and Social Sciences at Flinders University, Adelaide, Australia. He taught at universities in Bangladesh, Malaysia, Singapore, and the US before returning to his *alma mater*, Flinders University, in 2020. He has published numerous books and articles in American, Bengali, and Southeast Asian literature. His books on Malaysian anglophone literature include *Colonial to Global: Malaysian Women's Writing in English 1940s-1990s* (2003); *One Sky, Many Horizons: Studies in Malaysian Literature in English* (2014); and *Reading Malaysian Literature in English: Ethnicity, Gender, Diaspora, and Nationalism* (2021).

Grace V.S. Chin is Senior Lecturer in English Language Studies at Universiti Sains Malaysia, Malaysia. She specializes in postcolonial Southeast Asian literatures in English and has published journal articles and essays on writers and literary works from Malaysia, Singapore, Brunei Darussalam, Indonesia, and the Philippines. She has also published edited and co-edited volumes, the latest of which is *Translational Politics in Southeast Asian Literatures: Contesting Race, Gender, and Sexuality* (2021).

The Postcolonial Millennium

New Directions in Malaysian Literature in English

Edited by

Mohammad A. Quayum and Grace V.S. Chin

LONDON AND NEW YORK

First published 2024
by Routledge
4 Park Square, Milton Park, Abingdon, Oxon, OX14 4RN

and by Routledge
605 Third Avenue, New York, NY 10158

Routledge is an imprint of the Taylor & Francis Group, an informa business

British Library Cataloguing-in-Publication Data
A catalogue record for this book is available from the British Library

ISBN13: 978-1-032-66972-4 (hbk)
ISBN13: 978-1-032-66973-1 (pbk)
ISBN13: 978-1-032-66976-2 (ebk)

DOI: 10.4324/9781032669762

Typeset in Minion Pro
by codeMantra

Publisher's Note
The publisher accepts responsibility for any inconsistencies that may have arisen during the conversion of this book from journal articles to book chapters, namely the inclusion of journal terminology.

Contents

Citation Information

The following chapters were originally published in the *Journal of Postcolonial Writing*, volume 57, issue 5 (2021). When citing this material, please use the original page numbering for each article, as follows:

Chapter 1
China, Malaysia, and millennial diasporic identity in Tash Aw's The Face *and* Five Star Billionaire
Walter S.H. Lim
Journal of Postcolonial Writing, volume 57, issue 5 (2021), pp. 593–606

Chapter 2
Universalism and the Malaysian anglophone novel: Exploring inequality, migrancy, and class in Tash Aw's We, the Survivors
Angelia Poon
Journal of Postcolonial Writing, volume 57, issue 5 (2021), pp. 607–620

Chapter 3
Transnational re-memorialization in Preeta Samarasan's Evening Is the Whole Day
Ann Ang
Journal of Postcolonial Writing, volume 57, issue 5 (2021), pp. 621–635

Chapter 4
Interracial relations and the post-postcolonial future in Zen Cho's Spirits Abroad
Grace V.S. Chin
Journal of Postcolonial Writing, volume 57, issue 5 (2021), pp. 636–649

Chapter 5
Hyphenational poetics in Omar Musa's Parang *and* Millefiori
Weihsin Gui
Journal of Postcolonial Writing, volume 57, issue 5 (2021), pp. 650–664

Chapter 6
On not writing back: Cosmopolitan paradoxes in new diasporic Malaysian writing today
Jason Eng Hun Lee and Sreedhevi Iyer
Journal of Postcolonial Writing, volume 57, issue 5 (2021), pp. 665–679

Chapter 7

The ruins of referentiality: Allegorical realism and traumatic fragments in Scorpion Orchid *and* The Search
Augustine Chay
Journal of Postcolonial Writing, volume 57, issue 5 (2021), pp. 680–693

Chapter 8

Diffractive spaces: An analysis of Malaysian cyberpunk
Netty Mattar
Journal of Postcolonial Writing, volume 57, issue 5 (2021), pp. 694–708

Chapter 9

Satire and community in the time of COVID-19: An analysis of Ernest Ng's Covidball Z
Susan Philip
Journal of Postcolonial Writing, volume 57, issue 5 (2021), pp. 709–722

Notes on Contributors

Ann Ang is Assistant Professor in English Literature at the National Institute of Education, Nanyang Technological University. She researches contemporary anglophone writing from India, the Philippines, Malaysia, and Singapore. She is interested in tropicality and literary networks in Southeast Asia. Her research articles have previously appeared in *the Journal of Postcolonial Writing, the Cambridge Journal of Postcolonial Literary Inquiry and ELH.*

Augustine Chay is a PhD student at the National University of Singapore, Singapore. His research examines wartime literary production during the long Malayan Emergency (1948–60): a critical period of transition that was contemporaneous with the dawn of the Cold War and the birth of the Federation of Malaya.

Grace V.S. Chin is Senior Lecturer in English Language Studies at Universiti Sains Malaysia, Malaysia. She specializes in postcolonial Southeast Asian literatures in English and has published journal articles and essays on writers and literary works from Malaysia, Singapore, Brunei Darussalam, Indonesia, and the Philippines. She has also published edited and co-edited volumes, the latest of which is *Translational Politics in Southeast Asian Literatures: Contesting Race, Gender, and Sexuality* (2021).

Jason Eng Hun Lee is Lecturer at Hong Kong Baptist University, Hong Kong. He is a creative writer and scholar whose research and practice fields encompass global anglophone literatures, postcolonial and diasporic writing, and global Shakespeares. He serves as a literary editor for *Postcolonial Text* and is the current chief organizer of OutLoud HK, the Hong Kong's longest-running poetry collective.

Weihsin Gui is Professor of English and Director of the Southeast Asian Studies programme at the University of California, Riverside, USA. He is the author of *National Consciousness and Literary Cosmopolitics: Postcolonial Literature in a Global Moment* (2013) and an essay collection on Singaporean poet Arthur Yap titled *Common Lines and City Spaces* (2014).

Sreedhevi Iyer is Lecturer at RMIT University in Melbourne, Australia. Her research interests are interdisciplinary, including creative writing, postcolonial theory, discourse analysis, and cosmopolitanism. She is the author of *Jungle Without Water* (2017) and *The Tiniest House of Time* (2020).

Walter S.H. Lim is Associate Professor of English literature at the National University of Singapore. He is the author of *The Arts of Empire: The Poetics of Colonialism from Raleigh to Milton* (1998); *John Milton, Radical Politics, and Biblical Republicanism* (2006); and

Narratives of Diaspora: Representations of Asia in Chinese American Literature (2013). He also co-edited a collection of essays titled *The English Renaissance, Orientalism, and the Idea of Asia* (2010).

Netty Mattar teaches English literature at the International Islamic University of Malaysia (IIUM), Malaysia. She has also taught at National University of Singapore, Singapore, where she completed her PhD. Her current research interests include contemporary and global speculative fiction, literary representations of trauma, and new approaches to world literatures in English.

Susan Philip is Associate Professor in the English Department at the Faculty of Arts and Social Sciences, the University of Malaya, Malaysia. She has several publications in journals such as the *Asian Theatre Journal, World Literature Written in English, Journal of Commonwealth Literature, Kajian Malaysia*, and *International Journal of Indonesian Studies.*

Angelia Poon is Associate Professor of English literature at the National Institute of Education at Nanyang Technological University, Singapore. Her research interests include postcolonial theory and contemporary anglophone Southeast Asian literature with a focus on issues pertaining to globalization and gender, class, and racial subjectivities. She is the co-editor of *Singapore Literature and Culture: Current Directions in Local and Global Contexts* (2017) and one of the editors of *Writing Singapore: An Historical Anthology of Singapore Literature in English* (2009).

Mohammad A. Quayum is a full-time researcher and Professor in the College of Humanities, Arts and Social Sciences at Flinders University, Australia. He taught at universities in Bangladesh, Malaysia, Singapore, and the US before returning to his *alma mater*, Flinders University, in 2020. He has published numerous books and articles in American, Bengali, and Southeast Asian literature. His books on Malaysian anglophone literature include *Colonial to Global: Malaysian Women's Writing in English 1940s–1990s* (2003); *One Sky, Many Horizons: Studies in Malaysian Literature in English* (2014); and *Reading Malaysian Literature in English: Ethnicity, Gender, Diaspora, and Nationalism* (2021).

Introduction—The postcolonial millennium: New directions in Malaysian literature in English

Grace V.S. Chin and Mohammad A. Quayum

This book, based on the Special Issue of the *Journal of Postcolonial Writing*, casts a critical eye on new directions in Malaysian literature in English (MLE), exploring selected local and diasporic or transnational writings by established and new writers in the millennium and how they can potentially help us rethink and resituate postcolonial studies on Malaysia. Studies on MLE have flourished since the publication 20 years ago of the seminal volume of critical essays *Malaysian Literature in English: A Critical Reader* (Quayum and Wicks 2001), which helped lay the foundations of the field itself. Given Malaysia's history as a former British colony, it is not surprising to find that MLE scholarship has been dominated by postcolonial approaches to the analysis of local literary life and journey, which are entwined with the country's search for identity in the postcolonial, globalizing age. Since its humble beginnings in university productions of the late 1940s, MLE has been influenced and affected by the pivotal developments of decolonization, independence, nation-building, and globalization. History and the way it shapes the present have thus remained powerful concerns in the study of identity and literary expression in MLE as it involves the pressing question of what it means to be "Malaysian" – not by any means an easy question to answer.

Malaysian society is ethnically diverse, comprising Malays and indigenous groups (69 percent), Chinese (22.5 percent), Indians (6.8 percent), and Eurasians and other groups (1 percent) (Department of Statistics Malaysia 2021). However, it is also deeply polarized along the lines of race and religion, the roots of which can be traced back to the British divide-and-rule policy, used to maintain colonial order by segregating the Malays as well as the Chinese and Indian migrant labourers who worked in the tin mines and rubber estates at the turn of the 20th century in British Malaya, today known as West or Peninsular Malaysia. Over the succeeding decades, limited inter-ethnic contact and the essentializing discourses and practices of race promoted by the British tended to reinforce racial barriers and cultural insularity among the groups. Despite the formation of the Federation of Malaysia in 1963[1] and the achievement of independence from the British, inter-ethnic hostilities and tensions continued to escalate until the tragic day of May 13, 1969, when race riots broke out in Kuala Lumpur. "May 13" was a watershed event that led to the radical reshaping of Malaysia's sociopolitical landscape when the government moved to safeguard the position and special rights of "native" Malays – also defined as Muslims in the Constitution – by instituting key policies that inevitably affected the status of English-language and anglophone writing: the 1967 National Language Act, which mandated Malay or *Bahasa Melayu* (renamed *Bahasa Malaysia*) as the national language, in place of English, and the 1971 National Culture Policy, which conferred "national" status upon only "indigenous" cultural productions, including Malay literature. In line with these policies, English was downgraded to become the nation's second language, while anglophone writing, redefined as "sectional" or "foreign"[2] literature, languished for much of the 1970s and 1980s.

The rise of Malay ethnocentrism in the 1970s also had heavy consequences for non-Malay anglophone writers, who experienced a double marginalization in terms of race and language. The majority of the pioneering and second-generation writers in MLE were non-Malays and include the canonical names Lloyd Fernando (1926–2008), Lee Kok Liang (1927–92), Ee Tiang Hong (1933–90), Wong Phui Nam (b. 1935), Ghulam-Sarwar Yousof (b. 1939),[3] Cecil Rajendra (b. 1941), K.S. Maniam (1942–2020), Shirley Geok-lin Lim (b. 1944), and Kee Thuan Chye (b. 1954). Disillusioned and rejecting the state politics of race and language, Ee and Lim left Malaysia. Meanwhile, the writers who remained were, like all Malaysians, subjected to stringent censorship laws that prohibited statements about the privileged status of Malays as *Bumiputera* ("sons of the soil"). Such prohibitions extended to the discussion of *Bahasa Malaysia*, the monarchy, and Islam. Until today, the politics and practices of polarization, hierarchization, and exclusion have continued to thrive under the Malay-centric government as a result of which the racial and religious chasm between Malays and non-Malays has only widened.

In the 1990s, however, Malaysia began to transform under the auspices of late-capitalism and globalization, and the value of English as the international language of technology, finance, and commerce was increasingly recognized by the government. While still enforcing Malay/*Bumiputera*-first policies, the government also strengthened the use of English at the national level by, among other moves, incorporating the local anglophone literature in the English curriculum for secondary schools (Chin 2007, 268). The revival of English in Malaysia had positive consequences for the local writing scene, which saw the emergence of a "new generation" of writers (Chin 2007, 260) like Chuah Guat Eng (b. 1943; Malaysia's first female novelist in English), Marie Gerrina Louis (b. 1964), Charlene Rajendran (b. 1964), and Bernice Chauly (b. 1968). Of note, too, is the increased number of anglophone Malay writers such as Rehman Rashid (1955–2017), Che Husna Azhari (b. 1955), Karim Raslan (b. 1963), Farish A. Noor (b. 1967), and Dina Zaman (b. 1969); they represent the New Malays (*Melayu Baru*) who had "benefitted from the pro-Malay economic and cultural reforms of the 1970s and 1980s" (Chin 2007, 277). In the past, only a few Malay writers produced works in English, the most famous of whom are the poets Salleh Ben Joned (1941–2020) and Muhammad Haji Salleh (b. 1942).

Building on the creative momentum of the 1990s, MLE has enjoyed a relatively stable period of growth in this century. The award-winning US-based poet and author Shirley Geok-lin Lim published her only two novels *Joss and Gold* (2001) and *Sister Swing* (2006) in the first decade, as well as several volumes of poetry, while local writers K.S. Maniam, Chuah Guat Eng, and Bernice Chauly each published one or more novels. Though scarce, anthologies of poetry were also produced by established poets like Salleh Ben Joned, Cecil Rajendra, Wong Phui Nam, and Ghulam-Sarwar Yousof. Publications in drama have been more rare, although the theatre scene in Malaysia has remained active. Exceptions are the published plays of Jit Murad (b. 1960), Ann Lee (b. 1965), Huzir Sulaiman (b. 1973), and Kee Thuan Chye. Then there are the new writers of the millennium, whose fresh or different voices, viewpoints, ideas, and styles have also shaped recent trends and directions.

Without doubt, the development with the greatest impact over the last two decades has been the arrival of "global" award-winning Malaysian writers, including first-time authors Rani Manicka (b. 1964), Tash Aw (b. 1971), Tan Twan Eng (b. 1972), and Preeta Samarasan (b. 1976). The most prominent names here are Aw and Tan, whose respective first novels *The Harmony Silk Factory* (2005) and *The Gift of Rain* (2007) were longlisted for the Man Booker Prize; notably, Tan's second novel *Garden of Evening Mists* (2012) was not only shortlisted for the Booker Prize in 2012 but also adapted into a film in 2019. The literary scene has also been enriched by the works of other diasporic or transnational writers such as Chan Ling Yap (b. 1947), Tei Chiew-Siah (or Suria Tei) (b. 1963), whose first novel *Little Hut of Leaping Fishes* (2008) was longlisted for the Man Asian Literary Prize, Felicia Yap (b. 1980), Sreedhevi Iyer (b. 1977), and, more recently, Zen Cho (b. 1986), whose works have won awards in the fantasy genre. The writers mentioned thus far produce prose fiction, especially novels, but a very small group is focused on poetry, including Omar Musa (b. 1984) and Jason Eng Hun Lee (b. 1984). The global stature and significance of these writers, especially Aw and Tan, has also heightened Malaysia's presence on the world literary map.

That the majority of Malaysia's more famous anglophone authors are non-Malays residing abroad nevertheless speaks to the prevailing issues of race, place, and identity, not to mention the far-reaching effects of the country's neocolonial forms of divide and rule. It should be noted, too, that a few Malay writers, including Huzir Sulaiman and Farish A. Noor, have left Malaysia to make Singapore their home. The motivations compelling the migration of millennial diasporic writers may, however, be more varied, especially within the context of the globalized and decentred reality where multiple homes/centres and identities have become the norm while transconnections and mobility are increasingly valued. Regardless of the reasons, many of the diasporic authors – both past and present – still draw on Malaysia in their imagining and articulations of home, revealing in the process the intricate ties of attachment and belonging, in addition to the complexities of identity in the globalized era.

Within the glocalizing contexts of Malaysia, the literary terrain has witnessed similar positive movements in anglophone writing, many of which can be attributed to the efforts of local writers and publishers. Since the 1990s, local publishers have played a crucial role in creating a viable space for literary expression, especially for new voices in English. Silverfish Books has been particularly active, publishing the first novels of, among others, Rozlan Mohd Noor (b. 1953), Shih-li Kow (b. 1968), and Iskandar al-Bakri (b. 1974). Pelanduk Publications has produced the novels of Khoo Kheng-Hor (b. 1956), while Gerakbudaya has introduced its share of new writers such as Wong Ming Yook (b. 1960). In 2011, Malaysia's literary scene received a further boost with the launch of the George Town Literary Festival (GTLF). Held annually at the United Nations Educational, Scientific and Cultural Organization (UNESCO) World Heritage Site of George Town, Penang, the festival has attracted the attention of writers, literary aficionados, and artists from around the world. While spotlighting Malaysia's local and global luminaries like Muhammad Haji Salleh and Tan Twan Eng, GTLF has also promoted rising local talents like Shih-li Kow, Dina Zaman, and Iskandar al-Bakri.

Interestingly, literary output in the millennium has been dominated by prose fiction, with the global or transnational Malaysian novel by the aforementioned diasporic authors taking centre stage. Local publishers have also fostered new ideas, themes, genres, and styles among Malaysian writers. From 2001 to 2006, Silverfish Books contributed to the growth of contemporary short fiction by launching the Silverfish New Writing series. Another influential publisher is Buku Fixi, whose English-language imprint Fixi Novo helped expand the short story writing scene by tapping into the popular trends of pulp and speculative fiction, fantasy, horror, supernatural, noir, and crime. Queer writing, too, made its debut in Malaysia in the form of short fiction. Anthologized in *Body 2 Body: A Malaysian Queer Anthology* (2009) and *Mata Hati Kita/The Eyes of Our Hearts* (2016), these locally published stories of queer lives and experiences are all the more significant given the criminalization of homosexuality and the attendant stigmatization of Lesbian, Gay, Bisexual, Transgender, and Queer (LGBTQ+) by religious communities and conservative sectors of society.

The global recognition of local Malaysian talent is another important development. In 2011, Rozlan Mohd Noor's first novel *21 Immortals: Inspector Mislan and the Yee Sang Murders* (2010) was shortlisted for the Commonwealth Writers' Prize for Best First Book. Saraswathy M. Manickam's "My Mother Pattu" won the 2019 Commonwealth Short Story Prize (Asian region). More recently, Sharmini Aphrodite's "Ouroboros, Ouroboros" and Ling Low's "Weeds" were shortlisted for the Commonwealth Short Story Prize in 2020 and 2021, respectively. In 2019, too, Hanna Alkaf (b. 1985) made waves with her first novel *The Weight of Our Sky*, which won the Freeman Book Award in the Young Adult category, while her second novel *The Girl and the Ghost* (2020), aimed at young readers, was a Kirkus Prize 2020 finalist. Equally worth mentioning is the fact that certain international publishers have taken an interest in relatively unknown local authors. A good example of this development is Paul Gnanaselvam (b. 1975), whose *The Elephant Trophy and Other Stories* was published by Penguin in 2021. Monsoon Books has also published the works of new writers, including Golda Mowe's *Iban Dream* trilogy (2012–18). A Sarawakian, Mowe (b. 1970) represents one of the few new East Malaysian voices in a space largely overshadowed by West Malaysian writers.

Despite these promising achievements, writers in Malaysia undoubtedly face more challenges than most of their global counterparts. The overall limited output and sporadic publications that include one-off works attest to the difficulties experienced on the ground, which include the entrenched culture of (self-)censorship, insufficient publishing opportunities, and limited readership. This last concern can be attributed to linguistic divisions among Malaysian readers, the biased perception of local writings as "inferior" compared to internationally published works, and generally underdeveloped reading habits (Malaysians read an average of two books per year) due to varying influences, including the Internet, social media, video games, TV, and other forms of entertainment as well as the lack of motivation and peer pressure (Supramani 2021). Then there is the lack of state support for local English-language writing. With little funding, sponsorship, awards, or even infrastructure to encourage literary activities, budding local writers whose works have received scant recognition seldom last long or are soon forgotten. Consequently, new local writers have remained relatively little known outside Malaysia. This situation is reflected in MLE scholarship, where a considerable corpus of studies on famous transnational writers like Aw, Tan, and Samarasan can be found, alongside the studies of major or canonical writers; however, locally published and budding authors are seldom examined as a result of the above-mentioned factors. While the growth of MLE in the millennium has been positively influenced by global cultural flows, the constraints faced by local writers also highlight the diverse ways in which they are affected by state ethnocentrism and the attendant institutionalized barriers of race and language. Still, the developments discussed here underscore a growing local literary scene in the millennium, which is "nothing short of remarkable" and should "serve as an inspiring story of cultural tenacity" (Ng 2018, 6).

Given this steady growth of MLE, especially in the new millennium, in the face of many challenges from the state-authored policies in Malaysia, this book has been designed to highlight contemporary trends in the tradition, three of which can be identified as follows: (a) Malaysian anglophone literature has diversified into new genres such as fantasy fiction, science fiction, and webcomic; (b) it is flourishing more in diaspora, or among its transnational members, than at home; and (c) transnational writers tend to receive more critical attention than locally based ones.

It is, therefore, no surprise that six of the nine articles in this book deal with transnational or globally oriented writers, or writers who continue to write about Malaysia with an eye on the world outside, or the countries they have travelled to, sojourned in, or adopted as their new homeland. This list includes Tash Aw, Preeta Samarasan, Zen Cho, Omar Musa, Jason Eng Hun Lee, and Sreedhevi Iyer. All six now live outside Malaysia and write with a "double perspective" and deterritorialized consciousness. Because of the number of articles devoted to these writers, we table them first, followed by the articles on local writers. Moreover, the first group is sequenced both chronologically and according to genre: the first three are on canonical prose and fiction; the fourth is on fantasy fiction; and the fifth on poetry, while the final one is a reflective essay by two younger writers living in Hong Kong and Australia. The three articles on "local" writers are also arranged chronologically: the first examines two novels by earlier writers, the second a body of Malaysian cyberpunk short stories, and the last is an ongoing webcomic that caricatures Malaysia's handling of the current pandemic.

This volume opens with two articles on the works of Taipei-born Malaysian Chinese writer Tash Aw. The first, "China, Malaysia, and Millennial Diasporic Identity in Tash Aw's *The Face* and *Five Star Billionaire*" by Singapore scholar Walter S.H. Lim, focuses on Aw's third novel (from 2013) and his 2016 non-fiction essay to explore the author's representation of the overseas Chinese in Southeast Asia and how China's rise as a major economic and political power in the 21st century has transformed what was once a land of lack into one of new promise and opportunity for its migrant communities. Lim first investigates Aw's thematization of the cultural politics of Chinese identity in Malaysia in *The Face*, where the educated Chinese are no longer constrained by the demands and imperatives of the nation state but operate as cosmopolitans and world-travellers, enjoying the exhilaration of transnational mobility. Lim argues that, as a 21st-century writer, Aw has a different sociocultural and political frame of reference available as a result of the rise of China, compared to the material available to 20th-century Malaysian Chinese writers such as Shirley Geok-lin Lim. The discussion then pivots on *Five Star Billionaire* and the promise offered by millennial China, where several Malaysian Chinese subjects have gathered to pursue their dreams and ambitions, contrary to the familiar motif of east–west immigrant desire traditionally found in Southeast and Asian American literature. However, Lim suggests that Aw's portrayal of China in the novel is ambiguous; while he sees it as a land of new hope and excitement, it is also one of distrust, indifference, and horrific exploitation; a land of affluence, it is also a dog-eat-dog world.

Angelia Poon's "Universalism and the Malaysian Anglophone Novel: Exploring Inequality, Migrancy, and Class in Tash Aw's *We, the Survivors*" focuses on Aw's fourth novel, published in 2019. The article explores the motifs of inequality, migrancy, and class in a work that, Poon argues, is located in a pivotal space between national specificity and general universalism. She sees it as appropriating Darwinian ideas about survival, evolution, chance, environment, and competition to critique both Malaysian ethnic and class politics and global capitalism, as the two are interconnected, and the former operates within the orbit of the latter.

In "Transnational Re-memorialization in Preeta Samarasan's *Evening Is the Whole Day*", Ann Ang explicates Preeta Samarasan's debut novel from 2008, written purposely as a "more female" version of Salman's Rushdie's seminal work as a "*Midnight's Children* for Malaysia". Ang argues that the novel re-memorializes the marginalized history of the Malaysian Indians, especially following the violent riots of May 13, which entrenched the country's already racially hierarchic policies. However, Samarasan situates her narrative, firstly, from a Malaysian Indian perspective and, secondly, from a transnational locus since, like Aw, she is a transnationally mobile writer. While the novel offers a critique of Malaysia's oppressive race politics, it also exposes the class, gender, and caste injustices inherent in the Malaysian Indian community.

With "Interracial Relations and the Post-Postcolonial Future in Zen Cho's *Spirits Abroad*" by Malaysian scholar Grace V.S. Chin, we move from Malaysian canonical fiction to supernatural and fantasy fiction, as Chin investigates three stories from *Spirits Abroad* (2014) by Zen Cho, a Malaysian writer currently residing in the UK. Chin contends that although Cho breaks away from the "highbrow" literary aesthetics of earlier Malaysian authors by writing in a popular speculative genre, her work has significance within the tradition of resistance and inclusivity established by the older generation of writers. Chin maintains that Cho's fiction defies the ethnocentric boundaries of Malaysian politics and thus creates the possibility of a new Malaysia, or a post-postcolonial Malaysia, that is made up of interstitial spaces and hybridized identities, and where her human and supernatural characters mingle and interact without the traditional communal restrictions. This revisionary narrative makes Cho a progressive and futuristic writer who deconstructs the Malaysian race binary with a dialogic vision in which self and "other" are reconceived as different yet equal.

"Hyphenational Poetics in Omar Musa's *Parang* and *Millefiori*" focuses on the spoken-word poetry of Omar Musa, an Australian-born Malaysian poet of hybrid identity, who shares a complex mix of Malay, Kedayan, and Suluk heritage on his father's side and an Irish background on his mother's. US-based scholar Weihsin Gui probes two volumes of Omar's[4] poetry, *Parang* (2014) and *Millefiori* (2017), to bring home the argument that as a "doubly diasporic" and (multi-)hyphenated poet with a global consciousness, Musa recurrently uses the hyphen both as a bridge and as a parang (machete). His poetry critiques both Malaysia and Australia while creating connections between the two countries, as well as the multiple cultural elements in his life. "As parang", Gui argues, "the poem[s] offer incisive comments on national histories and political hypocrisies that have devastated and disenfranchised various groups of people around the world; as hyphen [they] bridge Omar's personal background and wider political consciousness [with] shared legacies of suffering". This complex texture of his imagination, expressed through a combination of English and Malay, induces Omar to write what Gui describes as "hyphenational poetics".

In "On Not Writing Back: Cosmopolitan Paradoxes in New Diasporic Malaysian Writing Today", two emerging Malaysian transnational writers, Jason Lee and Sreedhevi Iyer, who left the country several years ago and have only peripheral contacts with the homeland, reflect on how they see themselves as postcolonial writers, how they relate to the present state of Malaysian culture and politics, and how they perceive their identity in their deterritorialized state. They also deliberate on their choice of craft and the scope and function of their creativity. They argue that, unlike the previous generation of Malaysian post-independence anglophone writers, they are not interested in "writing back" either to the former colonial centre or to their condition as "sectional" writers in the Malaysian literary tradition. Iyer reflects on her short story collection *Jungle Without Water* (2017) and explains how she uses "Manglish", or the Malaysian variety of English, as a specific craft choice to transcend cultural explication and subvert the responses of the global/glocal English language reader. Lee, by contrast, draws on his poetry collection *Beds in the East* (2019) to suggest how a double perspective on Malaysia and the UK can strategically mediate the colonial/postcolonial gaze. In contrast to Iyer's resistance vernacular, Lee frames a dialogical interaction between a variety of local and cosmopolitan readerships, playing on their reflexive assumptions on the poet's identity as "other".

With "The Ruins of Referentiality: Allegorical Realism and Traumatic Fragments in *Scorpion Orchid* and *The Search*", we transition from the transnational writers to local writers or writers who wrote/write about Malaysia from home soil. There are three articles in this category: Augustine Chay's comparative essay on Lloyd Fernando's 1976 novel and T.J. Anthony's *The Search*, published in 1978; Netty Mattar's article on Malaysian cyberpunk short stories; and Susan Philip's appraisal of Ernest Ng's evolving webcomic based on Malaysia's response to the current global pandemic.

In his article, Augustine Chay explores the allegorical realism of *Scorpion Orchid* with its lesser-known contemporary *The Search*, by drawing on Walter Benjamin's theory of allegory. Chay argues that the two novels deal with Malaysian politics in the post-independence formative years and, in particular, the "nationalized cultural trauma" created by the pivotal interracial riots of May 13, which have come to define Malaysia's present identity as a nation. However, while *The Search* provides a literary archive of post-1969 memories that helps to illuminate the often-forgotten contingencies of the aftermath, *Scorpion Orchid* recontextualizes the traumatic events of 1969 through a narrative of the volatile political circumstances in Singapore in the 1950s.

In "Diffractive Spaces: An Analysis of Malaysian Cyberpunk", Netty Mattar investigates a group of three cyberpunk short stories from *Cyberpunk: Malaysia* (2015), the country's first anthology of this subgenre of science fiction, edited by Zen Cho, whose own fantasy short fiction from *Spirits Abroad* (2014) is the subject of Grace V.S. Chin's article. The stories studied are all set in a dystopian future Malaysia, reduced to an urban wasteland by the intrusions of global informational capitalism. Netty first illustrates the effect of colonialism and colonial reordering of space on Malaysian society and discusses the limits of postcolonial theory, with its ideas that address these issues – particularly those related to racial difference and contestation – through a process of negotiation, imitation, and assimilation. The article's argument then proposes a better way to read Malaysian literature, especially its cyberpunk stories, by adopting the concept of "diffraction" that allows readers to go beyond the Western binary system of thought and perceive non-dualistic patterns of difference. Diffraction allows us to be more attentive to how different cultural entities and ontologies impede, pass through, or interfere with one another, while observing how differences are upheld and strengthened. Netty applies this concept to her reading of the three stories and demonstrates how they offer an alternative spatial imaginary of Malaysia's identity outside Western binary frames of understanding.

In the final article, "Satire and Community in the Time of COVID: An Analysis of Ernest Ng's *Covidball Z*", Susan Philip provides a critique of Ernest Ng's evolving satirical webcomic that deals with the sloppy response of Malaysia and its political leadership to the COVID-19 pandemic. She explains how this webcomic, shared online via Facebook, lampoons the country's top leadership with carefully researched graphics and funny but caustic narratives and has created a strong community of readers united in their ridicule of themselves and their political leaders. Ng's webcomic is popular, first, because there is no outside control on its production, as in editorial cartoons in the mainstream media and, second, although satirical, Ng is strategic and measured in his criticisms of influential establishment figures, so that he does not violate the censorship laws. In other words, unlike the political cartoonist Zunar or graphic designer and street artist Fahmi Reza, Ng does not push too far his dissent against the government and ruling elites. Instead, he adopts a gentler and less biting approach and deliberately avoids exposing himself or his audience to the threats from Malaysia's Communication and Multimedia Act and the Sedition Act.

All in all, the articles demonstrate how much the Malaysian English language writers of the new millennium have accomplished and how much the anglophone literary tradition has advanced, notwithstanding the many challenges writers face in relation to their ethnicity and creative medium. It is evident that because of the government's increasingly Malay-centric policies, the centre of Malaysian anglophone literature is gradually moving outside the country's borders. More writers are becoming mobile and transnational and writing about Malaysia as their imaginary homeland from their adopted destinations. The writers at home, who are subjected to daily marginalization, are also finding new modes of expression, and because of the combined effort of the local and transnational writers, MLE is making strides and diversifying into new genres, increasingly making a mark on the global stage and bringing literary accolades to a country that, paradoxically, views them as a threat to its parochial vision of national identity and often relegates them to the category of "sectional" and "foreign" writers.

Notes

1. In 1963, the Federation of Malaysia was created with the merging of Malaya (which obtained independence from the British in 1957), Sabah, Sarawak, and Singapore. However, incompatible visions of the new nation led to Singapore's secession from the Federation in 1965.

2. Terms first used by Professor Ismail Hussein, a staunch Malay nationalist, in 1976 (Quayum [2007] 2014, 36).
3. A second-generation Punjabi Muslim in Malaysia, Ghulam-Sarwar Yousof is officially recognized as a Malay, but he prefers to identify himself as an Indian migrant rather than a Malay.
4. We have used the first name for Malay writers as per the practice in Malay culture.

Disclosure statement

No potential conflict of interest was reported by the authors.

ORCID

Grace V.S. Chin http://orcid.org/0000-0001-9292-4494
Mohammad A. Quayum http://orcid.org/0000-0002-3159-023X

References

Chin, Grace V. S. 2007. "New Generation Writings in English: Discursive Conditions and Literary Revival in Malaysia 1996–2005." In *English in Southeast Asia: Varieties, Literacies and Literatures*, edited by David Prescott, 260–289. Newcastle upon Tyne: Cambridge Scholars Publishing.

Department of Statistics Malaysia. 2021. "Demographic Statistics First Quarter 2021, Malaysia." https://www.dosm.gov.my/v1/index.php?r=column/cthemeByCat&cat=430&bul_id=aVlJRDAvbjhWWEhQa1YvSWhsSjF3QT09&menu_id=L0pheU43NWJwRWVSZklWdzQ4TlhUUT09

Ng, Andrew Hock Soon. 2018. "Reading Malaysian Literature in the Twenty-First Century: Familiar Concerns, New Directions." *Asiatic* 12 (2): 6–8.

Quayum, Mohammad A. [2007] 2014. *One Sky, Many Horizons: Studies in Malaysian Literature in English*. Singapore: Marshall Cavendish.

Quayum, Mohammad A, and Peter C. Wicks, eds. 2001. *Malaysian Literature in English: A Critical Reader*. Petaling Jaya: Pearson Education.

Supramani, Shivani. 2021. "Book Reading Culture Wanes with Rise of Technology." *The Sunday Daily*, April 20. https://www.thesundaily.my/local/book-reading-culture-wanes-with-rise-of-technology-FA7772142

China, Malaysia, and millennial diasporic identity in Tash Aw's *The Face* and *Five Star Billionaire*

Walter S.H. Lim

ABSTRACT
Chinese diasporic literature is alert to China's rise as a major political and economic power in the 21st century. In the novel *Five Star Billionaire* (2013), Chinese Malaysian author Tash Aw focuses on the megacity of Shanghai to capture China's economic and cultural vibrancy in the new millennium. Aw's novel shows that he is not only excited but also trepidatious about the implications of 21st-century China's emergence as a superpower. In his non-fiction essay *The Face: Strangers on a Pier* (2016), Aw represents the diasporic Chinese subject as a world traveller and cosmopolite, someone who embraces the exhilaration of transnational mobility. Unconstrained by the demands and imperatives of the nation state, Aw's *huáqiáo* (overseas Chinese) readily travels abroad to tap global opportunities as well as to meditate on the delineations of Chinese diasporic identity in the new millennium.

The presidency of Donald J. Trump from 2017 to 2021 has foregrounded international nervousness about China's rise as an economic and political power. Currently the second-largest economy in the world after the United States, China had engaged in activities that appeared to be underwritten by expansionist ambitions: claiming (almost) the entirety of the South China Sea as its historical possession, as well as rejecting the authority of the United Nations Convention on the Law of the Sea (UNCLOS) when it ruled in favour of the Philippines over China in their disputes over legal rights in this geopolitically significant body of water. Within this context of Chinese expansionist activities, Trump's America accused China of playing fast and loose with rules embraced by the international community for engaging in economic and trade relations with one another.

What does this familiar information about China and American international relations have to do with the writing of anglophone Chinese diasporic literature? For one, it enables us to consider some of the distinctive thematic and political foci of this literature produced in the first two decades of the 21st century, a time associated with China's rise as a major economic power. Books such as Jeff J. Brown's (2017) *China Rising*, David C. Kang's (2007) *China Rising*, and Denny Roy's (2013) *Return of the Dragon* – and their titles – resonate because the world has been made familiar with a discourse that implies that China, as a result of the size of its economic and political ambitions, is on its way to a collision with the US.

Anglophone Chinese diasporic literature has seized the opportunity to bring its readers into contact with seminal events of 20th-century Chinese history such as the Republican Revolution, World War II, the Communist Revolution, the Great Leap Forward, and the Cultural Revolution. From the vantage point of the 21st century, these historical events recall the political conditions of 19th- and 20th-century China that prompted many desperate Chinese to seek a new home in Nanyang ("South Seas"/ Southeast Asia) and the west. Reading literary representations of Mao Zedong's Great Leap Forward and Cultural Revolution reminds us of the political divide between the free west and the ambitions of expansionist communism, an historical memory that prompts us to compare the familiar narrative of Chinese authoritarianism with the 21st-century focus on the People's Republic of China (PRC) as an emerging superpower.

Chinese diasporic literature in the last decade of the 20th century and at the start of the 21st kept alive memories of life in China under Mao Zedong. First-generation Chinese American authors like Anchee Min (b. 1957), who experienced first-hand the Cultural Revolution, and Ha Jin (b. 1956), who served for five years in the People's Liberation Army (PLA), published literary works that capture the anxieties and trauma of social existence under Chinese communist rule. In *Red Azalea* ([1993] 2006), Anchee Min narrates the soul-sapping experience of living in an oppressive society in which individualism of any kind is prohibited. Ha Jin's (2002) *The Crazed* traces the source of the tragedy of the Tiananmen Square Massacre of 1989 to the oppressive and destructive spirit that inspired Mao's Cultural Revolution. Balancing literary narratives critical of Chinese communist rule are works that convey a more positive view of China. Chinese American author Yiyun Li's (2010) (b. 1972) *Gold Boy, Emerald Girl* is a collection of short stories that offers snapshots of a new China where characters are not trying to escape in search of a better life. Li evokes the setting of Beijing to highlight the changes that have taken place in the capital city's urban landscape as a result of China's modernization drive.

Millennial literature of the Southeast Asian Chinese diaspora also registers China's status as a major economic power in the 21st century. *Five Star Billionaire* (Aw 2013) and *The Face: Strangers on a Pier* (Aw 2016), two works written by Taipei-born Chinese Malaysian author Tash Aw (b. 1971), evoke the cultural politics of Chinese identity in Southeast Asia, an important region of the world settled by immigrants from the early Chinese diaspora. In his first-person non-fictional *The Face*, Aw thematizes the cultural politics of identity in the life of a diasporic Chinese subject educated in the west, who enjoys the exhilaration of transnational mobility. *Five Star Billionaire* grapples with the implications of China's rise as a major economic power for the *huáqiáo* (overseas Chinese) who live in Malaysia, by telling the story of five Chinese Malaysian characters who journey to Shanghai in search of a job, to gain access to the large Chinese market, and to reinvent the self. When we read *The Face* in conjunction with *Five Star Billionaire*, we encounter a Chinese Malaysian author who not only looks at millennial China as a land of opportunity, but also seeks to apprehend the country's geopolitical and cultural significance for overseas Chinese in the 21st century.

Diasporic beginnings and what it means to be Chinese

Aw's *The Face* takes the reader back in time to the presence of the Chinese in 19th- and early-20th-century Southeast Asia, focusing on his forebears' arrival in the Malay Peninsula. In the history of the Chinese diaspora, Southeast Asia is important because most of the Chinese who left Qing China in the 19th century to escape war, poverty, and political turmoil sought to settle down in this region to the south of China, as opposed to the US or any other country (Bernards 2015, vii–viii). This was partly because the different places in Southeast Asia which might prove conducive to work and settlement are geographically close (relatively speaking) to the ancestral homeland. The Malay Peninsula attracted Chinese labourers because of work opportunities in the tin mines of Perak and Selangor (Low 2014, 80–81). Early-20th-century Singapore, at whose port Aw's ancestors first landed in Southeast Asia, was a British colony and a city of free trade, "full of Chinese – laborers, dockside coolies, descendants of indentured workers in Malayan tin mines and plantations, but also merchants and tradesman, artists, writers" (Aw 2016, 17).

The journey of Aw's forebears to British Malaya to seek opportunities in a new land, start a family, and prepare for future generations to have a better life constitutes the diasporic context for the Chinese Malaysian author's meditations on his relationship with Malaysia and also with China. A descendent of the *huáqiáo* in Malaysia, Aw ponders the relationship between race, ethnicity, and culture in the construction of Malaysian national identity and definition of diasporic subjectivity. Not only does he focus on Malaysia as the controlling setting for his consideration of national belonging, transnational mobility, and the implications of being a person of ethnic Chinese descent born outside China, but he also thinks about the cultural politics of identity when coming into contact with peoples from other countries and societies.

Aw describes the early Chinese in Malaya and Singapore as "strangers lost on a pier" (2016, 19), dependent on a piece of paper to connect them with some distant relative or an unknown person who had come from the same home village in China. In Nanyang, these connections established between strangers enabled networking for employment opportunities, the creation of "adoptive families" (20) to help new arrivals with bed and food, and the development of clan associations (*kong si*) to lend support to Nanyang-bound Chinese who share a common dialect, surname, and village origin. This account of the travails of the diasporic Chinese in Nanyang equips the reader with an historical point of reference from which to measure the development and progress of the immigrant Chinese community in Malaysia across time.

Over the course of the 20th century, ties with one's adoptive families and relationships between clan members that were established in the early years of the Chinese arrival in British Malaya began to fray. Today, the younger generation "marry and move to Canada, Australia, the States" (Aw 2016, 21), identifying themselves with cities such as Vancouver, Melbourne, and Sacramento instead of with Chinese dialects such as Hokkien or Hakka (21). Members of this younger generation do not appear to be constrained by the need to start from scratch in a new land or to struggle for the means of survival that were laboriously sought by the pioneering *huáqiáo* of the late-19th and early-20th centuries. They enjoy things often made possible only through the struggles and travails of the pioneer and older generations. This younger generation belongs to a period of history when transnational mobility, as well as emigration to other countries, is more readily available, and even taken for granted.

In *Race, Education, and Citizenship*, Sin Yee Koh (2017) offers a sociological reading of migratory movements within and from postcolonial Malaysia, especially those inspired by overseas studies which entail physical separation from home country and exposure to foreign lands and cultures. For Koh, the Malaysian subject's capacity for transnational mobility is often intertwined with the opportunity for overseas studies. Both *bumiputera* (literally "son of the soil" and so often treated preferentially) and non-*bumiputera* go overseas for tertiary studies, the former often supported by government scholarships, the latter by familial sponsorship. The *bumiputera* who goes overseas to pursue a tertiary education might very well end up settling down as an immigrant in a foreign land. The same applies to the non-*bumiputera*, but with a difference. Whereas a foreign-educated *bumiputera* might reasonably expect to land a civil service job upon returning to Malaysia, the non-*bumiputera* is less likely to envision return to Malaysia as a particularly attractive option (Koh 2017, 161). This is because the overseas-educated non-*bumiputera* continues to be disadvantaged by the New Economic Policy (NEP) of 1971, a state-sponsored system of affirmative action aimed at improving the economic lot of the *bumiputera* at the expense of the country's minority subjects (Saravanan 2007, 151–176).

Chinese Malaysian literature valorizes transnational mobility. In diasporic Chinese literature, transnational mobility is supported by the possession of cultural capital, often assuming the forms of linguistic proficiency in the English language and strong academic credentials. Pierre Bourdieu has defined cultural capital as the (middle-class) possession of skills, knowledge, and norms that facilitate progress in education and enable advancement in life. Aw's Chinese community in Malaysia has ready-enough access to a good education and its benefits. The portrayal of young Chinese men and women securing admission to Ivy League schools and of Chinese families residing in gentrifying suburbs reinforces the narrative of Chinese immigrant success, one that elides accounts of the travail of early Chinese settlers struggling to make a new life in Nanyang.

Unlike the generation of Malacca-born and naturalized American author Shirley Geok-lin Lim, for whom studying overseas was a privilege afforded to only a select and fortunate few, Aw's cohort assumes that studying at world-class institutions such as Oxford, Harvard, and Stanford is not necessarily rare. Whereas Lim's (1996) *Among the White Moon Faces* depicts the minority subject's journey to the US for higher education as a breakthrough success story, *The Face* presents the ambition to study at prestigious universities in the US and Great Britain as a common enough phenomenon.

Aw's portrayal of the success of the immigrant Chinese community in Malaysia is balanced by the recognition that not everyone has equal access to a good education that might support upward social mobility. There are those who come from wealthy families, which means they can enjoy the benefits of tuition and enrichment programmes that increase their chances of getting into good schools. And then there are others who, due to circumstances or mixing with the wrong crowd, find themselves unable to move beyond a certain level in their education. The pursuit of education to fulfil one's aspirations encodes the cultural politics of class with the students who have been accepted into pedigree universities emanating a mystique which distances them from others attending less prestigious institutions or those who had to drop out of school.

In *Five Star Billionaire*, Aw evokes a similar theme when he describes a casual get-together party of friends who have completed their pre-university studies and are preparing to depart for university studies in the US, Great Britain, and Australia. Even though friends bound for Oxbridge and the Ivy League Universities "sort[ed] themselves out in a subtle hierarchy" (Aw 2013, 270), everyone at the party understands that they are members of an elite. To leave Malaysia for overseas studies is to belong to the privileged class. The age of globalization and era of transnational opportunities are obviously more hospitable to wealthy overseas Chinese who also happen to enjoy the benefits of cultural capital.

The story of the Chinese diasporic experience in British Malaya and in post-independence Malaysia has much to do with the narrative of moving from the condition of poverty to middle-class existence if not riches. When a Chinese family achieves middle-class status, the hard work undertaken and travail experienced to arrive at this social level are often excised from the cultural narrative and, where possible, historical memory. The purpose of erasing the history of poverty and hardship in the immigrant experience is to avoid the emotion of shame – shame about the shabby and impoverished condition of the diasporic subject forced to leave a humiliated China that is in a shambles for a better life. Immigrant Chinese edit their stories to focus on the terminus of their struggles and endeavours: the success of material possession and achievement of social mobility. They do not want negative history and inconvenient truths to affect the mythos of Chinese achievement and success: "In the story of modern Asia, [...] messy blotches don't sit well with the clean lines of our reinvention" (Aw 2016, 37).

Aw studied law at the University of Cambridge, worked as a lawyer in London, taught creative writing at Nanyang Technological University in Singapore, and spent time in Bangkok, Hong Kong, Shanghai, Nepal, and Patagonia among other places. He has also been to the US, Morocco, and Indonesia as well as travelling through South America and Europe (Lee 2016, para. 24). Aw's international travels reveal a transnational lightness of being, enabled by the forces of globalization and possession of economic and cultural capital. Celebrating the pleasures of international travel, Aw showcases the cultural vitality of modern Asia in cities such as Kuala Lumpur, Bangkok, Hong Kong, and Shanghai.

Aw brings an anthropological curiosity to his geographical excursions in Asia. In his visits, he discovers that he is often mistaken for a local or for someone who (most likely) has ancestral roots there. Embraced as someone indigenous to a location and culture when he is in fact only a tourist, Aw responds: "I wonder if, on some level, I enjoy being mistaken for a local as much as I am frustrated that no one seems to know, or care, where I'm from. [...] [M]y face is their face" (Aw 2016, 11). The experience of being one with the Other is enabled by perceptions of similarity based on physiognomy. Looking at a person and making inferences or assumptions about his/her ethnicity and even nationality can be misleading in a harmless, or even harmful, way. In the COVID-19 world, Asian Americans have been harassed, assaulted, and even killed in the USA because they are all seen as Chinese (presumably from the PRC) who exported the virus to the world. It matters not whether one is US-born or of Japanese, Korean, or Filipino ancestry. Typecasting physical features leads to the imposition of sameness on things radically different.

Aw's encounter with people in Asia who look like him but who have different nationalities, speak different languages, and have different cultures makes space for theorizing the relationship between national identity and diasporic subjectivity. If the outside world often looks at the Chinese as "a huge mass of people who look, think, and behave in largely the same way" (Aw 2016, 60), a conception that raises the terrifying spectre of a "single-willed horde of billions exerting its collective ambitions on the rest of the world" (60), Aw proceeds to dismantle "this image of One China" (60) by conjuring up the existence of multiple ethnic and dialect groups as well as different customs, cuisines, and dress in China.

If Chinese people, in whatever part of the world they are found, "presume a certain familiarity with one another, as if tied by an ancient kinship that defies nationality" (Aw 2016, 61), that familiarity belies a preoccupation with difference and categorization. People who speak a particular dialect and live in a particular area or region share a sense of kinship ties, differentiating themselves from other dialect communities and peoples from other regions. The Chinese who belong to one dialect group may have stereotypical views of those from other dialect groups, sometimes leading to tensions and friction.

When Aw considers the meaning of Chinese-ness by looking at physiognomy, spoken language, geographical setting, communal identification, and cultural affiliations, he seeks to position himself as a transnational and globalized subject whose sense of self cannot be dissociated from the larger experience of the historical Chinese diaspora. As an author writing in the 21st century, he finds he has a different sociocultural and political frame of reference from that available to Southeast Asian Chinese diasporic authors such as Shirley Geok-lin Lim in the 20th century. In the 21st century, this frame of reference is informed by the phenomenon of China as an economic power with the potential, it might appear, to threaten US economic pre-eminence.

Five Star Billionaire and the promise of millennial China

Five Star Billionaire depicts the experiences of five Chinese Malaysian subjects who find themselves in Shanghai pursuing their dreams and ambitions, seeking purpose in life and self-definition. From a humble background, Phoebe Chen Aiping, who works in a factory, is in China in response to the promise of a (non-existent) job. With little going for her, Phoebe seeks to reinvent herself in Shanghai, assisted by whatever advice she can glean from self-help books. Also of humble origins, Gary Gao of Kota Bahru is a pop star who, having impressed his Taiwanese fans, is now in Shanghai preparing for a concert. With ambitions to be a celebrity star, Gary finds himself involved in a drunken brawl, resulting in a tarnished reputation and the need to make a living by singing in shopping malls. Justin Lin is in China to help expand his family's real-estate business, while Leong Yinghui, the leftist-leaning daughter of a Malaysian government minister, is there to establish herself as a successful businesswoman. And then there is the enigmatic billionaire entrepreneur and self-help guru Walter Chao, whose plots and schemes bring the lives of the other four characters – Phoebe, Gary, Justin, and Yinghui – into contact, not always with their full knowledge. The reader is invited to consider the possibility that Walter Chao might be a conman instead of an entrepreneur.

The characters in Aw's novel come from different backgrounds. We learn about shameful family secrets, abusive guardians, impoverished upbringing, and loss of family wealth in Malaysia, all of which (it is hoped) can be more effectively managed or left behind in Shanghai, which promises that a person can be whoever or whatever he/she wants to be in China. When these characters navigate their way to China, they do so not because they are trying to escape a country locked in the throes of political turmoil and social unrest. They travel to China because China is the new millennium's land of promise and opportunity. The thematization of China not as a land of lack but of plenty represents a recent development in diasporic Chinese literature. If China, as observers have predicted, will, in the not-too-distant future, overtake the US as the largest economy in the world, that possibility is not lost on Aw.

Aw is alert to the phenomenal speed with which China underwent transformation into an economic and political power, evinced in the re-creation of the country's cityscapes, in its enticement of foreign businesses, and in the monumental ambition of its "Belt and Road" initiative. In *Five Star Billionaire*, the achievements of modern China are crystallized in the phenomenon of Shanghai, the shining city upon which is conferred the role of showcasing the country's economic success to the world. Home to China's largest companies and the key base for head offices of foreign companies stationed in the country, Shanghai is modern China's commercial and business capital. Shanghai is meant to impress. Resplendent in "all its twenty-first-century glory" (Aw 2013, 100), this megacity boasts a Bund where high-end western bars offer a magnificent "view of the wide sweep of the [Huangpu] river and the skyscrapers of Pudong" (52). From one's hotel room, one can enjoy a panoramic view of

> the Shanghai skyline, [...] the ribbons of elevated highways unfurling into the distance, twisting and curling into one another; [...] the brilliant gilding of Jing'an Temple amidst the blue-glass and chrome facades of the office blocks, [...] the crowds of people hurrying along the streets. (162)

This historic city draws attention to the disjunction between China's impoverished condition in the early decades of communist rule and its great economic transformation in the 21st century. Like other major cities of the world – London, New York, and Paris – Shanghai fascinates the beholder, partly because of its historical reputation as both the "Paris of the East" and "Whore of the Orient". Well known as a vibrant port and cosmopolitan city in the early 20th century, Shanghai was at the time also associated with opium, gambling, commercial sex, and interracial fraternization (Farrer and Field 2015, 180–184).

As both image and symbol, Shanghai enjoys an evocative presence in film and in the novel. Shanghai offers a rich historical setting for literary works as diverse as Lisa See's *Shanghai Girls* (2009) and Kazuo Ishiguro's *When We Were Orphans* (2000) as well as for films such as Ang Lee's *Lust, Caution* (2007), based on Eileen Chang's short story. In the James Bond movie *Skyfall* (2012), the audience encounters glamorous images of night-time Shanghai, resplendent with the lights of technology and bristling with the indefatigable energies of a great metropolis.

In Kevin Kwan's (2015) *China Rich Girlfriend*, a sequel to *Crazy Rich Asians* (Kwan 2013) and a novel about the lives of the supremely wealthy Chinese families of Asia, Shanghai is portrayed as the megacity in which the long-lost billionaire father of the central female character Rachel Chu lives. In Shanghai, Rachel and her newly-wed husband were picked up by a Rolls Royce at Pudong International Airport and driven to the Majestic Suite of the Peninsula Hotel where the bathroom alone is found to be larger than an entire apartment. "I just can't get over it", Rachel gushes at one point about modern China's great transformation, "all these megacities springing up overnight, this nonstop economic boom" (Kwan 2015, 535–536).

When the lives of China's uber-rich are portrayed in *China Rich Girlfriend*, such representation disrupts expectations of the familiar form and content of Chinese diasporic literature. The novel subverts stereotypical conceptions of the Chinese as a people who come from a land of lack by showcasing the uninhibited worship of Mammon in a communist state. Kwan's writing "revamps the image of Asia from one plagued by poverty and political turmoil to one characterized by hedonism and opulence, heralding the economic decline of Europe and America" (Ding 2020, 68). And it does so by means of a narrative that enables the functioning of "pride porn" (67), where the profligate lives of the wealthy in China and Southeast Asia are packaged for an audience's voyeuristic consumption. If Kwan's novels identify Southeast Asia and China as the controlling centre of focus in the 21st century for the accumulation of capital, Aw portrays changes taking place in China that have encouraged the Chinese who live overseas to return "home". Even when not portrayed with the kind of representational excess we find in Kwan, Aw's Shanghai nonetheless participates in the celebration of Asian capital by dilating China's economic success to the reader.

However, Shanghai's glamour and mystique do not tell the whole story. When we take a closer look at the setting of Shanghai in *Five Star Billionaire*, we encounter grit and grime, dark streets, dense markets, and ceaseless noise (Aw 2013, 74–75). Intertwining images of smog and skyscrapers point to the cost of China's modernization drive. The city is congested, with apartment dwellers living so close together they can literally peer into other people's dwellings. Daily existence for the ordinary individual is prosaic, in stark contrast to the glamour and energy found in advertisements showcasing Shanghai. Even though Justin may find the Pudong skyline and skyscrapers of Lujiazui impressive at night, he notes the contrast between this setting and that of daytime Shanghai "obscured by the perpetual haze of pollution" (22).

If Shanghai, the novel's synecdoche for China, is a gateway to the future, promising good things to those with the courage to dream, it is also portrayed as an alienating and "never-ending city" in which "if you stop for one moment, you fall, you disappear" (Aw 2013, 291). China, we learn, moves so quickly that "it [is] impossible to anticipate every development in advance" (35). If the novel represents China's economic and cultural vibrancy, it also shows Shanghai overwhelming in its immensity and in the speed with which things change. In Shanghai, "[e]veryone is busy preparing for tomorrow" (217). After barely three months in his apartment, Justin notes that Shanghai "seemed to have changed completely, the points of reference in his world rearranged and repositioned in ways he could not recognise" (210). "Nothing", Phoebe avers, "ever stood still in China, nothing was permanent" (17). While progress is exciting and to be embraced, it can also prove alienating and exhausting.

Shanghai is fast-paced, ruthless, and impersonal. Phoebe finds that the city "weigh[s] down on her with the weight of ten skyscrapers" (Aw 2013, 9), stifling and oppressive. One needs to be adept at meeting the myriad challenges thrown one's way or be crushed. Survival in the city requires street-smartness, quick thinking, and a willingness to compromise one's ethics and principles. Cultural norms and practices may need some getting used to, such as the view that, without a husband, a woman will not be successful in her work. Shanghainese society can be proud and condescending, such that you might be laughed at out loud should you apply too much make-up. Human relationships, which often involve mind games and manipulation, tend to be impermanent. Although characters demonstrate a capacity for determination, tenacity, and hard work, these virtues, typically associated with the work ethic, are compromised by a general lack of positive personal attributes.

Shanghai undermines dreams and aspirations:

> People say it is the size of a small country, but it is not, it is bigger, like a whole continent, with a heart as deep and unknown as the forests of the Amazon and as vast and wild as the deserts of Africa. People come here like explorers, but soon they disappear; no one even hears them as they fade away, and no one remembers them. (Aw 2013, 381)

These lines evoke Joseph Conrad's *Heart of Darkness* (1899), a novella about a British merchant seaman Marlow's journey up the Congo River to find the mad Kurtz, a Nietzschean character who represents the dark side of European imperialism. There is something defamiliarizing when reading a description of China that is based on a comparison with the Amazon and with Africa. Aw's evocation of the South American rainforest and the Sahara, Namib, and Kalahari Deserts associates China with both denseness and aridity, hostile conditions that invariably temper idealistic conceptions of the country's possibilities. Where *Heart of Darkness* grapples with the moral ambiguities of western imperial desire and with the consequences of the encounter between "savagism" and civilization, *Five Star Billionaire* considers China's inimicality to dreams of success because of its overwhelming size, lack or absence of order, and resistance to ready comprehension.

Shanghai may be a symbolically important setting in the novel, but the reader never loses sight of Malaysia, the birth country of Aw's characters. When these characters travel to China, they provide glimpses of Malaysia, described as "inherently Third World" (Aw 2013, 23). We encounter descriptions of village life in Malaysia, including modest living quarters, such as "one room above a tyre repair shop" (67), work life in a factory, and low-end shopping centres. Gary, barricaded in a hotel room following his altercation with a stranger at a bar, recalls life with his mother in Temangan, a rural town in Malaysia. The settlement is so small that it is difficult to say whether it even has "outskirts", unless one thinks of "outskirts" as "low rows of shop-houses and cheaply-built houses [bleeding] into the countryside, fading into the sparse jungle that stretched for miles until the next town" (164). The jungle can be relied upon in this novel as an image of wild and untrammelled nature that has yet to be tamed by the cultivational and civilizational forces of modernity.

Flashbacks to life in Malaysia capture the ethos of a bygone age and simpler past, an impression supported by images of rural settings, simple living quarters, and an old cinema built in the early 20th century and ironically named the New Cathay, that insists on forcing its physical and historical presence on the urban cityscape of 1980s and 1990s Kuala Lumpur. The debate on whether to demolish this movie theatre in the light of modern Kuala Lumpur's urban renewal and infrastructural renovation is suffused with considerations of the relationship between past and present, of the importance of history to one's sense of familial and cultural identity as well as national belonging. Should we preserve the New Cathay to protect Malaysia's cultural heritage, or try to get a healthy profit from its sale, given the current value of land and real estate?

Aw's portrayal of the *huáqiáo*'s return to China revises the familiar narrative of east-west immigrant desire in which the Chinese, overburdened by political turmoil, poverty, and social instability in China, seek to escape the country of their birth for the promises of new lands. It also adjusts a familiar narrative in Chinese Malaysian literature which identifies discrimination against the Chinese as an important reason for considering leaving Malaysia for other countries. An important work that tells the story of a young Chinese Malaysian student who decides to leave Malaysia for the US because of its race-based political system and social order is Shirley Geok-lin Lim's (1996) *Among the White Moon Faces*. Narrating the experience of growing up as a woman of Chinese descent in British Malaya and independent Malaysia, Lim's Bildungsroman provocatively engages with the cultural politics of British imperialism and race in the postcolonial nation.

In *Among the White Moon Faces*, Lim tells the reader that Malaysia does not recognize "merit [as] the main criterion for professional status", and that Malaysian society would always view her as someone "of the wrong gender and the wrong race" (1996, 197). With Malaysia's economic policies designed to discriminate against minority citizens, Lim decided that the country of her birth could only erect obstacles to hinder her aspiration to be an academic teaching literature at the university. When Lim's application for a lectureship at the University of Malaya was turned down despite her credentials, she realized that "the prejudices [she] had believed to be the product of small-town religious bigotry were systemic in Malaysian society" (197). When she left Malaysia for the US, Lim understood that she would henceforth view her natal country through the perspective of a traveller and a visitor.

It is interesting to note that Lim evokes the idea of "exile" (1996, 248) to describe her position in the US in *Among the White Moon Faces*. However, Lim's embrace of this exilic condition is framed by the opportunities for transnational mobility afforded her by the possession of cultural capital. Enabled by the privilege of choice, Lim's circumstance is not the exile of radical dispossession and dislocation but one of transoceanic crossing by an immigrant who has the freedom to choose between national homelands. If one insists on speaking about exile in the context of readily available transnational mobility, then at the very least one needs to qualify it as self-imposed or voluntary exile (Lim 2013, 123-124).

For Lim, the historical experience of the Chinese diaspora in Southeast Asia is fraught with tensions between host nation and the minority Chinese who came to settle there. Lim is sensitive to the politics of Southeast Asian nationalism and decolonization following World War II, a politics in which people of Chinese descent find themselves caught up as racial Others not yet accommodated by or fully assimilated into the nation state. The early years of post-independence Malaysia constituted the historical period during which the Chinese found themselves struggling with national belonging and diasporic identity.

The position of the *huáqiáo* in the historical experience of decolonizing Southeast Asia differs from the portrait of the Chinese as we move towards the latter part of the 20th century, when Hong Kong's handover to China in 1997 was imminent. Anxious about the political implications of the return of the British crown colony to China in the last decade of the 20th century, many Chinese in Hong Kong sought to emigrate to foreign lands. The 1990s was also the decade when the forces of globalization were powerfully unleashed, transforming the world into a network of technological, economic, and political exchanges. It was in the 1990s that Tash Aw went to the UK to study law at Cambridge University on a scholarship (Allardice 2019, para. 13). The globalized world that provides the framing context for Aw's experience as a university student in the UK is different from Malaysia's postcolonial context which informed Shirley Geok-lin Lim's decision to leave for the US in 1969 for doctoral studies.

Unlike Shirley Geok-lin Lim, Tash Aw does not register anxiety about the social existence of the *huáqiáo* in Malaysia. While Aw, like Lim, is familiar with the inhospitality and even hostility historically experienced by the minority Chinese community in Malaysia, he does not foreground this history in his representation of the millennial Chinese Malaysian experience. Aw's ambit is the 21st-century Asian world defined by globalization, smart technology, and the automation of old manufacturing and industrial processes. Aw does not evoke the outbreak of Chinese–Malay sectarian violence in Kuala Lumpur on May 13, 1969, or the implementation of the NEP in 1971. In *Five Star Billionaire*, he resists deploying the familiar motif of the Chinese Malaysian subject's encounter with state-sanctioned discrimination. Aw's characters are not in Shanghai to escape racially motivated hardships in Malaysia. Their presence in the city instead derives its significance from the larger context of 21st-century (post)modernity defined by ready transnational mobility, high-performing Asian economies, American populism, and disruptions of the existing global order.

Aw's novel represents the promise and allure as well as problems of China in the new millennium. Once we get past the glittering lights, the imposing skyscrapers, and the untameable energies of 21st-century China, we are confronted with an Asian power that can flaunt the success of its economy but is distrusted for its political ambitions. If Shanghai draws overseas Chinese by its allure of wealth, glamour, and adventure, it does not always afford the fulfilment that is much sought after. Aw's characters might have made individual gains of one kind or another and achieved a degree (even if limited) of self-knowledge, but their overall experience of Shanghai can be said to be chequered because the city is coldly indifferent to a person's needs and aspirations. Aw's Shanghai is a dog-eat-dog world. Unashamedly exploitative and callously indifferent to the emotional needs and mental health of both citizens and foreigners alike, Chinese capitalism appears to be unsupported by a resonating political philosophy or vision of ideals. Even as Aw represents the possibilities of China as the new millennium's land of promise, he portrays the fragmented and alienated nature of individual and social being fashioned by Asian capital.

Conclusion

Five Star Billionaire portrays modern China with excitement but also distrust. What, one wonders, is the basis for this ambivalence? Reading *Five Star Billionaire* in 2021, one can think of possible answers to this question, from contemporary China's pursuit of national interest and handling of foreign policy to the international community's perceptions of the country. In the 21st century, the desire of countries to engage in trade relations with China is complicated by actions of the PRC that have been viewed as coercive, authoritarian, and anti-democratic. China has in recent years been accused of flaunting its military muscle in the South China Sea, and of generating anxieties in Southeast Asia about Chinese hegemonic ambitions. Recently it passed a wide-ranging new security law for Hong Kong, undermining the city's autonomy and democratic institutions. China has also been criticized for mishandling the early COVID-19 outbreak in Wuhan, Hubei Province.

There are other issues as well. China has been accused of human rights violations against its minority Muslim subjects, the Uighur, in the autonomous territory of Xinjiang in northwest China. During the Trump presidency, the US argued that China's economic growth had been built on unfair trade practices such as high tariff barriers and forced technology transfer directed at American businesses that sought to gain access to the China market. Furthermore, the Chinese, it is alleged, were also seeking to undertake surveillance activities and enact other forms of espionage via the establishment of 5G wireless networks around the world.

However, criticisms of China such as these, led by the US and presented as having the support of the global community, do not necessarily present the full picture. In Southeast Asia, there are conflicting perspectives on China, with anxiety about Chinese hegemonic ambitions intertwined with a desire of countries to engage in trade with her. Malaysia's relationship with China is both fraught and cordial: fraught because both countries are claimants in the volatile South China Sea dispute; cordial because both recognize the importance of maintaining open trade relations in the face of an increasingly protectionist US. For Malaysia, China's enormous market makes it attractive as a trading partner.

The historical context for *Five Star Billionaire* and *The Face* is the rise of modern China in the new millennium. This phenomenon enables the Chinese Malaysian author to write the Chinese diasporic experience as one of opportunity and of becoming, enabled not by fantasies of western plenitude but by the possibilities of Asian capital. The characters in *Five Star Billionaire* are denizens of a globalized world generally unconstrained by the demands of the nation state or pull of familial obligations. When these characters looked overseas for opportunities, they turned their sight not towards the west, the familiar telos of Asian immigrant desire, but towards China. Aw's China is a land of opportunity, attractive especially to those with a spirit of adventure, who desire to be rich, or who simply want to escape the past.

In *The Face*, Aw's fascination with China's great transformation cannot be disentangled from a consideration of cultural roots and family history that leads us back to the ancestral homeland. A meditation on what it means to be Chinese in the 21st century with the opportunities it affords for travelling to different geographical settings and meeting other cultures, *The Face* is alert to the struggles of the early Chinese in Nanyang and to the opportunities for a better life they toiled to create for their descendants in diaspora. Aw does not rehearse the familiar narrative of Chinese desire to renounce Asia for a better life in the west. Instead, he presents the alacrity with which the diasporic Chinese subject can move from one country to another as a freedom readily available today through education and the possession of economic and cultural capital.

Engaging with the culture-specific conditions and political ethos of the 21st century, *The Face* and *Five Star Billionaire* afford the reader a vantage point from which to trace and apprehend the development of Malaysia's diasporic Chinese community over time. These works identify China as the land of promise and the world as a playground for exploration as well as a testing ground for considerations of race, culture, and diasporic identity. They also re-vision the familiar narrative of east–west immigrant desire found in Asian American literature by refocusing the thematic centre of the Chinese diasporic experience on Asia, that geopolitical region of the world reshaped by Asian wealth and by China's emergence as an economic and political power in the 21st century.

Disclosure statement

No potential conflict of interest was reported by the author.

References

Allardice, Lisa. 2019. "Tash Aw: It Used to Be that Asia Was Poor. 'Asians are Rich' Is the New Cliché." *The Guardian*, April 13. Accessed 14 April 2021. https://www.theguardian.com/books/2019/apr/13/tash-aw-malaysian-author-shining-light-on-immigration-stories

Aw, Tash. 2013. *Five Star Billionaire*. London: Fourth Estate.

Aw, Tash. 2016. *The Face: Strangers on a Pier*. New York: Restless Books.

Bernards, Brian. 2015. *Writing the South Seas: Imagining the Nanyang in Chinese and Southeast Asian Postcolonial Literature*. Seattle, WA: University of Washington Press.

Brown, Jeff J. 2017. *China Rising: Capitalist Roads, Socialist Destinations*. New York: Punto Press.

Ding, Yuan. 2020. "'Asian Pride Porn': Neoliberal Multiculturalism and the Narrative of Asian Racial Uplift in Kevin Kwan's *Crazy Rich Asians* Trilogy." *MELUS* 45 (3): 65–82. doi:10.1093/melus/mlaa028.

Farrer, James, and Andrew David Field. 2015. *Shanghai Nightscapes: A Nocturnal Biography of A Global City*. Chicago: University of Chicago Press.

Jin, Ha. 2002. *The Crazed*. London: Vintage.

Kang, David C. 2007. *China Rising: Peace, Power, and Order in East Asia*. New York: Columbia University Press.

Koh, Sin Yee. 2017. *Race, Education, and Citizenship: Mobile Malaysians, British Colonial Legacies, and a Culture of Migration*. New York: Palgrave Macmillan.

Kwan, Kevin. 2013. *Crazy Rich Asians*. New York: Anchor Books.

Kwan, Kevin. 2015. *China Rich Girlfriend*. Crows Nest, NSW: Allen & Unwin.

Lee, Jian Xuan. 2016. "Acclaimed Malaysian Author Tash Aw: 'Even though I Haven't Wanted To, I've Become a Role Model for Some Young People." *The Straits Times*, June 27. Accessed 14 March 2021. https://www.straitstimes.com/lifestyle/arts/acclaimed-malaysian-author-tash-aw-even-though-i-havent-wanted-to-ive-become-a-role

Li, Yiyun. 2010. *Gold Boy, Emerald Girl*. London: Fourth Estate.

Lim, Shirley Geok-lin. 1996. *Among the White Moon Faces*. Singapore: Times Editions-Marshall Cavendish.

Lim, Walter S.H. 2013. *Narratives of Diaspora: Representations of Asia in Chinese American Literature*. New York: Palgrave Macmillan.

Low, Kelvin E.Y. 2014. "Chinese Migration and Entangled Histories: Broadening the Contours of Migratory Historiography." *Journal of Historical Sociology* 27 (1): 75–102. doi:10.1111/johs.12037.

Min, Anchee. [1993] 2006. *Red Azalea*. New York: Anchor Books.

Roy, Denny. 2013. *Return of the Dragon: Rising China and Regional Security*. New York: Columbia University Press.

Saravanan, Vanithamani. 2007. "Linguistic Diversity: Asia." In *Handbook of Language and Communication: Diversity and Change*, edited by Marlis Hellinger and Anne Pauwels, 151–176. Berlin: Mouton de Gruyter.

Universalism and the Malaysian anglophone novel: Exploring inequality, migrancy, and class in Tash Aw's *We, the Survivors*

Angelia Poon

ABSTRACT

Tash Aw's 2019 novel *We, the Survivors* narrates the story of a convicted killer, Ah Hock, whose life serves as a lens to refract contemporary Malaysia's postcolonial history and its ethnic and class politics, as well as its location within the circuitry of global capitalism. This article examines Aw's representation of migrancy, class, and inequality in contemporary Malaysian society, reading the text as a critique of global capitalism through its tactical employment of a universalist idiom that appropriates Darwinian ideas about survival, evolution, chance, environment, and competition. The text also reflects on the ethics of novel-writing since Ah Hock's oral testimony is ostensibly mediated by a more privileged character. Aw locates his novel in the pivotal space between national specificity and general universalism while asking critical questions of his own position within the transnational literary marketplace, thereby underscoring the urgent need to re-world the world created by global capitalism.

There is an epiphanous moment in *The Face: Strangers on a Pier* (Aw 2016), Tash Aw's extended essay about his Chinese ancestry and childhood in Malaysia, when he encounters the boy who used to bully him in school. Aw relates how he had gone to a fast-food restaurant to celebrate a friend's admission to Stanford when he met his erstwhile bully:

> There, in a brown uniform and comically origami-like hat, will be my principal extortionist, a boy older than us who'd dreamed of being a big-time tai-kor [big brother] gangster, who'd boasted about slashing someone in the face while he was still at school. He will recognize me, and lower his eyes when he asks, Do you want fries with that? And I will not know why, but I am the one who feels embarrassed, almost guilty. (56–57)

It is a crushing moment of mutual recognition and self-realization that leads Aw to conclude that both of them were then in the process of being segregated by class. The meeting constituted a significant turning point, since school had previously been a common space where all students mingled in a kind of prelapsarian ignorance of their socio-economic and class status. In ten years, Aw notes, "when we are only in our mid-twenties, our paths can never cross again, not even in a fast-food joint. We don't know that yet, but we will, very soon" (57–58). What strikes me about this meeting is not just the emotional power of proverbial tables being turned but the sense of determinism it conveys – the use of the present tense and the modalities, "can never" and "will", within a retrospective narrative to enhance the inevitability of a foregone conclusion. Aw tries to pin this fatalistic determinism down: how is it that people's lives turn out the way they do – regardless of their dreams and desires – because of their class? This question lies at the heart of Aw's fourth novel as he explores the moral, existential, and affective implications of intractable economic inequality experienced at the level of individual subjectivity. *We, the Survivors* (Aw 2019b) narrates the story of a convicted killer, Ah Hock, whose personal circumstances serve as a lens to refract contemporary Malaysia's postcolonial history, and the dynamics of its ethnic and class politics, as well as its location in the world within the circuitry of global capitalism. An ethnic Chinese man from a poor working-class background, Ah Hock's life is a harsh one of physical labour and hard-earned wages, which leads ultimately to him killing a migrant worker. In this article, I seek to examine Aw's novelistic representation of migrancy, class, and inequality in contemporary Malaysian society, reading the text as a critique of global capitalism through its tactical employment of a universalist idiom that appropriates Darwinian ideas about survival, evolution, chance, environment, and competition.

Locating Malaysian anglophone literature: In search of universalism

Beginning with his first novel in 2005, Tash Aw has steadily gained international recognition for his fiction and is arguably the best-known among Malaysia's new generation of writers in English. "Malaysia" features significantly, if to varying extents, in all his novels: his third novel, *Five Star Billionaire* (Aw 2013), for example, is set in Shanghai but features a cast of Malaysian Chinese characters.[1] Since 2014, Aw has also contributed numerous opinion pieces to *The New York Times* on a variety of topical issues related to Malaysia and other parts of Asia. Mainly focused on urbanization, immigration, politics, and economic inequality, Aw's articles depict for the western or Global North reader what life and social attitudes are like in this increasingly affluent Southeast Asian country.[2] They serve as ethnographic and sociological snapshots of a multiracial postcolonial country, with a population of 32.7 million (Department of Statistics Malaysia 2021) and an ethnically Malay majority, navigating a globalized world and aspiring to scale the ranks into the top tier of developed nations. Aw documents Malaysia's reliance on migrant labour for its prosperity, often drawing a comparison between current labour flows and an earlier wave of immigration during British colonial times. With at least 3.85 million documented and undocumented foreign workers in Malaysia – many from countries like Bangladesh, Myanmar, Indonesia, and Nepal working in construction, manufacturing, and agriculture – the social and cultural impact of the presence of these workers on the country has been significant.[3] As Aw notes in an interview where he repudiates the cliché of all Asians as rich, the dream of migration to the west is but one story: "In fact, the more important story is about how Chinese people see Bangladeshis, how Malays see Nepalese. This is a story that needs to be told" (Aw 2019a, n.p.).

We, the Survivors allows Aw the fictional space to interrogate this historical moment as he trains his attention onto the segment of the local and foreign population in Malaysia whose lives and experiences collectively constitute what some scholars have called "globalization from below". The term captures "the transnational flow of people and goods involving relatively small amounts of capital and informal, often semi-legal or illegal transactions, often associated with 'the developing world' but in fact apparent across the globe" (Mathews and Vega 2012, 1). These workers and economic agents on the ground survive as best they can, often evading regulation while fulfilling needs and plugging gaps in the formal economy. Neither anti-capitalist nor counter-hegemonic, they operate within and between structures, amidst local and translocal networks. The often compromised agency of these individual actors stands in deliberate contradistinction to the forces of globalization from above, which is associated with official statistics, state directives, large transnational corporations, and supranational organizations. As anthropologist Gustavo Lins Ribeiro (2012) explains, globalization from below "provides a perspectival gaze, a subject position" (223), and, as a conceptual category, effectively captures the power differential between asymmetric forces in global capitalism.

In his novel, Aw examines the intersection between globalization from below within a Malaysian milieu and what Robert Young (2012) has called "postcolonial remains", that "ongoing life of residues, living remains, lingering legacies" (21) from the colonial era, that continue to define postcoloniality in many nations. The global chain of cheap migrant labour and refugees extending into Malaysia in *We, the Survivors* inflects the country's colonial and postcolonial scripts of economic and racial inequality, creating in the process new subalterns and forms of social invisibility. Aw's main characters in the novel are all members of the country's Chinese minority who form about 22.6 percent of the total population (Department of Statistics Malaysia 2021). On one level, the novel's exclusive focus on Malaysian Chinese characters reflects a cultural and ethnic insularity found, according to Andrew Ng (2018), in much of the "minority" or "minor" literature of Malaysia; that is to say, its non-Malay literatures, and, in particular, its anglophone and sinophone literatures. Ng argues that such "authorial singularity" is "a sophisticated resistive approach" (73) or an indirect and implicitly critical gesture on the part of such writers to resist the state's ethno-nationalism. Thus paradoxically insular and political, "Malaysia's minor literature reveals, in other words, another story unfolding within the nation's official story: a framed narrative that provides a different perspective from its framing discourse" (Ng 2019, 328).

While Aw's work is certainly meaningful within such parameters of the nation, I propose an analytical lens that draws upon recent debates in postcolonialism and world literature to explore another perspective of him as a globally oriented writer intervening in a wider public sphere. Unlike the work of an earlier generation of Malaysian writers in English, Aw's novels have all been published by international publishers and it is clear that he has always written for a global anglophone audience rather than solely for a local national one. Sarah Brouillette has noted the self-consciousness with which postcolonial writers market themselves and construct their authorial personae. She argues that postcolonial writers who have attained success or visibility in the global marketplace "do not seek to separate themselves from the commercial or economic spheres – the basis of those 'corporately owned' images – but rather to interact with various forms of politicized interpretation and reception that are imbricated with transnational culture and capital" (Brouillette 2011, 74). The self-consciousness that Brouillette has highlighted fully applies to Aw who, in his fiction and non-fictional writing, is fully cognizant of the political implications of his work and his place as a professional writer in the global capitalist economy. His *New York Times* opinion pieces about globalization, migration, poverty, and inequality constitute his extra-literary participation in a transnational public discourse and intellectual debate about pressing and topical global realities. The presence of a universalist rather than strictly national impulse in Aw's latest novel – as seen in his choice of an elemental Darwinian discourse to depict the imbrication of work, corporeality, and unequal competition, together with his self-conscious exploration of the writer's complicity in capitalist exploitation – further reinforces this impression of authorial self-consciousness. Indeed, *We, the Survivors* constitutes a useful site for the reconsideration of the idea of universalism which many in postcolonial studies have traditionally viewed suspiciously as an imperialist ruse. As Melissa Kennedy (2017) reminds us in *Narratives of Inequality*, wariness over totalizing universalism should not lead us to a disregard of all forms of the universal: "Incommensurability underpins the postcolonial emphasis on cultural difference as a rejection of universalism and Eurocentrism, but in doing so it overlooks the deeply similar structures of economic inequality portrayed in fictional representations of material lives" (13).

The critical postcolonial recuperation of universality is apparent in Neil Lazarus's examination of world literature. Lazarus describes "world literature" as literature of the last 200 years or so which "registers and encodes the social logic of modernity" (2011, 122) within a capitalist world-system. He proposes world literature "in the broadest sense as *the literature of the (capitalist) world system*" (122; original emphasis). Drawing upon the Marxist principle of combined and uneven development that also explains the unequal and differentiated but single world literary system where specific social experiences are represented differently yet are part of a whole, Lazarus maintains that there are "*only* local universalisms" and "local cosmopolitanisms" (134; original emphasis) which readers and literary scholars must delineate and situate carefully in order to explicate the text's manifold layers of meaning as fully as possible. We need to do this, he argues, rather than presume a stark dichotomy between the local and the universal. Aw's novel is exemplary in this respect as he depicts the relationship between economic inequality and migrant labour in terms of a primal struggle for survival so that contemporary Malaysia becomes the (local) site for a universally applicable existential meditation on humanity's capacity for both survival and cruelty. Put another way, the co-articulation of the local and the universal is a question of multidimensionality that is directed to variously located audiences – very possibly at different historical moments too – who are nevertheless all equally invited to contemplate a shared humanity.

Approaching universalism from a different angle, Mariano Siskind (2010) asks the crucial question of whether world literature "serves the cosmopolitan purpose that is supposed to be constitutive of its critical and pedagogical horizon" (351). While Siskind articulates this question out of a concern over how world literature is taught in US universities, maintaining that world literature as pedagogic practice needs to "[preserve] universality as the necessary horizon of cosmopolitan practices with an emancipatory purpose" (358), his point begs the question of writers themselves contributing to the discourse and imaginary of world literature either directly or indirectly through their writing. Contemporary writers who have attained some international prominence cannot be unware of their position in a global literary space. Besides fiction, many such authors also write non-fiction, essays, and book reviews, and, crucially, teach as university faculty or writers-in-residence in institutions of higher learning. Aw has done all of the above. Furthermore, writers like Aw who novelize globalization offer their work, I suggest, as part of world literature and also partake in designing a normative cosmopolitan ethic for it. In other words, they issue a call to readers through their writing and local universalisms, entering the literary critical fray concerning the responsible and ethical reading of world literature.

Like Siskind, the philosopher and literary scholar Pheng Cheah also stresses the need for a normative theory of world literature. Cheah's theory is based on an understanding of the world in terms of temporality rather than geo-spatiality. World literature, he argues, should be viewed as "an active power in the making of worlds, that is, both a site of processes of worlding and an agent that participates and intervenes in these processes" (Cheah 2016, 2). If Lazarus's proposition for understanding world literature places an accent on the local, Pheng Cheah calls more explictly for intervention in the battle against capitalist globalization. The reduction of the world to a global market erroneously predisposes us to think of world literature as a commodity or collection of things that circulate in empty global space. Cheah writes:

> Rethinking world literature solely in terms of global circulation intensifies globalization's unworlding of the world. Circulation is celebrated for its own sake as an inherently liberating process, when it merely retraces the closed sphericity of the globe. (193)

A world literature conceived only in spatial terms is deprived of any worlding force and the potential it has for imagining and envisioning alternative temporalities and worlds to challenge the time of capitalist globalization, and, relatedly, the notion that the excesses and unequal world created by capitalism are inevitable and necessary. Reading Aw's novel in the light of Cheah's conception of world literature allows us to approach it as a textual site in which to analyse the specific historical forces caused by national politics, the global capitalist order, and class-based interests as these coalesce or clash, in order to understand and question the "world" they produce as a necessary prelude to imagining other possibilities.

Although these theorizations have been only briefly sketched out, I have sought to situate Aw vis-à-vis such ideas in order to make meaningful sense of his writing as both Malaysian literature and world literature. For the rest of this article, I examine *We, the Survivors* to delineate Aw's "local universalism" and his attempts at "worlding" in his morally freighted novel as he depicts the intersectionality of class, nationality, and ethnic inequality within postcolonial and globalized Malaysia. I argue that he uses a Darwinian language of environmental determinism, evolution, and competition to evoke a universalism in his portrayal of the desperate lives of poor labouring subjects seeking to navigate specific postcolonial historical legacies and the ceaseless demands of a global capitalist world system.[4] It is worth remembering what the scholar of Victorian literature Gillian Beer wrote about Charles Darwin decades ago to explain the universal nature of the latter's thought and how his ideas have become part of public discourse and common knowledge:

> The unused, or uncontrolled, elements in metaphors such as "the struggle for existence" take on a life of their own. They surpass their status in the text [*On the Origin of Species*] and generate further ideas and ideologies. They include "more than the maker of them at the time knew". (1983, 9)

Beer's words help me to clarify that my aim here is not to map Aw's novel to Darwin's ideas in order to assess the accuracy of the former's use of them but rather to stress how Darwinian ideas have become so much a part of general cultural vocabulary and thinking that they afford Aw a universalist language for expressing capitalist exploitation and inequality in Malaysia. Employing Darwinian discourse, Aw seeks to locate his text in the pivotal space between national specificity and general universalism while asking critical questions of his own place within the transnational literary marketplace, thereby underscoring in these two ways the urgent need to re-world the world created by global capitalism.

We, the Survivors and its universalist idiom

We, the Survivors presents the story of Lee Hock Lye, better known as Ah Hock and once known as Jayden Lee – an unremarkable man noteworthy only because he killed a Bangladeshi migrant worker and is now the subject of a book by a young woman who is interviewing him for his story. In the novel, Ah Hock is cast as an Everyman figure, increasingly adrift in a world he seems perversely unable to fathom. With a discrepant sense of his life in a capitalist world system where he is at the mercy of a confluence of historical forces that feel like "laws", his ordinariness is emphasized numerous times as he is pressed into embodying symbolically the lives of thousands of small-town Malaysian Chinese born into hardship and poverty and destined to stay there. Hailing from a line of fishermen, Ah Hock explains how his family could not help but make a living from the sea after three of his grandparents moved from Indonesia to Malaysia in the early years of World War II. The history of his family in Malaysia is a tale of geo-economic determinism: "The country left us no choice – the river coiled around the village, blocking our route south towards the towns, forever nudging us towards the sea" (Aw 2019b, 22). The only alternatives to the river and the sea were the jungle and plantations. All the people who worked in the plantations were Indians, while the ones who fished were Chinese. As Ah Hock observes: "We never mixed with them – our lives were totally separate" (24–25). Encapsulated in Ah Hock's reflections about his family is the Malaysian nation's history of racial and ethnic segregation as a result of separate migration patterns, mutual communal prejudice, and the British colonial authorities' reliance on a divide-and-rule mode of governance to further their economic interests. In the late 19th century, South Asian indentured labourers were imported by the British to work in rubber plantations.[5] Contemporary globalization, as Ah Hock witnesses, brings new groups of workers to the scene, some of whom, like those from Nigeria, have no historical connection to Malaysia. To the locals, they were "Mat Hitam" or black people and few cared to know where they actually came from: "It's as if they all come from one big nameless continent" (6–7).

The text's depiction of the changing profile of migrant labourers occurs as part of broader economic development in the nation where asymmetries of power relations and privilege abound. The novel's globalized Malaysia is a specific social formation illustrating the Marxist principle of uneven and combined development within capitalism as a world-system. As E. San Juan Jr (2002) explains:

> Uneven development involves the inescapable polarization of the world into peripheral and central economies, tied with the intrinsic contradiction between labor and capital and the international division of labor whose boundaries were laid by the history of European colonialism and later by finance or monopoly capital. (230)

Uneven development takes place between countries and within countries. Throughout the novel, there are hints of prosperity far removed from the lives of migrant workers on the lowest rung of the economic ladder. These range from families who can afford to send their children abroad for an education to the day-trippers from the capital who patronize the seafood restaurant where Ah Hock worked. Alongside these visible signs of increased wealth are the parts of the country where time seems to have paradoxically stayed still. Thus there are the rural areas and moribund small towns where people cling on to their old ways of life and business, their shophouses in disrepair and overtaken by nature. Here, they subsist to the tune of a different temporal rhythm, as Ah Hock notes: "They're seventy-five, eighty years old. Still alive, but their business is being taken over by a tree. Imagine that" (Aw 2019b, 4).

Compared to *Five Star Billionaire*, Aw's previous satirical novel about the neo-liberal subject of self-help, there is little sense in this latest novel of the freewheeling atmosphere of individual entrepreneurial and mobile agents aspiring to remake their lives. Instead, a more raw and brutal social environment prevails as Aw depicts the exploitative nature of capitalism when observed up-close, on a smaller scale, and on the ground where workers whose only capital is their labour have their bodies destroyed and their lives crushed. He stresses the precarity of life for poor ordinary people like Ah Hock and his single mother, where capital accumulation is arduous if not practically impossible. Trapped in low-wage work, Ah Hock's mother moves from her fish-processing factory job to another job as a janitor. To Ah Hock, his mother's life "had run out of possibilities. Her life frozen. When she was not even forty years old" (Aw 2019b, 170). The jobs that Ah Hock himself takes on after deciding to leave his home town are low-paying, transient ones with few if any long-term prospects like being a waiter, a bottled-gas delivery man, and a night security guard. His life stabilized when he obtained a job at a fish farm in the Klang valley. There he worked for ten years and held the position of foreman before things spiralled out of control again.

Aw's desire for a universalist idiom to register his critique of capitalism leads him to focus on the gross materiality of the physical body. Thus he seeks to convey in a visceral way the suffering human body and its radical re-sculpting through work. Physical labour is depicted as bruising, backbreaking, and unrelenting; it turned people "from children to withered old creatures in the space of a few years" (Aw 2019b, 45). As Ah Hock explains, "[e]ven if someone pays you ten thousand a month, your body won't accept it. Your mind tells you to stay, to earn money for your kids back home, your old parents who need help. But your body says: *Run*" (45; original emphasis). In this way, he insists on a fundamental relationship between land, labour, and the body that potentially transcends the traditional specificities of identity like race, culture, and nation.

Yet physical labour is also not completely alienating. There are moments of satisfaction when manual labour is capable of affording one a sense of autonomy and self-sufficiency. When a youthful Ah Hock and his mother set up their own farm to grow vegetables and rear fish, they deliberately choose to live in a secluded part of town away from others in search of some form of economic independence. Of his mother, Ah Hock observes:

> She worked with a concentration so intense that it blocked out the rest of the world, and sometimes when I called out to her she wouldn't hear me, wouldn't stop until she had managed to slash all the branches from a bush. (Aw 2019b, 184)

Learning from his mother how to wield an axe and parang to clear the bush, Ah Hock soon becomes expert at it – "The tools became part of me" (185) – and he experiences physical work as transformative: "I could feel my body filling out, growing stronger and surer. I moved with the assurance of someone older, swifter" (185). Ironically, the repetition, monotony, and silence of such intensive labour also allow Ah Hock's imagination to take flight as he fantasizes about being a *wuxia* or martial arts storybook hero in a pre-modern world – battling monsters and bandits and saving oppressed villagers while roaming the countryside. It is only these short-lived moments, ironically enabled by physical labour, that link him most closely to creative labour including the act of writing itself.

Significantly, the interpenetration of body and imagination through labour also grounds Ah Hock as he explains his growing realization of a "feeling that I was connected to an unchanging place that belonged to me. A place that *owned* me" (Aw 2019b, 188; original emphasis). Of himself and his mother, he notes: "For once we had a sense of our place in the world" (196). Yet this bubble that mother and son create to eke out a living from the fruits of their labour – the closest the text comes to a romanticization of work – does not last. In a sign that they are always at the mercy of uncontrollable and inexplicable forces, floods eventually overwhelm their farm and fish ponds. In one startling scene, Ah Hock awakes in the middle of the night to the realization that "*[t]he sea is in my bedroom*" (200; original emphasis). The permanence and solidity of the land prove illusory: "The sea had erased everything we had thought unmoveable" (201). Nature, and geographical and environmental determinism create an atmosphere of grim oppression in the novel, a bleakly ironic twist since the possibility of extinction – an idea emphasized by Darwin as much as evolution and transformation – is the result of human-induced climate change. Faced with setback after setback, there seems no way out of this hard-scrabble life of continuous work and quiet desperation. It is a narrative in stark contradistinction to the coolie-to-tycoon story, that classic Chinese immigrant success story in Malaysia and other parts of Southeast Asia.

At the same time, one could read here a subtle critique of the national policy of preferential treatment for the *bumiputera* or "sons of the soil", a reference to Malays and other indigenous peoples of Malaysia.[6] The term *bumiputera* serves to distinguish particularly the non-Malay descendants of immigrant Chinese and Indian communities as having less legitimate claim to the nation, since it helps establish the primacy of Muslim Malays and Malaysia as a Malay homeland. As anthropologist James Clifford (1997) notes, people who claim natural or first-nation sovereignty "occupy the autochthonous end of a spectrum of indigenous attachments: people who deeply 'belong' in a place by dint of continuous occupancy over an extended period. (Precisely how long it takes to *become* indigenous is always a political question)" (254; original emphasis). His observation in parentheses is certainly applicable to the Chinese and Indian minority groups in Malaysia who have been there for generations.

Thus it is telling that *We, the Survivors* emphasizes the Chinese connection to the land through Ah Hock's story. The transference of agency to the land in the line above where Ah Hock felt that the land "owned" him suggests a unidirectional call he is powerless to resist. In short, working the land establishes roots. This sense of belonging privileges the claim of labour over that of birth and race but it remains only a tantalizing thought, one that merely underscores stark political reality as Ah Hock subsequently acknowledges the futility of trying to get compensation from the state when their land is destroyed: "We were the wrong race, the wrong religion – who was going to give us any help? Not the government, that's for sure. We knew that for no-money Chinese people like us, there was no point in even trying"

(Aw 2019b, 202). The claim to land through sweat and tears that Ah Hock is implicitly making is thus (and perhaps, merely) a moral one. It applies on the one hand historically to non-*bumiputera* Chinese and Indian minorities in Malaysia who worked the land. On the other hand, by logical extension, it also applies to the newer migrant labourers now working in the country's plantations and fish farms – the Indonesians, Bangladeshis, Myanmarese, Nepalese, and others – regardless of residency and legal status. What legitimizes this claim is the idea of physical labour as an equalizing force. Thus, as Ah Hock works alongside the migrant workers on the fish farm, he notes that although they would never be friends, there is a shared connection through exhausting labour: "During the day, those long, long days under the sun and rain, we experienced pain in the same way, and satisfaction and laughter too, but mostly hardship, and that is what bound us" (46). The act of working in synchrony creates a momentary sense of solidarity and equality.

The democratizing effects of physical labour are, however, quickly defeated by the inherently hierarchical and competitive nature of capitalism. Once Ah Hock gets "promoted" to a supervisory role, his local status giving him that one privilege and edge over the foreign workers, feelings of solidarity evaporate. Even as a waiter working in a restaurant, a younger Ah Hock had already experienced such a transformation. He "wielded power over them [the migrant workers], mysteriously and without me even asking, by virtue of being the same colour and race as the forty-something-year-old couple who owned the place" (Aw 2019b, 83). Through Ah Hock's musings over such arbitrary elevations, the text makes clear the inherent unfairness of the world and the random nature of privilege and good fortune. A microcosm of the capitalist system with all its inherent inequality and hierarchy is the multi-level marketing scheme selling skincare products which Ah Hock's wife, Jenny, joins, drawn to the prospect of higher income and social mobility. Essentially a pyramid scheme involving multiple layers of recruitment and ever-increasing sales, it allows only a few to make it to the top. Its sustainability rests on the constant availability of people desperate enough to start at the bottom. The text's critique of global capitalism, however, makes it further ask the question of who lies beyond that final but still economically productive layer. It turns out that this space is occupied by sick and traumatized Rohingya refugees – the "workers" Ah Hock and Keong, his Malaysian childhood friend, are desperate to find when faced with a labour crunch, and the people whose story remains ultimately untold.

Aw's portrait of capitalist competition is part of his deliberate invocation of a dark social Darwinian world. His use of a related rhetoric of survival, evolution, adaptation, change, and chance adds an elemental and primal quality to his characters' motivation in the novel. Like the tilapia fish that Ah Hock's mother rears, his characters seek to survive anywhere and any way they can. As Ah Hock observes of Keong: "We all have our own way of surviving, and telling stories was his" (Aw 2019b, 72). A trouble-maker at school and later small-time gangster, Keong sought to get ahead by operating in a shadow economy that involved peddling drugs, petty theft, and illegal work before eventually becoming a labour contractor and middleman procuring migrant workers for various companies. If Ah Hock is a rather passive and strait-laced character in the novel, Keong possesses the kind of energy that characterizes the economic agents of globalization from below, most likely not just to survive but to thrive. Theirs is a symbiotic relationship born out of mutual convenience and habit, and it is Keong whom Ah Hock makes the fateful decision to approach when his workers at the fish farm fall ill from cholera. Looking for a promised group of workers who have disappeared, they find instead Rohingya refugees. They confront a broker, Ashadul, a Bangladeshi migrant whom Keong accuses of cheating him of his workers – the man Ah Hock ends up killing. From this sordid mess, Keong emerges the more adept survivor. For in the three years that Ah Hock is imprisoned for his crime, Keong transforms himself, becoming a small business owner and family man. As Ah Hock bitterly admits, Keong "had taken hold of time and mastered it, I had let myself be crushed by it" (18).

By taking an unflinching look at poverty and class divisions, *We, the Survivors* hearkens back to a familiar 19th-century English and European novelistic tradition which established the genre's ethical credentials. There are significant differences, though. Unlike 19th-century bourgeois novels about the plight of the working class like those by Charles Dickens and Elizabeth Gaskell, Aw's text is unable to offer a steadfast moral compass, certainly not one undergirded by a faith in the ability of sympathy and greater understanding to solve the social ills caused by economic disparity. Furthermore, while the traditional realist novel tends to assume the developmental arc of the Bildungsroman and works to socialize and integrate the protagonist into capitalist society, Aw's novel takes a different tack. Through retrospective consideration of his own life, Ah Hock embodies the subject without much agency. Whatever hope one may have of climbing up the socio-economic ladder is always quickly dampened. Indeed, he bemoans the situation where one is led to believe in evolution only to discover its chimerical nature: "Evolution is a funny thing. For the longest time, you believe in the power of change – in your ability to mould your life through even the smallest acts" (Aw 2019b, 18–19). In Ah Hock's job as a foreman, incremental changes were enough to give him middle-class aspirations: "When life evolves like that, one small gift coming on top of another, you start to feel strong" (40). But his overriding sense of his life, ultimately established in terms of predestination and fate, means that these moments seem with hindsight nothing more than a cruel joke. Evolutionary change is in the end a repudiation rather than a justification of a linear, teleological narrative of progress for individual and society.

Besides the use of Darwinian concepts and evolutionary theory, the novel's attempt to construct a universalist imaginary is also apparent from its choice of epigraph. The novel's narrative is preceded by a quotation from Primo Levi's *If This Is a Man* (1947), also known by its American title, *Survival in Auschwitz.* Levi, an Italian Jewish writer and Holocaust survivor who wrote about his experiences in Auschwitz during World War II, had observed how inmates beaten in the concentration camp often felt no pain, only "a profound amazement: how can one hit a man without anger?" (Aw 2019b, n.p). Levi's work is, among other things, a meditation on survival. Its most obvious link to the novel's plot lies in Ah Hock's killing of Ashadul. Ah Hock's actions are presented as unintended, as self-defence that becomes unthinking, reflexive movement – "I remember raising my arm time and time again until it felt like the only thing my arm was capable of doing, that it had been created for that purpose and nothing else" (Aw 2019b, 320). The emotionless description of the murderous arm as mechanical tool resonates with the text's overriding sense of the individual's atomistic and baffled powerlessness against implacable forces set in motion by the self-running machinery of capitalism and inequality. In this inchoate universe, the ability to hit a man without anger speaks to a brutality and viciousness that seems inherent and systemic. How this occurs becomes the moral and existential question that overshadows the whole novel.

Perhaps most tellingly, the ethical dilemma raised by the deadly violence of seemingly unintended cruelty or exploitation is formally embodied in the narrative structure of the novel itself. Ah Hock tells his life story, from childhood to the point when he becomes a killer, to an interviewer, Su Min, who is writing a book about him. The novel begins in media res with Ah Hock addressing "you" – the as-yet unnamed interlocutor who turns out to be Su Min. As Ah Hock muses about things, we learn that he has been instructed to "just talk" (Aw 2019b, 10). The mediated nature of Ah Hock's oral testimony is revealed soon enough when his actions are detailed for the reader – "*sweeps hand theatrically over forehead, throws back his head in slightly camp fashion*" (17; original emphasis). The moment is meant to disconcert the reader, who is made to feel complicit in objectifying Ah Hock, as if he were a specimen being scrutinized. Ah Hock's story within the world of the novel is in effect a possibly edited transcript of Su Min's interview with him over a period of about three months. Appearing as testimony marked with dates in the novel, these pieces of Ah Hock's story are braided with his own first-person narration in the novel's narrative present. In this other account, he interacts with Su Min and makes his own observations and judgment of her.

Between the two characters, a wide age, class, and ideological gap exists, and the text repeatedly underlines their differences. Hailing from a privileged, upper-middle-class family and educated abroad, Su Min is working towards a PhD in sociology. She professes a progressive liberal politics that sees her taking part in *Bersih* demonstrations and agitating for political change.[7] Her convictions appear to Ah Hock as sheer naivety as he is unable to conceive of collective resistance to economic and social injustice. To burst her bubble and open her eyes to suffering, he admits: "I wanted her to be a part of that pain, to make sure that it seeped into her world, her clean, happy world" (Aw 2019b, 306). Su Min, on the other hand, is irritated with Ah Hock for colluding with the petty corruption that is a part of daily life in the country and annoyed by his unreconstructed views when he assumes she is heterosexual. In the novel, Su Min's intellectual labour is depicted as predatory and exploitative even as she assures Ah Hock: "We're here for your story. This is about you" (103). The tension between Ah Hock's "story" and Su Min's "book" is central to the text's moral economy as the nature of the book Su Min is writing remains a mystery. Su Min first describes it as "narrative non-fiction" or "true crime" (218). At her book party, it is described as a "novel" (324). The ambiguity seems deliberate, designed to emphasize Su Min's work as first and foremost a book – a physical commodity that can be circulated and sold. After all, a story has no economic value unless transformed quite literally into the book the reader holds in her hand. Thus, the novel throws up questions about the creative labour of Aw as a writer and the very status of fiction itself as it reflects on the ethics of storytelling. Clearly there is a reminder here that creative and imaginative work experienced by the author as unalienated labour is nevertheless still fundamentally exploitative of others – a related but different burden altogether from the epistemological and representational limitations articulated by Gayatri Spivak (1988) in "Can the Subaltern Speak?"

The novel concludes with Su Min's book party, celebrated on "an organic farm" – the choice of venue serving as ironic shorthand for the First World aspirations of the country. Out of place among the well-educated and affluent crowd, Ah Hock retreats to the periphery of the party, looking at the other guests as a silent outsider. There is no prospect here or anywhere else of bridging the gap between "[a] militant queer girl and a depressed felon" (Aw 2019b, 326), as Su Min describes them jokingly. Alone at the end, Ah Hock is a survivor but one whom a fast-moving and changing world will bypass, overlook and forget just as he "sit[s] on the concrete steps of a coffee shop, listening to the noise of the traffic from the highway nearby" (326), unable to catch a bus home from the party.

The novel's title – *We, the Survivors* – is hence undoubtedly significant. Presumably not just a literal reference to the characters who survive in the novel, the collective pronoun seems to gesture towards a universal and common humanity, making "us" complicit in the guilty politics of living and surviving. At the same time, the title also seems an indirect rallying cry for "us" to reflect and take action to dismantle – somehow – the inexorable binary logic of an inequitable and highly stratified capitalist system of winners and losers wherein those who survive are only alive because others die. In this way, the title underscores the universalist ambitions of Aw's text as seen in his use of Darwinian logic to express our interconnectness as humans through history, culture, and capitalism. By strategically claiming universalism, Aw also positions the Malaysian anglophone novel as part of world literature.

Notes

1. *The Harmony Silk Factory*, published in 2005, was Aw's first novel; it was followed in 2009 by *Map of the Invisible World*. The latter features a Malaysian subplot although the book is mainly set in Indonesia.
2. Examples of articles between 2014 and 2016 include: "Malaysia's New Immigrants", December 11, 2014; "A Return to the Malaysian Village", July 22, 2015; "Malaysia's Duty to the Rohingyas", May 27, 2015; "Malaysia's Welcome Wears Thin", August 26, 2015; "Malaysian's Immigrant Worker Debate", March 28, 2016.
3. See Lee and Leng (2018). It is likely that the actual number of foreign workers is higher, possibly 5.5 million.
4. Darwin's thinking spawned numerous related ideologies including that of social Darwinism by British philosopher and scientist Herbert Spencer, which sought to apply the same laws and principles from the natural world to human society and was popular in the late 19th and early 20th centuries. The term "survival of the fittest" was coined by Spencer.
5. See Harper (1999, 24). For the history of Chinese and Indian migration to Malaya in the 19th and early 20th centuries, see also Andaya and Andaya (2017).
6. See Milner (2008, 160).
7. Meaning "clean" in Malay, Bersih refers to the Coalition for Clean and Fair Elections. Formed in 2005, it is a social movement that has organized a series of mass rallies over the years pressing for electoral reform, anti-corruption, and greater democracy and inclusivity in Malaysia.

Disclosure statement

No potential conflict of interest was reported by the author.

References

Andaya, Barbara Watson, and Leonard Y. Andaya. 2017. *A History of Malaysia*. 3rd ed. London: Palgrave Macmillan.

Aw, Tash. 2013. *Five Star Billionaire*. London: Fourth Estate.

Aw, Tash. 2016. *The Face: Strangers on a Pier*. New York: Restless Books.

Aw, Tash. 2019a. "Tash Aw: 'Asians are Rich' Is the New Cliché." *Gulf News*, May 1. [Interview with Lisa Allardice]. https://gulfnews.com/entertainment/books/tash-aw-asians-are-rich-is-the-new-cliche-1.63362456

Aw, Tash. 2019b. *We, the Survivors*. London: Fourth Estate.

Beer, Gillian. 1983. *Darwin's Plots: Evolutionary Narrative in Darwin, George Eliot and Nineteenth-century Fiction*. London: Ark Paperbacks.

Brouillette, Sarah. 2011. *Postcolonial Writers in the Global Literary Marketplace*. London: Palgrave Macmillan.

Cheah, Pheng. 2016. *What Is a World? On Postcolonial Literature as World Literature*. Durham, NC: Duke University Press.

Clifford, James. 1997. *Routes: Travel and Translation in the Late Twentieth Century*. Cambridge, MA: Harvard University Press.

Department of Statistics Malaysia. 2021. "Official Portal." https://www.dosm.gov.my/v1/index.php?r=home/index&menu_id=OWNEc3U1QXJCQ1BuZVg0ZjcxTzlmUT09

Harper, Timothy N. 1999. *The End of Empire and the Making of Malaya*. Cambridge: Cambridge University Press.

Kennedy, Melissa. 2017. *Narratives of Inequality: Postcolonial Literary Economics*. London: Palgrave Macmillan.

Lazarus, Neil. 2011. "Cosmopolitanism and the Specificity of the Local in World Literature." *The Journal of Commonwealth Literature* 46 (1): 119–137. doi:10.1177/0021989410396037.

Lee, Hwok-Aun, and Khor Yu Leng. 2018. "Counting Migrant Workers in Malaysia: A Needlessly Persisting Conundrum." *ISEAS Perspective* 25: 1–11.

Mathews, Gordon, and Carlos Alba Vega. 2012. "Introduction: What Is Globalization from Below?" In *Globalization from Below: The World's Other Economy*, edited by Gordon Mathews, Gustavo Lins Ribeiro, and Carlos Alba Vega, 1–16. New York: Routledge.

Milner, Anthony. 2008. *The Malays*. London: Wiley-Blackwell.

Ng, Andrew. 2018. "Minority Literature, Performativity, Resistance: The Case of Anglophone and Sinophone Malaysian Writings." *Asiatic* 12 (2): 65–82.

Ng, Andrew. 2019. "The Novel of Malaysia." In *The Novel in South and South East Asia since 1945*, edited by Alex Tickell, 321–336. Oxford: Oxford University Press.

Ribeiro, Gustavo Lins. 2012. "Conclusion: Globalization from below and the Non-hegemonic World-system." In *Globalization from Below: The World's Other Economy*, edited by Gordon Mathews, Gustavo Lins Ribeiro, and Carlos Alba Vega, 221–235. New York: Routledge.

San Juan, E., Jr. 2002. "Postcolonialism and the Problematic of Uneven Development." In *Marxism, Modernity and Postcolonial Studies*, edited by Crystal Bartolovich and Neil Lazarus, 221–239. Cambridge: Cambridge University Press.

Siskind, Mariano. 2010. "The Globalization of the Novel and the Novelization of the Global: A Critique of World Literature." *Comparative Literature* 62 (4): 336–360. doi:10.1215/00104124-2010-021.

Spivak, Gayatri. 1988. "Can the Subaltern Speak?" In *Marxism and the Interpretation of Culture*, edited by Cary Nelson and Lawrence Grossberg, 271–313. Basingstoke: Macmillan.

Young, Robert. 2012. "Postcolonial Remains." *New Literary History* 43 (1): 19–42. doi:10.1353/nlh.2012.0009.

Transnational re-memorialization in Preeta Samarasan's *Evening Is the Whole Day*

Ann Ang

ABSTRACT

Preeta Samarasan's *Evening Is the Whole Day* (2008) traces the Rajasekharans' family history over three generations and re-memorializes the racial riots of May 13, 1969 from a Malaysian Indian perspective. Compared to an earlier phase of memorialization in Malaysia's national discourse about racial and cultural identity, the novel engages in the process of re-memorialization from a transnational locus, that brings together the material contexts of the Anglo American publishing industry as well as Samarasan's racialized belonging to her homeland as a mobile Malaysian. This doubly transnational frame is defined by a strong sense of injustice from a revisionist perspective, one that obscures the complex history behind Malaysia's public discourse on race and reproduces the essentialism of racial categories. The novel's regressive temporality is also a critique of Malaysia's non-progression on issues of race, as much as it forecloses other ways of rethinking racialization in Malaysia.

In an interview with *Fiction Writers Review*, Preeta Samarasan says of her debut novel: "I wanted to write a *Midnight's Children* for Malaysia – yet I wanted also to make a book that was in some ways more *female* than Rushdie's" (Samarasan 2008d, n.p.; original emphasis). *Evening Is the Whole Day* (Samarasan 2008c) is Samarasan's attempt to capture the troubled history of postcolonial Malaysia's divisive and pervasive discourse concerning race, by establishing an allegorical connection between the public sphere of the nation and the origins of a middle-class Malaysian Indian family, the Rajasekharans. Written at the distance of half a century after Malaya's independence in 1957 and the watershed racial riots of 1969, the novel is a revisionist presentation of the country's national history as well as an attempt, in Samarasan's own words, to "reveal that history [...] through individual lives" (Samarasan 2008d, n.p.). In order to depict through the lens of a Tamil household the psychological and emotional toll exacted by Malaysia's continued exclusion of non-*bumiputera* communities, the novel employs certain literary techniques that have become associated with the canon of anglophone postcolonial writing, such as allegory and a non-linear chronology. By reorienting these techniques towards a depiction of Malaysian history from this period, *Evening Is the Whole Day* re-memorializes the recent past for an international audience, as a critique of racial discrimination that is aligned with the perpetuation of injustice along other social axes, such as class, caste, and gender within the Malaysian Indian community.

This process of re-memorialization arises, firstly, from the context of the novel's production and publication for the US and UK book markets. *Evening Is the Whole Day* was, for the most part, written away from home and was first begun during Samarasan's Master of Fine Arts (MFA) programme in creative writing at the University of Michigan, where an earlier version of the novel won the Avery and Jule Hopwood Novel Award in 2006. Blurbs of Samarasan's debut novel by other literary authors positioned her work in relation to established Indian authors of the international set, with Peter Ho Davies describing *Evening Is the Whole Day* as "a magical, exuberant tragic-comic vision of post-colonial Malaysia reminiscent of Rushdie and Roy" and Ali Smith judging it to be as "furious, controlled, cool and urgent as Aravind Adiga's *White Tiger*" (Samarasan 2008c, n.p.). In an author interview, Samarasan also highlights this affiliation when she alludes to the epigraph to *The God of Small Things*, a quote from John Berger, that "never again will a single story be told as though it's the only one", so drawing an aesthetic connection between the fragmented and multiple histories of Roy's debut novel and her own (Samarasan 2008d, n.p.). Elaborating further, Samarasan lays claim to a longer tradition of English letters, specifically Charles Dickens's *Bleak House* for its focus on class and justice, and explains how she is influenced by the "big 19th-century narrator, the unapologetic prolixity, the somewhat formal, yet playful, diction" (n.p.). This underscores the positioning of Samarasan as a transnationally mobile author who can be read in relation to the larger anglophone canon, and for whom Malaysia remains a seemingly distant source of literary inspiration.

However, the novel's attempt at re-memorialization is further contextualized by Preeta Samarasan's status as a mobile Malaysian author who left the country due to social and economic barriers. In an autobiographical essay, Samarasan describes how she grew up as a member of the aspirational middle class in Malaysia in the late 1970s and early 1980s, with the keen awareness that non-Malays "would always be second-class citizens under the New Economic Policy (NEP)" (Samarasan 2020, n.p.). Her mother "took on the responsibility of making sure [she] would get out of Malaysia" (n.p.) and pushed Samarasan to excel academically to earn a scholarship, since the family was not affluent. When Samarasan finally left for pre-university in the USA, it was with a distinct sense of bitterness at the "institutionalized racism that had shaped [her] life" while continuing to feel strongly that she "had a stake in Malaysia's destiny" (n.p.), one that she expresses in her literary work as an extended critique of Malaysia's continued discrimination of non-*bumiputera*.

Hence, *Evening Is the Whole Day* is written from a doubly transnational locus, with its narrative shaped by allusions to a broader anglophone literary tradition and also textured by an exilic outwards journey from Malaysia. The present article will argue how both aspects are crucial to understanding the novel's re-memorialization of the Malaysian Indian experience of racial minoritization from a transnational locus. By first discussing the novel's paratexts in the form of its epigraphs, chapter titles, and end-matter against the Malaysian socio-historical context, I will show how the transnational circulation of Samarasan's novel also requires a translation of Malaysia's failures in social justice for a broader audience. In the second half, the article analyses the narrative's regressive temporality and its implications for Samarasan as a Malaysian author working transnationally.

Preeta Samarasan as a mobile Malaysian author

In *Evening Is the Whole Day*, Samarasan's literary project is to critique Malaysia as a nation where racialized identities are politically and economically mobilized. The plot of the novel centres on Chellam, a servant girl from the rubber plantations who goes up to the Big House, and who is subsequently framed for the death of the elderly Paati, when it is the paranoid selfishness of all other family members that results in a toxic atmosphere of indifference. Against the triumphantly progressive narrative of the first- and second-generation Rajasekherans' arrival into Malaysia, and their subsequent building of the Big House as a reflection of their increased wealth and status, Samarasan's portrayal of the middle-class Rajasekharan family is an allegory for the birth of independent Malaysia and the "selfish materialism" (2008b, 15) that resulted from a discourse of economic survivalism and interracial competition. Race, gender, and caste divisions intersect and Samarasan's novel highlights how the truly voiceless, like Chellam, bear the brunt of the hegemonic imposition of fixed identities.

In the public sphere, the experience of alienation and exclusion from the newly formed nation is focalized through Raju Rajasekharan. The eldest son of third-generation Tamil immigrants to Malaysia, he is the grandson of a shipping company magnate and the head of the Rajasekharan family at the peacock-blue Big House. Returning from Oxford to the town of Ipoh in the Malay peninsula, which had "begun to split its thin colonial skin" (Samarasan 2008c, 23), Raju is something of a cowboy figure, pondering "his place in the newborn nation" (28). While many Indians in Malaysia still regarded India as their homeland during this period and chose to return there (Vadivella Belle 2014, 282), others like Raju believed in the ideal of a "Malaya for all Malayans" (Samarasan 2008c, 44): a place where each Malaysian is a true citizen, regardless of race. After the 1969 racial riots, Raju's idealism becomes untenable and he falls into depression, "wondering if his life was over" (135). He is also especially incensed at Article 153 of the Malaysian federal constitution of 1957, which safeguards the special position of the Malays and acknowledges Malaysia as Tanah Melayu or Malay land, making them, as he points out, "the masters" (134) as opposed to Malaysian Indians who call it home.

By tracing the story of the Rajasekharan family from the time of their arrival in the peninsula in 1899 to their eldest daughter's departure in 1980 to attend university in the USA, *Evening Is the Whole Day* can be understood as portraying the psychic and social after-effects on Malaysians of Indian descent of Malaysia's public discourse on race. The present article employs the term "race" not merely as its popular English iteration of the Bahasa term *bangsa*, but also to highlight the ascriptive nature of such communal identities which have been imposed on individuals. Though processes of racialization within Malaysia have a much longer history, the bloody clashes between Malays and Chinese in Kuala Lumpur following the release of 1969 election results have been regarded as a watershed event that continues to ascribe and ethnicize the country's Malay, Chinese, and Indian communities on the basis of impermeable racial boundaries. An after-effect of such racial ascription was to obscure the internal heterogeneity and varied origins of these communities, with the Indian community, for example, comprising not just Tamils as the majority, but Malayalees and Telegus drawn through the *kangany* system, as well as Bengalis and Punjabis (Ongkili 1985, 7), while the Orang Asli were encouraged to convert to Islam and adopt markers of Malay cultural identity after they were grouped together with Malays as *bumiputera* in 1963 (Holst 2014, 106).

While it is not possible to discuss Malaysia's journey to independence in detail for lack of space, it is important to recognize that the "special position" of the Malays was part of official British policy as a form of trusteeship for indigenous institutions (Comber 2009, 13). The concept was alluded to in the decentralization debate of the 1920s, where the sultans and state councils were seen to be sidelined, thus forming the basis for a form of Malay nationalism known as *Ketuanan Melayu*, or Malay supremacy, through which the Malay race was bound inextricably to the concept of *bumiputera* or indigenous rights (Shamsul 2004, 324). The term *bumiputera* (literally "son of the soil") has a political and legal dimension in Malaysia since it refers to a group of people construed as "native" and therefore deserving of preferential treatment, although it was already in use in colonial times (Holst 2014, 33). In contrast, the term also "foreignizes" Malaysian Chinese and Malaysian Indian citizens, who are seen as "immigrants", *pendatang* (newly arrived) or *penumpang* (transients, squatters, or trespassers) (Gabriel 2015, 785–800), while the Orang Asli tribes were seen as Malay and hence *bumiputera* despite undergoing a gradual process of Malayanization.

In this complex intermingling of colonial policies amidst clashing doctrines of nativist primacy, now equated with *Ketuanan Melayu*, and the need for coexistence in the emergent Malayan nation, race was conceptualized in public discourse as an exclusionary difference between *bumiputera* and non-*bumiputera* communities that was expressed in the implementation of the NEP, as well as in the National Culture Policy (1971) which stipulated the centrality of Islam and "indigenous culture" to the nation (Holst 2014, 126). The National Language Act of 1967, designated Malay, though rightfully the pre-colonial language of the region, exclusively as the sole national language and the basis of a national literature. In a historical moment where language, race, and religion were perceived as synonymous, the non-Malay English-language writer was increasingly marginalized. Well-known poet Ee Tiang Hong sought to migrate because he "could no longer accept, intellectually or emotionally, the official and Malay definition of the Malaysian nation and culture" (Ee 1988, 36), while fellow poet Wong Phui Nam stopped writing all together in the 1970s, finding himself linguistically and culturally exiled in his own home (Wong 2007, 39).

Born in 1976, and growing up in the early 1980s, Preeta Samarasan would have experienced the political and social rubric of the NEP as racial discrimination, combining political and cultural marginalization of their ethnic group in the public sphere with policies that presented barriers to social and economic mobility. The exit strategies of non-*bumiputera* during this period are well documented, such as through higher education (Brooks and Waters 2011, 33), while the notion of "transnational exit" was present in everyday discourse (Nonini 2015, 248). Folded within such mobility was Samarasan's inheritance of the marginal status of English which was subsequently transformed into a site for a transnationally inscribed politics of protest by the subsequent publication of *Evening Is the Whole Day* in the larger anglophone book market.

Hence there is a transnational dimension to Malaysia's race discriminatory policies in the form of an escape from Malaysia, one that is registered through Samarasan's own life-trajectory and development as a writer and expressed in *Evening Is the Whole Day* as a dual address of Malaysian and international readers. Samarasan can be seen as a "mobile Malaysian", for whom Malaysia continues to be home, despite the continued understanding of race as an exclusionary state discourse mobilized as Malay ethnic nationalism. A term coined by the Malaysian sociologist Koh Sin Yee, the "mobile Malaysian" designates one who migrates abroad; such people often continue, nonetheless, to evince a strong sense of loyalty to Malaysia based on affective communal or place-based experiences (Koh 2017, 197). Typically well-educated and affluent, the mobile Malaysian Indian or Malaysian Chinese labours under racialized notions of citizenship, compounded by personal experiences of discrimination as a non-*bumiputera*. A culture of migration in search of social or economic opportunities allows mobile Malaysians to navigate structural obstacles in education, employment, and opportunities for enterprise (137). Yet, as Koh elaborates, such survivalist attitudes are frequently coupled with a discourse of disloyalty to the nation when a Malaysian relocates permanently (8). Such migration overseas to more affluent nations such as Australia and Canada in the 1970s and 1980s should not be confused with Aihwa Ong's (1999) concept of flexible citizenship (19), where multiple citizenships are a wholly pragmatic strategy for relocation and transnational capital accumulation. Instead, the prevailing view is to keep one's Malaysian citizenship "just in case" (Koh 2017, 206), thus evincing a continued racialized identification with being Malaysian Chinese or Malaysian Indian.

Existing scholarship on the novel, however, does not fully register this crucial sociohistorical context undergirding the transnational positionality of a Malaysian author, whose mobility is anchored in a racialized belonging to Malaysia, and how this context is further registered in literary representations of the past. Critics have read *Evening Is the Whole Day* as a diasporic critique of national consciousness, which testifies to how "anticolonial nationalism has not so much failed as it has not been given a chance to succeed or properly take shape" because colonial racial differences persist as a residue in terms of social and economic inequalities (Gui 2013, 182). The novel's leaping back-and-forth between different decades has also been understood against the figure of Walter Benjamin's Angel of History, whose fixation on "lost potentials that disallow the amelioration of conventional narrative closure" points to the inadequacy of cosmopolitical mobility, since Uma's departure from Malaysia does not effectively protest against the power politics of her home (Erwin 2014, 215).

Building on these approaches, the present article registers both the localized politics of race for reading *Evening Is the Whole Day* and the implications of Samarasan's transnational positioning for literary techniques in the novel as further framed by the novel's paratextual materials. More importantly, the novel's transnational address makes a claim for re-memorializing the racial discrimination of Malaysian Indians as a retelling of recent Malaysian history in the world's eyes – a claim that this article will discuss as unprecedented as well as subject to certain distortions from a temporally and spatially distant perspective.

The transnational address of *Evening Is the Whole Day*

According to Nielsen Bookscan data, *Evening Is the Whole Day* had by May 2019 sold 9668 copies in the UK, South Africa, Australia, and New Zealand, which is a not insignificant number. Moreover, as a work that is "circulating out into a broader world beyond its linguistic and cultural point of origin" (Damrosch 2003, 6), Samarasan's novel may be interestingly considered as world literature for its "mobility", though its circulation occurs amidst the cultural politics of literary gatekeeping, where Malaysian writers, in writing about their homeland, are perceived as translating and reinventing material from a lesser-known cultural location for a broader audience. With the further marketization of the postcolonial brand in the second millennium, the Anglo American publishing industry functions as a conduit for the circulation of literary works from authors on the cultural periphery. Sarah Brouillette (2011) has written at length about how these writers "face the expectation that their fiction will comment on their own locales for a larger, more diffuse audience" (8) amidst the growing corporatization and professionalization of the publication industry.

Reviews of *Evening Is the Whole Day* in the international press praise the novel for its richly realized and multilayered presentation of Malaysian history, conveyed with an emotionally charged depiction of character and situation. While commentators recognize that Samarasan's debut novel deals squarely with the racial politics of her home country, what emerges distinctly is a continuous likening of Samarasan to major Indian writers in the international arena, as part of a growing cross-cultural canon of literary fiction. *The New York Times* lauds Samarasan for "her ambitious spiraling plot, her richly embroidered prose, her sense of place" while asserting that readers will "immediately compare her to Kiran Desai" (Goodman 2008, n.p.), while *The Independent* notes that her publicists continually compare Samarasan's *Evening Is the Whole Day* to both Desai's and Arundhati Roy's first novels "as if being a young, photogenic woman of Indian origin, she shares something with them" (Tripathi 2011, n.p.). Curiously, reviews in the Malaysian newspapers have criticized *Evening Is the Whole Day* for its stock characters and stereotypical plot (*New Straits Times* 2008, 13), while another proudly reports that the novel has been well received abroad, and notes that the lack of a glossary for untranslated Malay and Tamil terms would result in an inaccurate understanding of local nuances (Mehta 2008, 62). Both sets of responses point to an assumed responsibility towards cultural and national representation, one that is further complicated by the perception, in the international press, that Samarasan's novel is part of "the quiet emergence of new Malaysian writing" into the world (Tripathi 2011, n.p.)

For a broader audience, the transnational address of *Evening Is the Whole Day* thus possesses the quality of being unprecedented, in its extended representation of the racial troubles encountered by the Malaysian Indian minority, which is itself a re-memorialization in literary form of events in Malaysia up to the 1980s. The earlier memorialization of racial unrest leading up to the May 13, 1969 incident occurred amidst national debates about the cultural and linguistic fabric of the nation, undergirded by tribalist loyalties that situated language usage within the framework of ethno-linguistic nationalism (Leow 2016, 180).

Though Malay could potentially have been a language of national inter-communication, it became a "a static, highly exclusionist expression of Melayu hegemony" (Leow 2016, 180). A significant moral majority continues to demonstrate a "passion for race" as proof of communal loyalties (Lim 2008, 3). As an after-effect, English-language literary works from the 1980s demonstrate a focus on the ethnic community of the author and "a noticeable withdrawal from engagement with multi-ethnic and multi-religious issues" (Ng 2019, 328).

By contrast, the re-memorialization in *Evening Is the Whole Day* is constructed from an important transnational locus that brings together the material contexts of the publishing industry as well as Samarasan's racialized and diasporic belonging to her homeland. As part of a wider and more complex circuit, Samarasan's literary representation is equated with the making of a truth-claim to a new audience about the racialized injustice encountered by Malaysian Indians throughout the years. This positioning of Samarasan and her novel as historically revisionist is also supported by the epigraphs to the novel, which provide the preliminary framing of the narrative. An extract from *Waterland* by Graham Swift pays tribute to an aesthetics of fragmented narrative style and the importance of prolepsis and analepsis in revealing the root causes of contemporary events through the reconstruction of the past. "History begins only at the point when thing go wrong", the quote begins; it concludes with the wistful query "if only we could have it back. A New Beginning" (Samarasan 2008c, i). The second epigraph is an English translation from the classic Tamil love-poem cycle, the Kuruntokai, and laments how the "pain grows sharp", while "evening is the whole day / for those without their lovers" (Samarasan 2008c, i), as a gesture of interminable and endless waiting in the twilight in a divided community. Both quotes point to the novel's protest against the deep historical roots of racialization in Malaysian history, and the ongoing, undisrupted racial minoritization of ethnic Indians. Yet equally, these epigraphs establish an affiliation with a wider tradition of contemporary letters, of which Swift is a representative, and to which classical Tamil poetry belongs via translation, and so indicate how *Evening Is the Whole Day* adopts a transnational address that transcends the hegemonic discourse of race and public ethno-nationalism in Malaysia's public arena.

The transnational address of *Evening is the Whole Day* is also present in several stylistic allusions that pay homage to the broader anglophone canon, while marshalling these literary techniques in service of an intergenerational tale about the Rajasekharans during the decades immediately before and after Malaysia's independence in 1957. In its account of the Tamil immigrant's in-journey and the loss of cultural identity amidst independent Malaysia's first years of economic development, Samarasan's novel features subject matter that has already been depicted in K.S. Maniam's classic trilogy of *The Return* (1981), *In a Far Country* (1993), and *Between Lives* (2003). In contrast to Maniam's work, however, *Evening Is the Whole Day* is made accessible to a broader audience through strikingly recognizable tropes, with the Big House of the Rajasekharans a parallel to the Caribbean plantation house and the English country mansion. Individual chapter titles, such as "After Great Expectations", situate class concerns of marrying-up in Samarasan's novel within a Dickensian frame, while "What Aasha Saw" alludes to Henry James's *What Maisie Knew*, as a further intertext featuring a precocious girl growing up amidst her parents' failing marriage. In the *Fiction Writers Review* interview (Samarasan 2008d), *Midnight's Children* is explicitly cited as a "big influence" (n.p.), and Samarasan taps into the earlier work's hyperbolic depiction of a nation's birth amidst a dazzlingly erratic chronology, to make a claim to representing Malaysia's birth not as the moment of political independence in 1957, but as the crisis of May 13, 1969, where aspirations to racial equality were stifled.

In the chapter "Power Struggles", the events of that evening are depicted as equivalent to the birth of Malaysia as a nation defined by racial grievance. During the violence, Suresh, the second child of the Rajasekharans, is born "wet with the brave blood of life and hope, while so near and yet so far away the heroes of Malay Land soared through the skies, soaked with a seamier blood" (Samarasan 2008c, 133), that of the victims, both Chinese and Indian, of ongoing racial clashes in the streets. When Suresh's mother goes into labour on "that night of bloodshed and bedlam, of dreams sent up in flames and ideals abandoned in dirty back alleys" (133), her sister and brother-in-law attempt to take her to the hospital in a taxi, but their way is blocked by armed Malay rioters. They are spared from further violence because they are "Orang Keling" and "mere bloody Indians" (132) rather than the Chinese, who are being targeted that night. The boy is born in the back seat of the car, in full view of a disintegrating society where "Rumour and Fact fornicated openly" (127). Unlike Rushdie's Saleem Sinai, who was born at the stroke of midnight when India became independent, and whose mistaken identity is an occasion to trace the "excess of intertwined lives events miracles places rumours" (Rushdie 2005, 9) and the "consumed multitudes" (9) celebrated as part of the India's multifarious genealogies, Suresh was born into his racialized identity as a Malaysian Indian, which is inscribed through an act of fearful submission to Malay ethno-nationalism.

By orienting a famously allegorical scene away from *Midnight's Children* towards a depiction of the injurious racial grievances of Malaysian Indians, *Evening Is the Whole Day* can be usefully considered a form of multidirectional memory constructed from Samarasan's transnational position, which exists in competition and dialogue with public discourses on race within Malaysia's national space. Though originally theorized by Michael Rothberg (2009) in the context of the Holocaust, multidirectional memory is "subject to ongoing negotiation, cross-referencing, and borrowing; as productive and not privative" (3), and builds on Jan Assman and John Czaplicka's (1995, 129) distinction between two types of cultural memory, the fluidity and intimacy of everyday communicative memory and the external objectification of collective memory in its temporal distance. As discussed above, a scene filled with the bloodied screams of rioters and the ventriloquizing of the crudest anti-*bumiputera* views in phrases such as "No means please shaddup your mouth" and "Go back where you came from" (Samarasan 2008c, 134) is powerfully vivid, and therefore can be seen as exercising the immediacy of communicative memory through stylistic techniques. The literary text, therefore, becomes a site of vibrant re-memorialization, with the potential to intervene in collective memory and to re-imagine the enunciative frame of race as public memory in Malaysia.

The extended work of multidirectional memory can also be perceived in the postscripts to the novel's main narrative, which comprise an interview with the author titled "Only the Past Has It" (Samarasan 2008a) and a reflective essay by Samarasan (2008b) herself on contemporary Malaysia, "The Deepest Wounds". The pernicious effects of racial discourse in Malaysia are again brought to the attention of an international audience by these paratexts that question the dominance of Malay interests. Reminiscent of the supplementary content of many novels that ply the international arena, these paratexts frame the text for readers less familiar with Malaysia and set out not only the basics of Malaysian culture and history, but also a clear oppositional stance to general attitudes towards race in Malaysia, which Samarasan terms "legalized racism" (2008b, 15). It is impossible for an anglophone reader experiencing Malaysian writing for the first time to read the novel apolitically, without a sense of the country's troubled inheritance of racial identities, including those that minoritize the Indian community, and yet it is worth querying further if the transnational locus from which Samarasan writes might lead to certain distortions of historical understanding that hinder a more transformative critique of race.

In "The Deepest Wounds", Samarasan singles out "apathy" as her "country's most insidious epidemic" (2008b, 12) – the metaphor of disease underscoring her accusation. She draws a connection between the materialism and self-absorption of Malaysia in the 1980s and the structure of racial difference inaugurated by the 1969 riots. Traced across the generations, the fate of the Rajasekharan family is a microcosm of events in the nation. "Quietly, at home", Samarasan elaborates,

> we teach our children that we have to step on others to rise, the Malays on the Indians and Chinese, the Chinese on the Indians, and the Indians, to whom is left the smallest piece of the pie, even on each other. (2008b, 15)

However, against the gradual emergence of Malaysia's racialized appellations, it appears that Samarasan has inherited, and is in turn reinforcing, the homogenized racial identities which have been perpetuated since the Alliance of 1953. In the lead-up to independence in 1957, racialized political parties representing the largest ethnic groups, namely the Malaysian Chinese Association (MCA) and the Malaysian Indian Congress (MIC), became part of an electoral coalition with the United Malays National Organization (UMNO). Known as the Alliance, it was an expedient bargain to ensure a political majority and has for the most part succeeded in doing so since the country's municipal elections in 1952. Frederik Holst has discussed extensively how the Alliance resulted in a further a manifestation of homogenized "Malay", "Chinese", and "Indian" racial identities, which became further polarized following the May 13 incident in 1969, thus allowing the Alliance, later renamed the Barisan Nasional (BN) in 1973, to solidify its role as an arbitrator of racial relations. By viewing race relations as occurring between the ascriptive identities of "Malay", "Chinese", and "Indian", and according to a rather simplified hierarchy of one racialized group trampling upon another, Samarasan's commentary obscures the complex processes by which racialization intersected with political and economic formations of the time. Additionally, the varied composition of these racial communities is erased, and, in the course of *Evening Is the Whole Day*, the story of upwardly mobile Tamil immigrants, refracted by caste distinctions within their community, such as the denigration of Chellamservant for her rubber-estate origins and Amma for her dark skin (Samarasan 2008c, 91), is taken as representative of the Malaysian Indian experience without mention of other minority Indian communities such as the Gujaratis or Assamese. Ironically, Samarasan's narrative reinforces external views on the Malaysian Indian community as Tamilian, further evinced in the novel when an overly friendly Malay man addresses young Uma in the train as "thangggachi" or Tamil for "little sister" (116).

A similarly problematic attempt at a transnational address occurs when Samarasan describes the NEP of 1970 as "apartheid with a tarted-up face" (2008b, 15), in an attempt to translate Malaysia's racial discrimination into a larger cultural idiom. However, by comparing the NEP with apartheid in South Africa, Samarasan equates its pro-*bumiputera* stance with the disproportionate ownership and domination of economic and social assets by South Africa's white minority, thus effacing earlier developments under the British administration, which had effectively kept many ethnic Malays from acquiring capital and participating in a modern industrial economy (Comber 2009, 6). A further context that would be apparent to contemporary readers is the role of South Africa's Truth and Reconciliation Commission (TRC) in reframing the history of apartheid's brutal segregationist policies as part of the country's transition to democratic constitutionalism. Beginning in 1994, the task of the Commission was to "foster and repair what its report refers to variously as 'national memory', 'public memory', and 'social memory' " (Sanders 2007, 36). At the heart of the TRC process was a process of mournful witnessing and memorialization through the act of confession, as part of a larger effort to "redeem that suffering in its telling and in the contribution of that truth to the production of a new moral order" (Posel 2008, 128). As a literary text, *Evening Is the Whole Day* is engaged in a parallel, though not identical, effort, as an act of imaginative witnessing. The novel is an attempt to redress the grievances of the Malaysian Indian community but, unlike the TRC, offers little reconciliation by way of depicting what a more egalitarian Malaysia might be like, except in allusions to a Malaysian Malaysia, articulated through Raju's failed political ambitions.

On the whole, Samarasan's re-memorialization of Malaysia's formative years through a transnational address is heavily invested in reorienting a narrative of racialized non-*bumiputera* exclusion towards a broader audience beyond Malaysia and as part of a longer anglophone literary tradition. Yet in facilitating the narrative's cross-border circulation, Samarasan does simplify the complex historical origins of race and racialized hierarchies in Malaysia. Her novel paradoxically relies on race as an essentializing category while critiquing it as the cause of disempowerment for non-*bumiputera* in Malaysia. As a form of multidirectional memory from a transnational locus, *Evening Is the Whole Day* would seem to invite comparisons with global memory studies, which refuse a national methodology by questioning the "unalienable inheritance that binds groups to a particular identity fixed in the past" and recognize the generative horizontality of transnational memory production (De Cesari and Rigney 2014, 9). But in yoking the history of Malaysia to a recounting of the racialized injustice encountered by Malaysian Indians, Samarasan's debut work ironically binds itself to race as a site of righteous redress, and to the Malaysian nation with its foreignizing discourse on the non-*bumiputera*.

Racialized belonging as regressive temporality

Despite the complexities of representing Malaysia's cultural politics via a transnational address, *Evening Is the Whole Day* can nonetheless be read as a trenchant critique of race in Malaysia, one all the more striking when historical progress, rendered as a movement towards egalitarianism and away from the claustrophobic discourse of race, and other hegemonic identity discourses, such as class, caste, and gender, is presented as well-nigh impossible. Samarasan's novel is distinctive for its non-chronological structuration, which shuttles between the 1960s and the 1980s as separate time periods, while the narrative progresses in a deceptive forward movement towards Uma's departure from Malaysia for university. A transnational exit from Malaysia, as implied by the narrative's insistence on the home country as a setting, does not mean leaving one's origins behind, and the novel's temporally regressive structure reflects both an indictment of Malaysia's non-progress on issues of race, and how Samarasan's umbilical connection to her homeland requires a sad acceptance of her racialized exclusion as a non-*bumiputera*. For Samarasan as a mobile

Malaysian author, the outward journey from her country is negated by the all-consuming need to return, via a historically revisionist perspective, to the root causes of racial discrimination.

In a more recent interview, Samarasan speaks about her process of arriving at telling the "Now story backwards" (2018, n.p.), as alternating between two timelines would allow readers to focus on the "why and how" after hearing about the plot-ending at the start. After first learning about Paati's death in the first chapter, readers experience the continued splicing of episodes contrasting the younger and happier Rajasekharans with their disillusioned and older selves, which results in a slow revealing of the psychological processes that have led to the entire household demonizing Chellam. At the same time, this narrative technique of juxtaposing past and present junctures from public history makes readers feel keenly how the aspirations of multiracial Malaysia have been sidelined by racist attitudes and individualistic and unprincipled ambitions. As an anti-national allegory, the novel enacts the process of false progress as a critique of Malaysia's growing material prosperity, while Malaysian Indians, especially the displaced working classes on the rubber plantations, continue to be excluded from full participation in the Malaysian national imaginary and a more equitable distribution of wealth. The last two chapters in the novel, titled "The Golden Descent of Chellam, the Bringer of Succor" (dated chronologically before Paati's death) and "The Glorious Ascent of Uma the Oldest-Eldest" (dated after), offer the illusion of hope by presenting characters analeptically before the tragedy, and, just as Uma is about to leave Malaysia, pitting the mythic register of these chapters against the novel's investment in critiquing but also portraying race, class, and gender in Malaysia as deeply rooted social discourses.

While none of the novel's characters break free from the historical events that inexorably limited and shaped their lives, much of the unwarranted violence in the novel is directed against Chellam, a term of endearment in Tamil, meaning "darling", which serves to underscore ironically both her namelessness and the minimal affection she receives from either her drunken, exploitative father or her employer's family at the Big House. A lower-caste servant girl from the rubber plantations who goes up to the Big House, Chellam is subsequently framed for the death of the elderly Paati, the grandmother of the house and Raju's mother. Predictably, most of the abuse that she receives is at the hands of Raju. As soon as Aasha identifies Chellam as the cause of Paati's death, he unleashes a vitriolic outburst, calling her a "shameless prostitute" and a "killer" (Samarasan 2008c, 163). While his character showcases the racial discrimination experienced by a Malaysian Indian despite the privileges of education and wealth, his actions foreground a further intersectional alignment of such discrimination with the way he treats a female Indian from a lower socio-economic class. Dashini Jeyathurai (2012) reads Chellam's labouring self as also the female body exposed and abused. Her broken English and unsanitary habits, which the Rajasekharan children make fun of, are markers not merely of class and caste differences, but also of "disturbing cultural and national narratives that many wish to forget" (311). In particular, Chellam is a living embodiment of Malaysia's failed decolonization, which has kept the economic apparatus of the British plantation system intact, forming an underclass of Indian rubber-tapper families who remain resident on these estates in a cycle of impoverishment.

The non-chronological temporality of *Evening Is the Whole Day* fills Chellam's tale with added poignancy, when her return from the Big House to her abusive father is contrasted with the flashback to her hopeful arrival at a new place of work in the book's second-last chapter. Only Aasha's morbid and vague speculations permit the presence of "Chellam Future" as a suicide, "her eyes wild as she screams to them from her funeral pyre [...] whole bitter planets orbiting at the back of her gaping mouth" (Samarasan 2008c, 9). Implausible as these fantasies may seem, such fiery and vivid imagery nonetheless expresses the injustice of omitting such narratives from Malaysia's history. These references to ghosts in the first pages of the novel foretell the tragedies to come, while functioning as a *récit* to highlight the arrested futurities implied by ghosts. Their continued haunting hints at a deep mourning over the lack of political action that makes Chellam a subaltern-victim (Spivak 1988, 80) at the intersecting discourses of violence of race and class. "Life will go on as it did before Chellam ever arrived", the omniscient narrator observes with barely concealed sarcasm, "or even better, except there'll be new ghosts in the house" (Samarasan 2008c, 9). As a story of arrested social mobility, Chellam's trajectory might be first understood as the tragic counterpoint to Uma's outwards journey, except that her doomed "golden descent" into the Rajasekharan household, chronicled against Uma's "glorious ascent", reads as an ominous foreboding about this second, new beginning.

If there is one character who stands a chance of escaping the regressive temporality of the novel's obsessive critique of race, it would be Uma. Before winning a scholarship to go to New York for university study, young Uma was precociously intelligent and bright-eyed for her age, her "supernal brilliance" (Samarasan 2008c, 105) capturing the attention of her parents and Paati sufficiently to distract them from their mutual animosity, so that "they all imagined exactly the same thing" (106) as they fed her with Scott's Emulsion and lavished her with Fisher-Price toys. "They watched her grow as if she were a hero-child in a folktale" (105), which quickly turns out to be a fairy tale, when Uma turns out to be adored less for her character and talents than as war booty in the ensuing household rivalry, with her grandmother encouraging Uma to dismiss the doll-games and pretty clothes as indicative of her mother's superficiality. This brief and transient period of hope where the Rajasekharans "wondered if they might now be an almost normal family" (105) is allegorized to the "afterglow" (106) of Malaysia's early years as a nation. After her own father molests her in a drunken episode, which Paati witnesses but keeps silent about to protect her son above her granddaughter, Uma descends into a period of enraged muteness, playing Simon and Garfunkel on loop. Like Chellam, the forestalled temporality of Uma's growing up has its root cause in the intersectional violence enacted as the pathological control of the female body. To escape these toxic realities of gender and class, for which the Rajasekharan household is a microcosm of the nation, Uma has no option but to escape from Malaysia.

A further effect of this continuous retreat into the past, despite Uma's departure, is to present the notion of transnational exit as only a temporary departure from the country's hold on one's origins. Uma never writes back to her family, and the only scenes that depict her newfound freedom in America are present in the narrative through Raju's imaginary tales about his eldest daughter and the fantasies of Aasha, his youngest child, who is pining for Uma's affection. The closing pages of the novel feature Raju in the home of his Chinese mistress and surrounded by his mixed-race children, where he dreams out loud about the "Ghost of Uma Future" in a country where "you can go there a nobody, a no-name orphan, and tomorrow find yourself a United States senator" (Samarasan 2008c, 339). The visual fantasy of Uma striding down New York's pavements in a stylish trench coat embodies Raju's own deep desire to reinvent himself outside race as a historically entrenched category. This unrealistic aspiration is described further as a fairy-tale "Happily Ever After in which Appa's Chindian children, and his awestruck mistress, and Appa himself, can believe" (339). Likewise, Aasha's fantasies about her sister's new life are equally nebulous and function as an intense envisioning of life outside Malaysia's restrictive subject positions for a Malaysian Indian woman. "With a psychic's clarity", Aasha sees how the "Ghost of Uma Future" will be "many different someone elses" including Uma as "an American girl buying hot dogs from a stand" (326). Dressed, like any other girl, according to the changing seasons in New York, "her head [is] held high, because emptied of old faces, it's lighter than anyone else's" (326). These visions haunt a novel exclusively anchored in Malaysia's historical chronotope, which Mikhail Bakhtin (1981) defines as an organizing centre "for the fundamental narrative events of the novel" (57), and convey a strong yearning for an identity free from the historical inheritance of racialized categories – a yearning that is never fulfilled, though amply expressed through Aasha's imagination. With neither Uma nor Chellam able to transcend their beginnings, *Evening Is the Whole Day* in its regressive temporality rejects the possibility of growth or change, and, by extension, the viability of an alternative future.

Conclusion

As Samarasan herself says in an interview, there was never "a *substantial* post-Malaysia section" (Samarasan 2008d; emphasis in original). Though her text may be seen as an example of the Malaysian novel as "a uniquely disembedded literary form" (Holden 2012, 52) that is easily transported across geographies, *Evening Is the Whole Day* demonstrates how a literary work produced on the transnational circuit, and stylistically shaped by its transnational address of a broader audience, can remain resolutely situated in the cultural politics of an author's origin. In large part this is due to the nature of Samarasan's re-memorialization of the racial discrimination faced by Malaysian Indians as an unresolved and ongoing grievance, which in turn highlights how her diasporic relationship to her homeland remains racialized according to Malaysia's historical formations.

While Samarasan's debut novel effects a powerful critique of the racialized exclusion of non-*bumiputera*, its transnational re-memorialization may not fully depict the complex origins of race as a contemporary social formation in Malaysia, or the varied composition of the Malaysian Indian community. By favouring an idiom of protest that circulates beyond Malaysia, *Evening Is the Whole Day* is indelibly shaped by Samarasan's transnational leave-taking from her homeland as a non-*bumiputera* excluded from full participation in the national imagination, and who remains Malaysian through her narrative's continual return to the historical roots of such exclusion.

Disclosure statement

No pontential conflict of interest was reported by the author.

ORCID

Ann Ang http://orcid.org/0000-0002-5954-2459

References

Assmann, Jan, and John Czaplicka. 1995. "Collective Memory and Cultural Identity." *New German Critique* 65 (65): 125–133. doi:10.2307/488538.

Bakhtin, M. M. 1981. *The Dialogic Imagination: Four Essays*, Edited by Caryl Emerson and Michael Holquist. Austin, TX: University of Texas Press.

Brooks, Rachel, and Johanna L. Waters. 2011. *Student Mobilities, Migration and the Internationalization of Higher Education*. Basingstoke: Palgrave Macmillan.

Brouillette, Sarah. 2011. *Postcolonial Writers in the Global Literary Marketplace*. Basingstoke: Palgrave Macmillan.

Comber, Leon. 2009. *13 May 1969: The Darkest Day in Malaysian History*. Singapore: Marshall Cavendish Editions.

Damrosch, David. 2003. *What Is World Literature?* Princeton, NJ: Princeton University Press.

De Cesari, Chiara, and Ann Rigney. 2014. *Transnational Memory: Circulation, Articulation, Scales, Media and Cultural Memory*. Berlin: Walter de Gruyter GmbH.

Ee, Tiang Hong. 1988. "Literature and Liberation: The Price of Freedom." In *Literature and Liberation: Five Essays from Southeast Asia*, edited by Edwin Thumboo, 11–42. Manila, Philippines: Solidaridad Publishing House.

Erwin, Lee.2014. "Class and the Time of the Nation in Preeta Samarasan's *Evening Is the Whole Day*." *Ariel* 45 (1–2): 195–220. doi:10.1353/ari.2014.0002.

Gabriel, Sharmani P. 2015. "The Meaning of Race in Malaysia: Colonial, Post-colonial and Possible New Conjunctures." *Ethnicities* 15 (6): 782–809. doi:10.1177/1468796815570347.

Goodman, Allegra. 2008. "'What Aasha Saw': Review of *Evening Is the Whole Day*, by Preeta Samarasan." *The New York Times*, July 27. https://www.nytimes.com/2008/07/27/books/review/Goodman-t.html

Gui, Weihsin. 2013. *National Consciousness and Literary Cosmopolitics*. Columbus, OH: Ohio State University Press.

Holden, Philip. 2012. "Global Malaysian Novels: Prospects and Possibilities." *Kajian Malaysia: Journal of Malaysian Studies* 30: 47–59.

Holst, Frederik. 2014. *Ethnicization and Identity Construction in Malaysia*. Abingdon and New York: Routledge.

Jeyathurai, Dashini. 2012. "Labouring Bodies, Labouring Histories: The Malaysian-Indian Estate Girl." *The Journal of Commonwealth Literature* 47 (3): 303–323. doi:10.1177/0021989412450703.

Koh, Sin Yee. 2017. *Race, Education, and Citizenship*. New York: Palgrave Macmillan.

Leow, Rachel. 2016. *Taming Babel: Language in the Making of Malaysia*. Cambridge: Cambridge University Press.

Lim, David C. L. 2008. *Overcoming Passion for Race in Malaysia Cultural Studies*. Leiden and Boston: Brill.

Mehta, Manik. 2008. "Putting Malaysia on the World Literary Map: Review of *Evening Is the Whole Day*, by Preeta Samarasan." *Malaysia Business*, October 1.

New Straits Times. 2008. "Oh, Such Drama." August 23, p. 13.

Ng Soon Hock, A. 2019. "The Novel of Malaysia." In *The Novel in South and South East Asia since 1945*, edited by Alex Tickell, 321–336. Oxford: Oxford University Press.

Nonini, Donald Macon. 2015. *Getting By: Class and State Formation among Chinese in Malaysia*. Ithaca, NY: Cornell University Press.

Ong, Aihwa. 1999. *Flexible Citizenship: The Cultural Logics of Transnationality*. Durham, NC: Duke University Press.

Ongkili, James P. 1985. *Nation-building in Malaysia 1946–1974*. Singapore: Oxford University Press.

Posel, Deborah. 2008. "History as Confession: The Case of the South African Truth and Reconciliation Commission." *Public Culture* 20 (1): 119–141. doi:10.1215/08992363-2007-019.

Rothberg, Michael. 2009. *Multidirectional Memory: Remembering the Holocaust in the Age of Decolonization, Cultural Memory in the Present*. Stanford, CA: Stanford University Press.

Rushdie, Salman. 2005. *Midnight's Children*. London: Vintage.

Samarasan, Preeta. 2008a. "Only the Past Has It: Travis Elborough Talks to Preeta Samarasan." In *Evening Is the Whole Day*, 3–11. London: Fourth Estate.

Samarasan, Preeta. 2008b. "The Deepest Wounds." In *Evening Is the Whole Day*, by Preeta Samarasan, 12–16. London: Fourth Estate.

Samarasan, Preeta. 2008c. *Evening Is the Whole Day*. London: Harper Perennial.

Samarasan, Preeta. 2008d. "Interview with Preeta Samarasan, *Evening Is the Whole Day* [With Anne Stamekhin]." *Fiction Writers Review*, October 4. https://fictionwritersreview.com/interview/preeta-samarasan-evening-is-the-whole-day/

Samarasan, Preeta. 2018. "Robert Raymer Chats with French-based Malaysian Writer Preeta Samarasan." *Borneo Expat Writer* Blog, January. http://borneoexpatwriter.blogspot.com/2018/01/interview-preeta-samarasan-robert.html

Samarasan, Preeta. 2020. "Malaysian Writer Preeta Samarasan on How Her Country's Systemic Racism Forced Her to Move Abroad and How She Still Mourns the Loss of the Nation Which Never Quite Accepted Her." *The Culture Review Mag*, April 23. https://theculturereviewmag.com/2020/04/23/malaysian-writer-preeta-samarasan-on-her-countrys-systemic-racism-why-she-moved-abroad-and-how-she-still-mourns-the-loss-of-her-country-who-never-quite-accepted-her/

Sanders, Mark. 2007. *Ambiguities of Witnessing: Law and Literature in the Time of a Truth Commission*. Stanford, CA: Stanford University Press.

Shamsul, Amri Baharuddin. 2004. "History of Identity, an Identity of a History: The Idea and Practise of 'Malayness' in Malaysia Reconsidered." In *Contesting Malayness: Malay Identity across Boundaries*, edited by Timothy P. Barnard, 135–148. Singapore: Singapore University Press.

Spivak, Gayatri Chakravorty. 1988. *Can the Subaltern Speak?* Basingstoke: Macmillan.

Tripathi, Salil. 2011. "Review: *Evening Is the Whole Day*, by Preeta Samarasan." *The Independent*, October 23. https://www.independent.co.uk/arts-entertainment/books/reviews/evening-is-the-whole-day-by-preeta-samarasan-846082.html

Vadivella Belle, Carl. 2014. *Tragic Orphans: Indians in Malaysia*. Singapore: ISEAS Publishing.

Wong, Phui Nam. 2007. "Getting to Speak without a Language." In *From the Inside: Asia Pacific Literature in Englishes*, edited by Edwin Thumboo and Rex Ian Sayson, 33–45. Singapore: Ethos Books.

Interracial relations and the post-postcolonial future in Zen Cho's *Spirits Abroad*

Grace V.S. Chin

ABSTRACT

Malaysian supernatural and fantasy fiction typically belong to culture-specific mythologies that stay within the limits and boundaries of race and ethnicity. Zen Cho's collection of fantasy short fiction *Spirits Abroad*, however, defies these limits and boundaries – and indirectly the ethnocentric politics of Malaysia – through representations of interracial and interspecies relationships. Exploring the emotional connections between human and magical or supernatural beings in selected stories, this article examines Cho's subversive vision and articulation of an *other*-Malaysia that is made up of interstitial spaces and hybridized identities, and where the hierarchies and boundaries between native and migrant, self and other are dissolved. Her revisionary narratives not only contribute to the decolonizing of postcolonial Malaysia's binary discourses and narratives of race and ethnicity, but are also essential to the imagining of a post-postcolonial Malaysian future.

Introduction

The ethnocultural divisions and boundaries found in Malaysian literature in English (MLE) are well established (Chin 2006; Quayum 2008, 2018). Rooted in the historical systems of colonial divide-and-rule, these divisions and boundaries were exacerbated by the state's authoritarian implementation of pro-Malay policies in the early 1970s, notably the New Economic Policy (NEP), the National Education Policy, and National Culture Policy, which were aimed at the political advancement of the majority Malay ethnic group, Malay language, and Islam in the nation space. By continuing the colonial epistemological legacies of race, the postcolonial state has created a fractured society that is organized around the binary politics of identity, with the Malays established as masculine *Bumiputera* (sons of the soil) while the non-Malays/non-*Bumiputera* are feminized as racial – and, increasingly, religious – other, especially the Chinese and Indians who, even today, are labelled *pendatang* (immigrant) by ultra-Malay politicians. Tapping into these historical and sociopolitical developments, MLE has produced important works that interrogate, critique, resist, and reject the divisive discourses of race and ethnicity by espousing inclusivity, hybridity, and plurality – especially those by the older-generation writers like Lloyd Fernando, Shirley Geok-lin Lim, Lee Kok Liang, and K.S. Maniam (Quayum 2007). However, these very same discourses have also taken their toll on the literary scene, which has become "fragmented", carrying perspectives and voices that are "culturally insular, rather than encompassing, in their imagination" (Quayum 2018, 1). These polarizing effects can also be traced in the works of transnational or diasporic Malaysian authors – the majority of whom are non-Malay – who have retained the idea of a divided nation, with Malaysia viewed as the site of marginality, exclusion, exile, and loss (Chin 2006; Quayum 2008; Boey 2018). This situation thus begs the crucial questions: can MLE move past or beyond the polarizing and binary politics of postcolonial Malaysia? And what might that future look like?

Since the 1980s, works by Malaysian writers who have migrated abroad have opened up new scholarly avenues of pursuit as they espouse a global, diasporic, or transnational and inclusive perspective that also challenges Malaysia's culturally insular gaze. Zen Cho not only belongs to this diasporic group of writers but her collection of short fiction, *Spirits Abroad*, offers a different direction in the study of MLE. Inspired by supernatural and fantastical tales from Malaysia and Europe, Cho's stories of interracial and interspecies relationships defy conventional notions and discourses of otherness and marginality that have been established as part of the MLE tradition and its attendant scholarship. Although Cho works within the tradition of resistance and inclusivity established by the older generation mentioned earlier, she also breaks away from it by writing in the popular and speculative genres of science fiction and fantasy, which do not readily fit the "highbrow" literary aesthetics associated with the canonical works and authors of MLE. Published under the aegis of Fixi Novo (an imprint of the local publisher Buku Fixi, which specializes in anglophone writing in popular genres like noir, thriller, and speculative fiction), *Spirits Abroad* and other Fixi Novo publications appeal to the culturally contemporary and globally conscious generation of urban and tech-savvy anglophone Malaysian readers. While representing a departure from the MLE tradition, such publications are nonetheless a welcome development as they present new Malaysian voices, viewpoints, and visions, including Cho's.

A relative newcomer to the MLE scene, the Malaysian born-and-bred but UK-based Cho has been awarded the Crawford, British Fantasy, and Hugo Awards for her works in fantasy and science fiction, which to date include three novels, two novellas, and a collection of short stories (https://zencho.org/). Cho has stated that these genres have opened up new symbolic territories through which she can imagine and express that "what the ordinary Malaysian believes about the world is true"; more importantly, they have become "part of [her] process of decolonisation" (https://zencho.org/faq/). This process of decolonizing the postcolonial Malaysian racialized self is, I contend, reflected in her forward-looking vision and articulation of an *other*-Malaysia; in this case, an alternative fantasy world system inhabited by human, magical, and supernatural beings and non-human species. Through stories that depict this *other*-Malaysia, Cho articulates one possibility of a future post-postcolonial Malaysian society and what it can be: an inclusive, pluralistic, and intercultural world where the native and migrant as well as self and other are entangled and mixed. In this manner too, her vision is distinct from that of the older-generation writers who, while upholding an inclusive vision of Malaysia, still work within the more realistic frames of race and ethnicity, based on history, nation, culture, and society (Quayum 2008; Raihanah 2009). Tapping into the "what-if" and "what-can-be" possibilities offered by the fantasy genre, Cho's decolonizing gaze can be seen in her wilful and subversive acts of critiquing, destabilizing, and transgressing the established boundaries, binaries, and divisions of race and, occasionally, gender and sexuality. In this *other*-Malaysia, difference and diversity are celebrated through interracial relationships that not only resist and rewrite the ethnocentric narratives and binary polemics of postcolonial Malaysia, but are also vital to the imagining of a post-postcolonial future.

Post-postcolonialism? Interstitiality and the idea of "beyond"

The question of what lies beyond postcolonialism was raised as early as the 1990s (see Maes-Jelinek 2004, 9). More recently, scholars have proposed "post-postcolonialism" and what it entails as a concept or theory. Engaging with recent developments in European literature, Dirk Göttsche (2017) defines post-postcolonialism as involving "new discursive formations" that are "too distinct to still be usefully subsumed under the 'postcolonial'" (120). These new formations are found in the popular contemporary discourses of diaspora, transnationalism, globalization, and cultural hybridity, which are moving the focus and discussion beyond the postcolonial framework. Eyoh Etim (2019) similarly argues that post-postcolonialism involves a paradigm shift; however, her perspective is based on the need to redefine, reassess, and reposition Africa's postcolonial discourses, in particular African literature, which she claims has "met its aporia, that is, its dead end" (1). For Etim, post-postcolonialism is a "periphery-searching and margin-centering theory" that "creates a centre out of the Otherness of Africa" (5) while binaries – self/other, centre/periphery – are "jettisoned so that the focus can be on the Other and the Periphery" (6). Here, clearly, post-postcolonialism is conceived as a decolonial strategy that can be used to move the conversation "forward" (4) or even "beyond" (1) the (neo)colonial systems and epistemes that have been maintained in the construction and development of Africa's postcolonial societies.

While sharing Göttsche's and Etim's views that post-postcolonialism posits a new critical way of thinking about and looking at postcolonialism, my discussion is specifically based on the sociopolitical and cultural contexts of postcolonial Malaysia and, more pertinently, how post-postcolonialism as a concept enables us to move the critical conversation *beyond* the postcolonial hermeneutics and binary frames that have dominated the MLE scholarship for more than two decades. To date, a significant portion of the scholarship revolves around the critique and analyses of the inherited burdens of race, seen in the preoccupation with colonial/national history and the past, and their continued influences and effects on the present realities. Studies on the identity politics of race and ethnicity within the context of the nation/local often highlight the differing articulations and representations of othering and otherness (see Chin 2006; Quayum 2008), even when exploring narrative strategies that include resistance, deconstruction, and revision, or concepts of multiculturalism, hybridity, and plurality. However, the limitations of these studies also underline the paradoxes and troubling issues presented by the state constructs of multiplicity and hybridity, as Malaysians – despite living in a heterogeneous society – have developed a compartmentalized view of themselves as "racially distinct and culturally separate" (Kwok and Ali 1998, 116), while the hybridity of creolized or hyphenated identities is still subjected to the essentializing and homogenizing forces of the state. It is noteworthy that more recent studies are pushing the boundaries in MLE through the lenses of diaspora, transnationalism, and globalization (see Holden 2012; Gabriel 2016), but, by and large, the MLE scholarship has not been able to move past the divisive polemics and discourses that have continued to drive and shape Malaysia's postcolonial conditions.

It is not my intention to detract from the important work that is still being done in the field of MLE. Critical and interrogatory, the ongoing investigations into the postcolonial concerns and issues that beset the Malaysian nation state remain as urgent and relevant as ever. However, few studies have considered the potential offered by speculative fiction for the rethinking of race. Indeed, Malaysians who have grown up in a divided society have need of a new vision to look forward to: in particular, the possibility of a post-postcolonial Malaysian future based on what the society can be, instead of what it is or what it could have been. Cho's *Spirits Abroad*, I contend, offers this vision with its depiction of interracial and/or interspecies relationships. Defiant and transgressive, Cho's decolonizing gaze insists on moving beyond by disturbing, blurring, or crossing the discursive and ideological boundaries of race, culture, gender, and sexuality. Emphasizing culturally mixed or hybrid identities and bodies – both material and immaterial – her stories not only engage the development of interstitial spaces and identities in a glocalizing Malaysian society, but also reject their constructed racial and cultural otherness and marginality. In so doing, her writing contributes to the decolonizing of postcolonial Malaysia's binary discourses and narratives of race and ethnicity.

Interstitiality, then, is key to Cho's rebellious vision and fiction. Developed by Homi K. Bhabha (1994) in his analysis of the "beyond", the notion of interstitiality lays the critical groundwork for the framing of post-postcolonialism as a concept. The prefix "post", Bhabha writes, does not necessarily imply temporal sequentiality; instead, it is an insistent "gesture to the beyond", with the potential to "transform the present into an expanded and ex-centric site of experience and empowerment" (6). The path to the beyond, moreover, lies in the interstitial space, which interrogates and disrupts the linear narratives of postcolonial history and nation by opening "up the possibility of a cultural hybridity that entertains difference without an assumed or imposed hierarchy" (5). Constituting the site of intervention through which cultural hybridity and difference as well as new identities and articulations are initiated and negotiated, the interstital space and its liminal and interrogatory properties are notably captured by the metaphor "borderlines". Porous, tenuous, and shifting, the "borderlines of the 'present' " (1) signify the faultlines and thresholds where the binaries and boundaries of self and other are vexed, breached, blurred or crossed by individuals and communities continually on the move as a result of diasporas and migrations. Through the cultural hybridity of the borderlines, the "social imaginary of both metropolis and modernity" (9) is thus reinscribed and renewed by the "unknowable" and "unrepresentable" (6) albeit revisionary possibilities of the beyond.

Interstitial and interracial: Imagining a post-postcolonial future in *Spirits Abroad*

In Malaysian narratives, the spirits featured in Cho's collection typically belong to culture-specific mythologies. The *pontianak* (female vampiric ghost), *toyol* (undead foetus or infant), and *orang bunian* (invisible beings of the forest) are, for instance, associated with Malay folklore while "hungry ghosts" and *kuang shi* (hopping vampire) are from Chinese spiritual and supernatural realms. In *Spirits Abroad*, however, the Malaysian spirits are rendered culturally mixed or hybrid, with a few European magical beings thrown into the mix: there are "Chinese" *pontianak* and *orang bunian* while a European dragon turns out to be a dark-skinned man of undefined origins with a Chinese name. Refusing to stay within the stereotyped confines of race and culture, Cho's transgressive and fluid spirits both elude and unsettle the state and social constructs of identity by mingling with humans or other species in the interstices of their shared territories. The fantasy genre thus enables the imagining of an alternative world system that undergirds the social reality of Malaysia, through which Cho is able to critique the state-mandated discourses by using the subversive elements of humour, irony, and satire to undermine the commonly held expectations and stereotypes of race and culture. By exploring the "what-if" and "what-can-be" possibilities of the genre, Cho offers a playful vision of an *other*-Malaysia as well as revisionary narratives that highlight the fluidity and resilience of the interstitial space of hybridity.

The shifting and resistant energies of Cho's spirits are moreover captured by the organization of the collection. Divided into three sections titled respectively "Here", "There", and "Elsewhere", the collection plays with our understanding of time and space: "Here" denotes the present or "now", with the stories located in Malaysia; "There" moves the stories to an unspecified distant time in the UK, while the stories in "Elsewhere" take place anytime, anywhere. However, the ambiguity of these headings also highlights the elusive and unsettling meanings and properties of time and space/place, which are always fluid and shifting and thus difficult to fix or pinpoint. In short, the restless energies of the collection underscore the potential for change and transformation, which does not necessarily involve an outward shift/move but an inward one. At the same time, Cho's exploration of the discursive dynamics of race and ethnicity across these differing tempo-spatial contexts also reveals the pervasiveness of racism as a global discourse and reality: the interracial relations in "First National Forum on the Position of the Minorities in Malaysia" and "The House of Aunts" in "Here" spotlight Malaysia's race politics, while "Prudence and the Dragon" in "There" gestures at the historical fear evoked by blackness in the western context. "Elsewhere" too explores racial tensions and biases in stories like "The Earth Spirit's Favourite Anecdote" and "The Four Generations of Chang E", albeit through the representations of interspecies relations set in fantastic realms where humans and/or magical, non-human, and supernatural beings reside.

Focusing on the following selected stories that speak to Malaysia's race politics in "Here" and "Elsewhere", I trace the development of interracial relations in differing tempo-spatial contexts to reveal how each narrative involves the shifting borderlines and transitions in time and/or space/place that progressively move the narration *away* from the preoccupation with Malaysia's past and present burdens of race in the articulation of "beyond" and the post-postcolonial future.

Boundaries and foreclosure

In "First National Forum on the Position of the Minorities in Malaysia", hilarity ensues when the titular forum is disrupted by an *orang bunian* named Tan Chor Seng, who appropriates the raced and gendered bodies of the delegates to voice his indignation at being ignored by the government, simply because he belongs to the "invisible minority" (Cho 2014, 47). The occupied human bodies represent the multiculturalism and diversity of Malaysia; they include the "sandalwood" (47) colour of the lawyer, Abner Ignatius; a Malay scholar of Islam, Farid; a Chinese woman who runs a breast cancer support group, Annabella Lim; and the unnamed secretary of the Pahang Consumer Association whose "skin [is] so dark it was almost blue" (49). Incongruous and unsettling, the voice of "a middle-aged Chinese" man (49) emerging from the mouths of racially and, for Annabella, biologically different bodies causes confusion among the delegates, who are "taken aback" (47). More consternation is caused when it is revealed that the Chinese male voice belongs to an *orang bunian* from the jungle. Responses range from disbelief ("orang bunian aren't real!" [50]) to rejection ("it's all heathenish superstition" [50]), but the majority are directed at ethnicity: "But why are you a Chinese?" (51); "Orang bunian is a Malay folktale" (52); "I always heard that orang bunian are supposed to be devout Muslims" (52).

Based on the prescriptions of race, culture, and religion, the contestations about what/who an *orang bunian* is invariably tap into the country's polarizing forces and the endemic issues of bigotry, discrimination, and insularity. As Datin Zainab, an elderly Malay woman who once had a love affair with Chor Seng, exclaims, "This is what is wrong with our country! [...] You younger generation do not know how to accept. You don't know how to live together" (Cho 2014, 52). Nostalgically recalling the multicultural harmony of the "beautiful" 1970s and the even "more beautiful" 1950s (53), a time when Malaysian children of different ethnicities – "Chinese, Malay, Indian, Orang Asal, Sikh, Kristang, anything" (52) – used to eat and play together with "no division" (52), the older delegates long for a lost (albeit romanticized) past, especially in the face of the problematic present: "Now people have grown intolerant. They only want to see their own race. The state of the country has become bad, very bad" (52). The juxtaposition between past and present also reveals those who have been marginalized in the process: the "invisible minority" (47). The invisibility of Chor Seng's character thus serves as an important talking point since Malaysia's discourses of identity, as elsewhere in the world, are premised on the visible differences of race, gender, and class, as well as the corresponding productions of inequality, subjugation, and exclusion.

Being both invisible and the minority, Chor Seng the Chinese *orang bunian* and his species symbolically represent the minority ethnic communities – including the non-Malay/non-Muslim groups like the Chinese, Indians, Eurasians, and indigenous peoples such as the Orang Asli – whose voices and rights have been ignored by the pro-Malay/*Bumiputera* state: "Nobody ever did a survey of our opinions. Nobody wants to know what we think. We are being marginalized!" (Cho 2014, 51). In contrast, his ex-lover, Zainab, enjoys the political privileges accorded by her ethnic and class identity. The honorific title "Datin" signifies not just an elevated social position, but also belonging to the "elite or middle class of Malay society" (Hamidon 2014, 65) that had emerged as a result of the NEP. Enjoying the opportunities provided by racial privilege, Zainab experiences upward mobility as well as a politically active life as a Member of Parliament (MP) and founder of a woman's organization. Chor Seng, on the other hand, has remained hidden and invisible in the margins of human society: the jungle.

While critiquing the postcolonial state's prejudicial policies and parochial vision of the nation, the story of Chor Seng and Zainab also demonstrates how the established boundaries can be turned into interstitial spaces where interracial and interspecies encounters, interactions, and connections are engendered. As such, the spaces that straddle human territories and the margins of the jungle can be reinscribed as the interstitial borderlines, which can be breached, blurred, or crossed, and where "what is real and what is not real is not always clear"

(Cho 2014, 50). Abutting the jungle, the hotel where the forum is held is one such liminal space that enables Chor Seng to cross over and make contact with humans, and even appropriate their bodies. Transgressing the laws of physics as well as the norms that regulate the way Malaysians perceive the material (visible) world of race and gender, these moments of disruption not only constitute a symbolic break from linear history and the ruling discourses, but also represent the intervening spaces that produce the possibility of cultural hybidity. By inhabiting varying human bodies and using them as his mouthpiece, Chor Seng generates the confusing blend of identities that also destabilizes the essentialized categories of race and gender in Malaysia: Malay, Chinese, Indian, man, woman.

Symbolizing the "unknowable" and "unrepresentable" space of invisible spirits and magical beings, the jungle as a liminal space defies human laws and understanding; it is "not safe" (Cho 2014, 51) to humans. Simultaneously however, the jungle as the intervening site of human–spirit encounters can engage the revisionary possibilities and creative potential of the beyond. Significantly, the jungle is where Chor Seng and Zainab met and fell in love. Although already married, the rebellious Zainab nonetheless violates religious and racial injunctions in order to to live with Chor Seng in the jungle for a year; they even had a child, Boon Yi, before she returned to the human world. Raised as a Muslim in accordance with Zainab's wishes, the interracial and interspecies Boon Yi embodies the culturally hybridized identity that underscores the symbolic crossing of boundaries while also bridging differences and divisions between the human and non-human worlds, visible and invisible, Chinese and Malay. Fusing different races and cultures, the truly mixed Boon Yi reminds Malaysians of their once "beautiful" past when social and cultural interactions and exchange have led to the creation of heterogeneous, syncretic, and acculturated communities – evinced by the hybridized roots of the Malays as well as creolized identities such as the Peranakan Chinese (mixed Chinese and Malay descent), Jawi Peranakan (mixed Indian Muslim and Malay descent), and *Kristang* (mixed Portuguese and Malaccan descent), among others – that have unfortunately been made less visible under the ethnocentric government and the Malay-dominated *bumiputera* privileges.

While Boon Yi offers a path out of Malaysia's postcolonial predicament by representing the possiblity of what can be in the beyond – a glimpse into the post-postcolonial future – the story also suggests that this hope cannot be realized as long as the boundaries and divisions of race and culture remain entrenched. Chor Seng and Zainab's bittersweet reunion at the story's ending presents a scenario of what could have been, but the intimation that this is their final meeting reveals the difficulties of crossing or transgressing the formidable barriers of race and species. The foreclosure of the potential and possibilities of the interstitial space thus speaks of the damaging effects of the country's racist discourses and practices inasmuch as it is an indictment of the cultural insularity that attends them.

Negotiating and crossing boundaries

The next story to be discussed, "The House of Aunts", continues with the thematic exploration of interracial and interspecies relations when a Chinese teenage girl-turned-*pontianak*, Ah Lee, falls in love with her new Malay classmate, Ridzual, who has recently moved to her village, Lubuk Udang. Constituting the interstitial space where the different worlds of human and spirit collide, the small and insular village of Lubuk Udang subverts expectations with its hidden depths, thanks to a powerful all-female family of Malaysian Chinese *pontianak* to which Ah Lee belongs. Read through the restrictive lenses of Malaysia's binary discourses, Lubuk Udang, or "prawn's depths" in English translation, should symbolize the subaltern space of the marginalized other – represented by Ah Lee and her relatives who belong to the triple minority identity categories of woman, Chinese, and (non-human) *pontianak*. However, this view is challenged when one realizes that the story upholds matriarchal authority and female resilience and agency through the women's shared experiences of personal hardship, "suffering", and "sorrow" (Cho 2014, 116) in the patriarchal spaces of Confucian Chinese culture and Malaysian society. In a reversal of gender identities and roles, Ah Lee and her matriarchal family form the formidable centre of Lubuk Udang; they are strong, powerful, and frightening, and men are their prey.

Apart from subverting the gendered structures and expections of culture and society, the story also critiques Malaysia's problematic race relations. By opposing the privileged discourse of Malay *bumiputera* masculinity, the text implicitly resists the violent rhetoric of othering used by Malay politicians who label Malaysian Chinese and Indians "*pendatang*" by introducing Ridzual, who – in another subversive twist – becomes the "migrant" figure from the capital city and metropolis of Kuala Lumpur, also known as KL. Dismantling the established Malay/non-Malay hierarchy in this *other*-Malaysian world, "The House of Aunts" shows how Ridzual is the outsider who has to adapt to Lubuk Udang and its people. An educated, urbanized young man who speaks with a "strong Western accent" (Cho 2014, 67) and wears expensive trendy sneakers, Ridzual is comically likened to a fish out of water. His difference or foreignness, moreover, raises rumours about his having been born in the US, or that he studied at an international school. Such speculations are based on his western accent and fluent English, as Ridzual uses mostly standard forms of English and only occasionally code-switches to Malay. Unlike Ridzual, Ah Lee speaks colloquial Malaysian English, which makes her appear more "local" than him; she code-switches more frequently and uses non-standard forms that include Malay and Chinese slang. However, the text also emphasizes that Ridzual is as Malaysian as Ah Lee, since their linguistic differences do not imply the forces of hierarchization or division at work; instead, they highlight the multiplicity of Malaysians through the development of different varieties of English within the nation space. As Ridzual explains, his so-called western accent is simply his urbanized "Bangsar accent" (84) – a reference to the affluent, trendy, and cosmopolitan Bangsar suburb in KL.

By emphasizing their different, albeit equal, status, "The House of Aunts" demonstrates that Ah Lee's and Ridzual's relationship does not conform to the usual understanding of power relations in the postcolonial Malaysian context as they rewrite the narrative of Malay/masculine/self and non-Malay/feminine/other by following the desires of their hearts. However, the process of rewriting the narrative is not an easy one. There are ideological lines and discursive boundaries that must be negotiated – a process that also depends much on the individual acts of agency and accommodation. The portrayal of Ah Lee's and Ridzual's budding feelings for each other, for instance, involves the act of exploring the potential of their relationship and what it can be. Ridzual is tempted to cross religious boundaries when he curiously wonders what pork might taste like, asking "What is life if you don't taste everything that the world has to offer?" (Cho 2014, 87). Ah Lee, however, counters by reminding him that certain boundaries are important, and must be respected: "In this country we must accept other people's customs [...] Not just tolerate, but respect. That is how to live together" (87). Of significance here is how their relationship opens up the critical space of negotiation and dialogue – one that accommodates their individual viewpoints while fostering the understanding and bridging of cultural difference. In this way too, we find that the interstitial is not just formed through the liminal space as in the story "First National Forum on the Position of the Minorities in Malaysia", but also through the symbolic territory engendered by interracial bondings and cross-cultural communication, where difference is mediated.

At the same time, "The House of Aunts" highlights the tensions and anxieties underlining the complex process of negotiation, especially within the postcolonial context of Malaysia where the discourses of difference are embedded within historical and (neo) colonial epistemologies of race. The assumption of Ridzual's "western" background in Lubuk Udang, for instance, reveals how difference can quickly become the basis of differentiation. But when fear, prejudice, and the binary politics of self/other enter the picture, the act of differentiation can also lead to discrimination, contention, separation, and exclusion, while boundaries may prove difficult, even impossible, to cross. When Ridzual finds out that Ah Lee is a *pontianak*, he gives in to fear and prejudice, and attempts to "nail" her throat (Cho 2014, 100) in the belief he can turn her back into a "beautiful woman" (101). Ridzual's inability to accept Ah Lee's irreconcilable *pontianak* otherness thus results in the couple's break-up, while their differences are reinforced by the lack of communication after he attacked her with the nail. But as Ah Lee angrily points out to Ridzual, her "otherness" is in fact inextricable from her "self" and identity, even her existence; she is *both* human and *pontianak*: "There is no Ah Lee the vampire and Ah Lee your friend […]. I am just one person. If you make me not a vampire anymore, means there is no me anymore" (101). Further exclaiming that she is "already a beautiful woman" (101), Ah Lee rejects Ridzual's parochial perspective and binary thinking about humans and *pontianak*.

Countering the essentialist views that often accompany the prescriptions of race, "The House of Aunts" insists that identity is not carved in stone but is fluid, continually adapting and always hybridizing. It also reminds us that, despite the divisive politics and practices of race and religion, Malaysia is an acculturated space where new hybrid identities and articulations have taken shape – one which, apart from racially mixed communities, should also include the country's rich food culture and multilingual scene. Ridzual's westernized and urbanized Malay anglophone character and Ah Lee's Chinese and human-*pontianak* identity are not only differing embodiments of Malaysia's cultural hybridity, but they also attest to the changes and transformations occuring in the shifting and intervening borderlines of Malaysia's contemporary and glocalized society. Defying self/other binary and boundaries, "The House of Aunts" reimagines an *other*-Malaysia by showing the potential of how race relations can be, if only one is willing to negotiate difference and change, while engaging the challenges and obstacles involved in the process of rewriting the narrative. When Ah Lee rescues Ridzual from her angry aunts, and Ridzual – realizing his own "horrific" (Cho 2014, 108) action and that Ah Lee has not hurt him (and, in contrast, that he is the one hurting her) – asks to "talk" (114), they symbolically open up the space of communication that leads to reconciliation. Ridzual's overcoming of his fear of otherness and his acceptance of Ah Lee for who she is mark the start of their relationship and the symbolic resetting of their story. By breaking down barriers and crossing the boundaries of race and species, Ah Lee and Ridzual's relationship opens the path to the beyond while nudging the narrative closer to the possibility of a post-postcolonial future.

The promise of "tomorrow" – and beyond

The final story analysed here, "The Earth Spirit's Favourite Anecdote", also celebrates the interstitial borderlines through the meeting between a 53-year-old migrant female earth spirit and a 2467-year-old indigenous and gender-neutral forest spirit in Kuala Ketam. True to its name, Kuala Ketam – with "kuala" referring to the confluence of rivers while "ketam" means "crab" – represents the liminal site of cultural hybridity where "everybody new and mix up together" (Cho 2014, 238) has the chance to do "different-different things" (238) and be different. While filled with potential and new oppportunities, Kuala Ketam is also a place of bristling energy and tension as everyone has to learn "how to get along" (240). Still, the rich plurality represented by "all kinds of spirits – gods, ghosts, monsters" (238) and the "many-many voices" (244) of Kuala Ketam attracts the earth spirit, who decides to settle down in this new land by digging a hole/home. For the earth spirit to stay in her new hole/home however, she must receive permission to have "freedom of the land" from the forest spirits, "the first people at Kuala Ketam, before all the immigrants came" (239). She then meets the forest spirit in charge of the land where her hole/home is located, and, although the latter likes her, comic miscommunication and misunderstanding occur as a result of their opposing differences.

Maintaining the diasporic motif of "crossing boundaries", "The Earth Spirit's Favourite Anecdote" allegorizes the troubled Malay–Chinese relations in Malaysia, and – like "The House of Aunts" – interrogates the notion of difference between the native/indigenous and the new migrant, with the former represented by the feckless teh tarik-drinking forest spirit who has authority as the "true owner of the land" (Cho 2014, 239) while the earth spirit is "small" and has "no power" as a mere "renter" (239). Already separated by age, gender, and race/species, the two spirits are also culturally distinct: the earth spirits are industrious, "neat, sensible" and "like to have everything clear" (243), while the forest spirits are "lazy people" who "don't like to follow rules" (241); the latter are also "very messy" since "they cannot even decide whether they are boy or girl" (241). Even their speech styles differ. Although both use the particles and colloquialisms associated with Malaysian English, the elements of Chinese in the earth spirit's voice are inescapable, thanks to particles like "loh" (238) and "Aiyah" (244) as well as slang words like "Chau chibai" (246) and "kau-kau" (248). Their communicative styles, moreover, clash; the earth spirit likes clarity whereas the forest spirit favours indirection: "It never said no. It was never so straightforward" (245). Walking "different path[s]" (246), both spirits indeed appear to be incompatible in every way. While the forest spirit is fond of saying "*tomorrow also can*" (245; original italics) – alluding to the Islamic phrase *Insha'Allah* (God willing) that the Malays commonly use in order to "procrastinate and offload responsibility" (Imtiaz 2021), the earth spirit disagrees: "My life is not long. Every tomorrow you give me means another today is wasted. Tomorrow won't do!" (Cho 2014, 246).

Divided by irreconcilable differences as well as boundaries that draw on the cultural stereotypes and racial imbalances in Malaysia, the spirits' problematic relationship can easily be interpreted through the polarized lens of the lazy native Malay self and the industrious migrant Chinese other. However, Cho's subversive humour can be seen here too, as she overturns prevailing assumptions not only of race, but also of gender and sexuality by feminizing the Malay/forest spirit through depictions of indirection, indecisiveness, and sexual confusion, while the straightforward and decisive Chinese/earth spirit is virilized. While this comic reversal serves its function in destabilizing binaries and equalizing the relations between the indigenous landlord and migrant renter, the story more importantly highlights how difference can quickly become a point of contention and division when fear and prejudice are involved, as in "The House of Aunts". Wary and suspicious of the "too alien" (Cho 2014, 246) forest spirit and its "strange" (242) ways, the earth spirit is more prepared to draw the line between them: "I didn't know how forest spirits think. I didn't understand that forest spirits are not sensible. They are not like us earth spirits" (244–245). Unable to "read its expression" (246) and confused by its indirect communicative style, the earth spirit is also unable to understand the purpose behind the forest spirit's indulgence in social niceties like drinking tea, which is its way of being sociable and initiating dialogue. When the latter keeps deferring its decision to give permission until "tomorrow" (244, 246), the earth spirit loses her temper at this show of procrastination and inefficiency. It is only later that she realizes this was the forest spirit's oblique way of getting to know her better each time she returns "tomorrow".

The idea of "tomorrow" is in fact key to the movement of the plot and narrative, as it is the promise of receiving the forest spirit's permission the next day, or "tomorrow", that keeps the earth spirit returning every day. And over time, the earth spirit's perspective of the forest spirit begins to change. Previously viewing the forest spirit's smile as "dangerous" (Cho 2014, 243), she now "quite liked its smile" (247). When she is angered by the *toyol* sent by the forest spirit to her hole/home, she deliberately confronts the latter while it is still asleep, noting that "I [had] spent so many days waiting for the forest spirit to give me my freedom, I even knew its habits" (250). As the earth spirit learns to read the ways and expressions of the forest spirit, the divide between them begins to close. Realizing "it's just a matter of getting use to the difference" (255), she begins to see the forest spirit in a new light: it is merely "shy" (255) as it tries to woo her. Overcoming the barriers of self and other, the two spirits negotiate their differences with the understanding that boundaries can be resisted, even crossed: "you don't always have to draw line or follow rule" (257). Certainly, the development of interracial relations in the interstitial space is "messy" (257) as misunderstanding and miscommunication will continue to occur. Like "The House of Aunts" however, "The Earth Spirit's Favourite Anecdote" makes it clear that the ongoing dialogue and communication are necessary to the mediation of boundaries, and the understanding of each other as different yet equal in the interstitial space. And once difference is accepted, life can be "quite interesting" (257).

While sharing several striking similarities with "The House of Aunts" in its portrayal of interracial relations, "The Earth Spirit's Favourite Anecdote" is able to explore the idea of beyond more explicitly by espousing a forward-looking mindset, which is vital not only to the successful negotiation of difference and boundaries in the interstitial, but also to the idea of the post-postcolonial future. One reason for the earth spirit's decision to leave her parents and "kampung" (village; Cho 2014, 239) is because they "always look Back" and "keep thinking: go Back lah, go Back" (238). Unlike them, she is "not the kind of person who likes to go Back" (238) and rejects their backward mentality and insistent gaze to the past as the only way to live. By looking forward to each "tomorrow" and moving forward, the earth spirit not only learns to overcome the barriers of race/species, gender, and age, and embrace difference, but also marries the forest spirit. The phrase the forest spirit is fond of saying – "*tomorrow also can*" (245) – thus takes on new significance as each "tomorrow" opens up the "unknowable" space that is filled with the revisionary possibilities and creative potential of the beyond, not to mention the hopeful possibilities of a post-postcolonial future.

Conclusion

As the critical site of inquiry into Cho's decolonizing gaze, interstitial borderlines are reflected in the title *Spirits Abroad*, which envisions border-crossing, rule-breaking spirits who venture "abroad" or beyond and mix with humans in their shared societies and territories with little fear of or regard for binaries and boundaries. As I have shown, the stories analysed here not only support interracial and interspecies relationships, but also contain the restless and revisionary forces of the borderlines, which enable new ideas and inscriptions as well as transformations that point the way forward to the post-postcolonial beyond as the site of possibilities and progress. Manifested not only through the shared territories between humans and spirits in fluid "watery" spaces symbolized by Kuala Ketam and Lubuk Udang, but also through native–migrant encounters and interracial relationships, the interstitial space of cultural hybridity thus constitutes the intervening site where the boundaries between self and other, native and migrant, are dissolved, while the binary politics and cultural insularity that attend these boundaries are criticized and rejected. Advocating a forward-looking perspective and an inclusive attitude, Cho reimagines an *other*-Malaysia where the margin becomes the new centre, where differences are resolved through dialogue and communication, and where self and other are reconceived as different yet equal.

At the same time, my analysis also reveals a dialogic engagement with the idea of "beyond" through the depiction of interracial relations set in the various tempo-spatial contexts of "Here" and "Elsewhere". The story "First National Forum on the Position of the Minorities in Malaysia" offers a more realistic reflection of Malaysia's polarized society through Chor Seng's and Zainab's failed relationship, which underscores the foreclosure of interracial potential and possibilities as a result of the entrenched boundaries of race and ethnicity. "The House of Aunts" and "The Earth Spirit's Favourite Anecdote", on the other hand, convey a more optimistic and hopeful vision of the future, and what it can be, by emphasizing the importance of dialogue and negotiation, which enable the couples to bridge difference and cross the boundaries of race and species. The future, then, lies in one's own hands. Despite their differences (which at first seem to be irreconcilable), the interracial couples in "The House of Aunts" and "The Earth Spirit's Favourite Anecdote" are able to move forward in their relationships due to their individual acts of agency – reflected in the mediation and making of personal choices as well as their articulations of desire and free will. As both stories highlight, these acts of agency not only effect vital changes at the private level of everyday life, but can also reshape views and atititudes towards the perceived "other".

Notably, each story analysed here contributes to the elucidation of a post-postcolonial future in the Malaysian context. Visualized as a narrative progression, or an evolutionary process, that involves the decolonizing of Malaysia's embedded epistemologies and binaries, the post-postcolonial future as a concept adopts a forward-looking mindset and agency-based philosophy that upholds the individual's potential for adaptation, hybridity, change, and transformation. At the same time, such a philosophy also implicitly criticizes or rebukes individuals who simply toe the line or blame the system for their present sociopolitical reality while remaining complacent or apathetic. Embracing an encompassing vision of Malaysia via the representations of *other*-Malaysia, the stories repeatedly highlight Malaysia as an acculturated space that has, to a certain extent, embraced heterogeneity and difference – seen in the liminal spaces where culturally hybridized identities and polyglossic communities have emerged, in addition to the rich fusions found in the food, music, and fashion cultures. The road towards the post-postcolonial future is undoubtedly filled with many challenges and obstacles, but Cho's imagining of interracial friendships and relationships and how they are fostered in the interstitial borderlines is nonetheless key to the narration of race relations in Malaysia, as they herald the hope of a better "tomorrow" and what it can be.

Disclosure statement

No potential conflict of interest was reported by the author.

ORCID

Grace V.S. Chin http://orcid.org/0000-0001-9292-4494

References

Bhabha, Homi K. 1994. *The Location of Culture*. London and New York: Routledge.

Boey, Kim Cheng. 2018. "'We are All Exiles': Exile and Place in the Poetry of Ee Tiang Hong, Wong Phui Nam and Shirley Geok-lin Lim." *Asiatic* 12 (2): 23–45.

Chin, Grace V. S. 2006. "The Anxieties of Authorship in Malaysian and Singaporean Writings in English: Locating the English Language Writer and the Question of Freedom in the Postcolonial Era." *Postcolonial Text* 2 (4): 1–24.

Cho, Zen. 2014. *Spirits Abroad*. Petaling Jaya: Fixi Novo.

Etim, Eyoh. 2019. "Post-Postcolonialism': Theorising on the Shifting Postcolonial Paradigms in African Fiction." *IOSR Journal Of Humanities And Social Science* 24 (5): 1–12.

Gabriel, Sharmani Patricia. 2016. "'Local' and 'National' Transformations: Cultural Globalization, Heterogeneity, and Malaysian Literature in English." *The Journal of Commonwealth Literature* 51 (1): 145–164. doi:10.1177/0021989414566517.

Göttsche, Dirk. 2017. "Post-imperialism, Postcolonialism and Beyond: Towards a Periodization of Cultural Discourse about Colonial Legacies." *Journal of European Studies* 47 (2): 111–128. doi:10.1177/0047244117700070.

Hamidon, Syahira. 2014. *The Development of Malay Entrepreneurship in Malaysia*. Kuala Lumpur: ITBM Institut Terjemahan & Buku Malaysia.

Holden, Philip. 2012. "Global Malaysian Novels: Prospects and Possibilities." *Kajian Malaysia* 30 (Supp. 1): 47–59.

Imtiaz, Aysha. 2021. "You're Probably Using the Arabic Phrase 'Inshallah' All Wrong." *Vice*. February. 17. Accessed 3 March 2021. https://www.vice.com/en/article/7k9j3q/arabic-phrase-inshallah-biden-arabic-culture

Kwok, Kian Woon, and Mariam Ali. 1998. "Cultivating Citizenship and National Identity." In *Singapore: Re-Engineering Success*, edited by Arun Mahizhnan and Lee Tsao Yuan, 112–212. Singapore: Oxford University Press.

Maes-Jelinek, Hena. 2004. "Post-Colonial Criticism at the Crossroads: Subjective Questionings of an Old-Timer." In *Towards a Transcultural Future. Literature and Society in a 'Post'-colonial World*, edited by Geoffrey V. Davis, Peter H. Marsden, Bénédicte Ledent, and Marc Delrez, 1–19. Amsterdam and New York: Rodopi.

Quayum, Mohammad A. 2007. "Self-fashioning a Plural Society: Dialogism and Syncretism in Malaysian Post-colonial Literature." *New Zealand Journal of Asian Studies* 9 (2): 27–46.

Quayum, Mohammad A. 2008. "Interrogating Malaysian Literature in English: Its Glories, Sorrows and Thematic Trends." *Kunapipi* 30 (1): 149–168.

Quayum, Mohammad A. 2018. "Malaysian Literature and Beyond." *Asiatic* 12 (2): 1–5.

Raihanah, M. M. 2009. "Malaysia and the Author: Face-to-Face with the Challenges of Multiculturalism." *International Journal of Asia Pacific Studies* 5 (2): 43–63.

Hyphenational poetics in Omar Musa's *Parang* and *Millefiori*

Weihsin Gui

ABSTRACT

This article examines two poetry collections by Omar Musa (b. 1984) and his hyphenated identity as a Malaysian Australian. Extending Jahan Ramazani's concept of transnational poetics, it draws on Omar's comments about the importance of the hyphen in his personal and artistic self-fashioning to argue for the presence of a "hyphenational poetics" in his work. This poetics functions as both hyphen and parang (machete), enabling transnational connections and sociopolitical critique. It is evident in the mixture of Malay language and Malaysian cultural details, African American hip-hop rhythms and aesthetics of spoken-word or slam poetry in Musa's anglophone poems. His poetry performs a simultaneous critique of the sociopolitical status quo of both his ancestral homeland of Malaysia and his country of birth and citizenship, Australia. His hyphenational poetics offers one way of thinking beyond the national–sectional division in Malaysian literature, focusing instead on in-betweenness and cross-cultural borrowings and exchanges.

Although he was born and raised in Australia, Omar bin Musa and his work can be considered part of Malaysian literature in English because he maintains an abiding connection to Malaysia both personally and in his two published poetry collections, *Parang* (Musa 2014) and *Millefiori* (Musa 2017a). As Omar explains, Malaysia is part of the "complexity" of his Australian identity: his "mother is of Irish extraction", his "father is from Borneo and is himself a Suluk-Kedayan hybrid", and Omar uses "poetry as a way to access and understand" his "Malay side" (Musa 2013). The mixture of Malay, Suluk, and Kedayan influences comprises the Malaysian part of Omar's self-identification as "Malaysian hyphen Australian", with the hyphen being a corrective to the ignorance of racial discrimination and inequalities in Australia. Such a hyphenated identity should also prompt white Australians to "acknowledge the concept of race, and accept that they are Anglo hyphen Australian" (*The Pin* n.d.). For Omar, the hyphen functions poetically as both parang (machete) and bridge; his poetry critiques both Malaysia and Australia while creating connections between the two countries and also the multiple cultural elements in his life.

Omar's writing is both a continuation and a departure from existing paradigms within Malaysian literature in English. Other scholars have discussed the problems of Malaysian literature and the divisions within it. As Mohammad A. Quayum (2018) notes in a special issue of the journal *Asiatic* on 21st-century Malaysian literature, since the 1970s the "pegging of literature by race" leads to "writers generally choos[ing] to write in their respective languages and about their ethnic experiences" and prevents "the growth of a holistic national literature mirroring the nation life" (3). Others have discussed how elevating Malay-language literature to the status of national literature and treating literature in other languages (including English) as sectional literatures has affected Malaysians' sense of their ethnic and national identities (Gabriel 2014; Leng 2017; Lim 2015); there are also considerations of how cultural globalization may create opportunities to contest the national status quo (Gabriel 2016; Holden 2012).

Where can we locate Omar in this conversation? On the one hand, his poetry does not evince a deep sense of exile akin to that expressed by earlier anglophone Malaysian poets such as Ee Tiang Hong, Wong Phui Nam, and Shirley Geok-lin Lim (Boey 2018). Contrary to notions of exile and estrangement, since 2019 Omar splits his time between Australia and the East Malaysian state of Sabah where his father and paternal grandparents live (Van Neerven 2019). Omar's double consciousness of and connection to other countries besides Malaysia can be considered within an existing strand of anglophone Malaysian writing. For example, we might read Tash Aw's (2013) novel *Five Star Billionaire* as a critique of China's economic boom, and some stories in Beth Yahp's (2017) latest collection *The Red Pearl* are about France and Australia. Omar can thus be grouped with more recent anglophone Malaysian writers who are "doubly diasporic" (Gabriel 2016, 153). These writers foreground "the multiplicity of Malaysian national-cultural identity, rather than its false unities" and "use their situatedness in the interstices of the local and global to explore the fundamental instabilities in the meaning of the 'national' ", and they sometimes do so "by deploying self-reflexive techniques of narrativization" (153). In Omar's poetry there is a similar element of self-reflexiveness as he often writes from deeply personal perspectives or interpolates himself into a poem. Omar is also doubly diasporic because his identification with Malay language and culture is qualified by his Kedayan and Suluk lineage; in fact, in his interviews Omar often brings up his grandparents' Kedayan and Suluk backgrounds but only once (Musa 2013) mentions the term "Malay". In this, Omar might be associated with writers such as Rehman Rashid and Dina Zahman, whose anglophone life-writing and creative nonfiction have variously interrogated what Malayness means beyond a narrow racial-religious definition. Finally, as a slam poetry performer, Omar represents a new aspect of Malaysian literature in English that has not received much scholarly attention even though there are anglophone spoken-word artist performers such as Melizarani T. Silva and Alana Azlan based in Malaysia.

By Omar's account, his father was very religious during Omar's childhood but Omar now considers himself to be more "culturally" rather than faithfully "Muslim" (Van Neerven 2019). Omar learned from his father (himself a poet) that "in Malaysia the best poetry [is] spoken, verbalised out loud" and studying the Koran made him realize it was not only a religious but also a literary text (Musa, n.d.a). Besides canonical British poets he read at school, Omar was also inspired by African American rappers who produced "living, breathing poetry" he admired from Malaysia (Musa n.d.a). This cultural and aesthetic admixture crystallized, as Omar recounts in *The Moth* (Musa n.d.b.) when he visited his grandparents and also performed one of his poems at a cousin's wedding in Malaysia. After his performance, Omar's grandmother commented that his rhythmic spoken words reminded her of the pantuns she composed in her head as a child surviving on the streets (Musa n.d.b., 10:33). This was an epiphany for Omar: "I realized that I found my own parang, my own machete. My words that could cut through worlds, time, and even generations" (Musa n.d.b, 10:33–11:17). When Omar accompanies his grandfather into the jungles of Borneo, he sees Grandfather "wielding a parang" to cut away undergrowth, "forging a lane [...] to this old dilapidated hut in the jungle" where their ancestral lands were. Just as his grandmother's memories of her childhood pantuns led to an epiphany, Omar saw how his grandfather's parang, instead of being "a dangerous thing", could be "a constructive tool" that "forges a path between places that don't usually connect" or "communicate" (Musa n.d.b., 6:33–7:04).

Omar's epiphany about the parang as both a cutting and connective symbol and his own stress on the power of the hyphen in his hybrid identity suggest that parang and hyphen are two sides of the same blade. They help him to incise and connect, to critique and communicate, to bridge the personal and the political and multiple cultural elements using what I call a hyphenational poetics. I am extending Jahan Ramazani's (2015) conceptualization of a transnational poetics, which describes poems that "cross between the oral and the literary, interanimate foreign and indigenous genres, span distances between far-flung locales, frame discourses within one another, and indigenize borrowed forms to serve antithetical ends" (4). For example, Black British poets such as Grace Nichols "dislocate England from itself by casting it into translocational conversation with its 'others' " (172) and represent the nation as "a changed space, nonhierarchically intermapped with Caribbean spaces once ruled by Britannia" (174). My preference for the neologism "hyphenational" stems from Omar's own emphasis on the hyphen as an important ingredient in his self-fashioning and literary craft. Furthermore, hyphenational is also distinct from hyphenated as an adjective, because it preserves the *national* in its spelling. Omar is in dialogue not only with Australia but also Malaysia, especially if one remembers his insistence on being Malaysian hyphen Australian and his acknowledge of his Malay, Suluk, and Kedayan background. Not only does Omar's poetry interrogate Australia's sociopolitical status quo, it also imagines a "varied subjectivity" of Malayness that accords with what Maznah Mohamad (2011) calls, in her study of five modern Malay intellectuals, "a constant movement towards dissent and diversity" (36). This broader understanding of Malayness has been obscured by "the hegemonic project of a singular-unitary Melayu" propagated by "the dominance of racialized state policies" in Malaysia (37). Malayness in this singular-unitary form has been promoted by "UMNO [United Malays National Organisation], the dominant party serving Malay interest" as having an indigenous "continuity of belonging on national soil"; this political distinction categorizes Malays as "bumiputera" and "ethnic Chinese and Indians" as "quintessential others – the pendatang and penumpang, 'newcomers' and 'squatters' " (Gabriel 2014, 1215).

The situation in Sabah, where Omar's father and grandparents live and where he now spends much of his time, is different from Peninsular Malaysia because there Malays are a minority. In 2011, Sabah's *bumiputera* population of 2 million consisted of 184,000 Malays compared to 568,500 Kadazandusun, 450,000 Bajau, 102,393 Murut, and 659,865 from other ethnic groups (Barlocco 2013, 468). In terms of Omar's own heritage, his grandmother is Kedayan and his grandfather is Suluk. The ancestors of the Kedayan (numbering about 30,000 in Sabah) are believed to have originated from Java in

Indonesia (Ros and Sa'ari 2015, 454). The Suluk, on the other hand, "are located throughout the Sulu archipelago in the southern Philippines" (where they are known as the Tausug) and "Suluk people motivated by trade had begun to settle in Sabah about 200 to 300 years ago" (Quintero and Nor 2016, 2). My point in noting the overseas provenance of Omar's Kedayan and Suluk heritage is to stress that when Omar employs Malay language and cultural elements – such as tattooing his right forearm with the words *penglipur lara* – he is interanimating them with and through Sabah's multi-ethnic and multicultural milieu rather than affirming a hegemonic Melayu identity rooted in national soil. While *penglipur lara* may be a Malay term that specifically refers to the "storytellers of old Malaya, who wandered from kampung to kampung", Omar explains that he also cherishes the literal meaning of the term – "reliever of sorrows" or "dispeller of worries" – because he sees this as a key artistic and poetic role (Toh 2014). Writing as a diasporic subject situated in Australia, Omar does not regard Malaysia as an ethno-racial fountainhead. His invocation of hybrid Malay, Suluk, and Kedayan linguistic and cultural elements functions as both parang and hyphen, as a hyphenational poetics that helps him slice into sociopolitical problems while also building bridges towards a more expansive sense of being Australian and Malaysian. Omar sees being Australian as inseparable from being Malaysian, and being Malaysian means acknowledging and performing the Malay, Suluk, and Kedayan aspects of his self.

Parang

This can be seen from Omar's collection *Parang*, which opens with a couple of epigraphs: first, a quotation from Chilean author Roberto Bolaño, "every hundred feet the world changes"; second, two definitions of the parang as "a broad, heavy knife used as a tool or weapon" and "a Malay machete" (Musa 2014, ix). The concluding definition of the parang as a distinctively Malay object is qualified by the initial epigraph from Bolaño about change wrought by distance and the other definition about the large knife's use as either a tool or a weapon rather than a cultural symbol. This resignification of the parang is elaborated in two of the collection's poems. In "Parang", the name of the eponymous blade is anaphorically invoked by the speaker, like a sequential chant, in the poem's second stanza:

> *Parang,*
> guardian angel of gangsters and pirates
> headhunters and thieves.
> *Parang,*
> patron saint of mob rule and blood bath,
> of the man who runs amok through the village.
> *Parang,*
> guiding spirit of the housebuilders, the tool carver
> and the opener of paths (4)

The speaker, most likely an extension of Omar, acknowledges that the parang has a historical association with colonial-era racial stereotypes of indigenous people on Borneo: "gangsters and pirates", "headhunters and thieves" who are prone to running "amok" and causing a "blood bath" with their parang. However, the sequence ends with the parang becoming a more proactive and uplifting presence as a "guiding spirit" who inspires "the opener of paths" rather than a "patron saint" who hears supplicants' pleas.

In "The Parang and the Keris" there is a similar disavowal, this time of heroism rather than villainy. The speaker declares: "This parang is not sensuously curved / immortalised in a *Hikayat* / by a brave hero's hand" (Musa 2014, 20). The speaker goes on to claim that "it is mine. / *I* / made it" (20), forging the parang "into the Italic font / *I* / sharpened the blade / and carved my history in its handle" (21). The italicized "*I*" correlates the speaker's sense of self with the visual image of the parang's straight and slanted blade, as opposed to the keris's curved and wavy edges. Here we might remember that Omar has the words *penglipur lara* tattooed on his right forearm, invoking "the wandering story-tellers of old Malaya" (Toh 2014). The contrast between the parang and the keris, then, may also be read as a contrast between Omar's errant or excentric verse and the classical hikayat, a literary genre from the Malay world that often recounts epic stories of folk heroes. The most famous is arguably *Hikayat Hang Tuah*, "a strongly national example of the artificial historical-heroic epic, in which history, in the medieval Malay sense of the term, is unfolded as a biography" (Braginsky 1990, 410). Thus, when the poem ends with the speaker's wielding of the parang

> to clear a lane through the jungle,
> to tap rubber from a tree
> or with swish calligraphic
> take a head
> clean
> off
> (Musa 2014, 21)

We see echoes of the collection's epigraphs where there is a new understanding of the parang as a tool or weapon instead of a cultural artefact. Like a hyphen, the blade can clear lanes to connect people and places; as a weapon, the parang's calligraphic flourish can be poetically incisive about matters of politics and society.

The first section of *Parang* contains poems about Omar's relationship to his father's home country of Malaysia and his grandparents who reside in Sabah. As the poem "A Homeland" expresses, visiting Malaysia quickly dispels any romanticized images such as "a brown shouldered woman / twisting water from her hair" surrounded by "hibiscus flowers" and "kampungs full of the wise and noble poor" (Musa 2014, 18). Instead, the speaker sees a modern country replete with virtues and vices. Malaysia's booming economy is shown by ubiquitous markers of consumerism and urban entertainment such as "Prada and mirror-balls", and from the "mosques and malls built from the same bricks, / and just as full of faithful" (18), the faithful here referring to adherents not only of a religion, but also of materialistic lifestyles. There are also sharp racial and class divisions emphasized by the visual scenes of "races dining separately / and skyscrapers as sheer as knives" (18). The speaker's epiphany in the middle of the poem brings home his recognition that he had a "second generationer's hope and despair! / To syphon stories from those who left [Malaysia] years ago" and incorrectly assume the country would remain in a pristine state untouched by "modernity churned" (19). Instead of a pastoral paradise, Malaysia as "a homeland is a bastard thing, / a chimera, shapeshifter" (19). For the speaker/Omar, as a second-generation Malaysian Australian, Malaysia cannot be a homeland to which one can return and retrieve culturally or racially pure roots. Instead, contrary to official state pronouncements emphasizing Malay ethno-cultural nationalism, the country's mutable and shapeshifting character is "a bastard thing" and its shapeshifting character poses an epistemological challenge: "to confuse to enlighten to confuse to enrich?" (19). This line, with its lack of punctuation, shows how confusion and enlightenment bleed into each other, and it will take some critical distance (signified by the white space after the second "confuse") before the diasporic subject's understanding of Malaysia can be enriched. Some other poems in this section of the collection do indeed show how Omar develops a deeper understanding of Malaysia.

In "FELDA", the speaker confronts the dilemmas of Malaysia's national development project. The Federal Land Development Authority (FELDA) was created in 1956 "to resettle and employ the rural poor in the palm oil industry" and "grew to become the world's largest state-run palm oil agency" (Chow and Sipalan 2019). The poem's speaker regards "the palm oil plantation" as a "[g]reen desert, / perfect pattern of oil-rich trees, / minting money" (Musa 2014, 12), with the alliteration of "p" and "m" sounds in these lines emphasizing the commodity nature of these cash crops. In contrast, there are more rolling vowel sounds and assonance when the speaker remembers what the oil palms replaced, suggesting an underlying sense of regret and loss: "There was jungle here once, / fecund, / loud with orangutan and sunbear, / gibbon and bul bul" (12). But the speaker's interlocutor, who presumably owns this palm oil plantation and is a blood relative, argues "why should we care about monkeys in trees / when our children cannot eat?" and even the speaker cannot deny that "a plot of soil sent three of my cousins to university / who might otherwise have drifted" (12). The speaker summarizes the situation in a tercet: "Poor man employed / Empty plate filled / Rainforest destroyed" (12). While unable to offer a clear solution, the tercet's rhyming first and third lines link the livelihood of cash crop farmers under FELDA with the devastation of Malaysia's natural flora and fauna. The poem raises an implicit question about the efficacy of state land development initiatives and also, like a hyphen, links this to political questions about indigenous identity: how can an Antaeus-like connection with the soil be claimed as the basis for *bumiputera* identity if the very soil and land are not respected and cherished?

This same regret about the destruction of nature and degradation of traditional bonds between humans and the environment is also expressed in the poem "*Sunyi*", which is Malay for quiet. The speaker describes how his grandmother and grandfather "*Nenek* and *Datuk*" pay a visit to the family's ancestral lands:

> *Parang* in hand,
> they wade through swathes of green,
> vines and grass,
> where green caresses
> and hides worn paths
> (Musa 2014, 14)

This scene comes from Omar's personal anecdote from *The Moth*. As his grandparents cut through the undergrowth they appear to be in harmony with the jungle's greenery, which "caresses and hides" the paths they walk. The "old house" on the ancestral land is "now home to chattering monkeys. / A family", but the grandparents treat the noisy occupants as "friends, / who fill the air with soft prattle, / . . . so the jungle is never truly / *sunyi*" (15). The auditory conviviality between humans and monkeys is underscored when "*Datuk* crouches in the lalang grass / and sings a song for them. / Man and monkey watch each other, / at ease, intrigued" (15–16).

Their harmonious relationship is threatened, however, by "the men who come with guns" and "return" (Musa 2014, 16) even after the grandfather lies to them that there are no monkeys in the area. The hunters' cruelty is emphasized as they seem to be killing off monkeys for amusement rather than sustenance: "world falls out of love with itself – the men carry something away / for sport for food for sport?" (16). Playing on the auditory and orthographical similarity between "for sport" and "forget", the speaker laments that the monkeys' deaths mean that people "forget that loss is stitched on branch on leaf on human hearts" and "the silence now is louder than our own remorse" (16). The slaughter of monkeys is more than just the killing of wildlife; it represents a loss of humanity's conscience, also a breaking of the bond between humanity and nature. Like "FELDA", this poem illuminates how the brutal treatment of Malaysia's natural environment undermines claims to national progress and an official indigenous identity anchored in soil.

In contrast, Omar maintains sustainable cultural bonds with the country through his father and his grandmother as seen in "Lost Planet". In the midst of a dream-like sequence the speaker encounters his father "sitting cross-legged / beneath a banyan tree" (Musa 2014, 28). Father and son "played chess and once I captured his king, / we ate durian, / and shared *kretek* cigarettes. / We spoke of ancestral heroes and water from the moon" (28). The competitive chess game ends with the speaker's victory, leading to a reconciliation as they eat and smoke together, discuss their shared past ("ancestral heroes") and fantasize possible futures ("water from the moon") as equals. Unlike the scene with his father where there is no obvious dialogue, the speaker's encounter with his grandmother, "a woman in a sarong" who is "still very strong and very beautiful" (28), has an entire benedictory stanza spoken by her in Malay (quoted below is the English translation at the end of the poem):

> *Waves. Waves. Omar, your ancestors come from the waves.*
> *Their house is this ocean. Now you sail on ocean, desert and sky.*
> *Your words have sails. It doesn't matter how far you go,*
> *do not forget your origins, that flow in your blood.*
> *We may be poor but we are kind.*
> *I know that you can only speak a little bit in Malay.*
> *Don't worry, don't worry Omar.*
> *We are united not just by blood, but by soul* (30; italics in original)

Unlike the speaker's meeting with his father that is anchored in soil ("beneath a banyan tree"), in the grandmother's speech the dominant metaphor linking past and future is that of oceanic "waves" from whence Omar's Kedayan and Suluk "ancestors" came. This departs from the Malaysian state's official designation of Malays and other indigenous peoples as *bumiputera* ("sons of the soil") and instead configures the relationship between the speaker, his grandmother, and their history and heritage through a fluid metaphor that extends outwards instead of turning inward ("your words have sails"). In the second half of the stanza an ethical openness becomes as important as ties of blood and land. The grandmother suggests that their family "origins" that "flow in [the speaker's] blood" come from a sense of kindness even in the midst of poverty. What has "united" their "souls" across generations is not only the fact of being blood relatives, but also an active choice to be "kind" to others. This poem underscores Omar's doubly diasporic position as an anglophone Malaysian poet. He is diasporic on one level as an Australian who claims Malaysia as an integral part of his identity; on another level, he understands Malaysia through a hybrid Malay, Suluk, and Kedayan cultural matrix that is also diasporic. The Kedayan and Suluk settled in Borneo after travelling across the waves from Java island and the Philippines archipelago; Malays also have a history of transoceanic travel to and settlement in places such as South Africa and Sri Lanka (Haron 2002; Nordhoff 2012).

The oceanic metaphor articulated by the grandmother in "Lost Planet" appears in the first lines of Omar's spoken-word poem "My Generation": "My generation / sat on the brim of the ocean, / waiting for the tide to bring something in" (Musa 2014, 45). The poem moves swiftly from this opening moment of quiet anticipation to a fast-paced account of what members of the speaker's generation indulge in:

> the ones who drop out of college to get collagen,
> hoping to hook up with popped-collar Gen Y men
> with copycat tattoos,
> footy contracts and right-angled jaws,
> hoping to ride
> amphetamine horses and red Porsches
> into clubs (45)

This stanza reveals some striking verbal flourishes: the expanding wordplay of "college", "collagen", and "popped-collar Gen Y men"; the zeugma coupled with assonance and slant rhymes of "to ride / amphetamine horses and red Porsches". They emphasize the get-rich-quick, materialistic desires together with the self-destructive behaviour of the speaker's generation (the riding of Porsches *into* instead of to nightclubs suggests a drug-induced vehicular crash). As the poem unfolds we learn that this behaviour could be in part due to generational disillusionment with Australia's politics and society. There are "[h]ushed coups in the halls of parliament, / heads rolled over bad polls, tongues lolled, / drums rolled as newspapers harmonised like baying wolves" (45–46). The alliteration of "h" sounds throughout these lines and the internal rhymes of "rolled", "polls", and "lolled" all underscore how comically ineffectual the country's government appears to the speaker.

Worse still, "[w]hile the traditional custodians of the land / sweated in the concrete gizzards of govvo flats, / left wing activists sipped red wine / and talked of reform" (Musa 2014, 46). The reference to "traditional custodians of the land" and the use of the colloquial phrase "govvo flats" place this poem squarely within the Australian context. That Indigenous Australians are living in uncomfortable "concrete" government housing likened to the hot entrails of a dead animal while "activists sipped red wine" highlights the disparity between the rhetoric of socio-political "reform" and its reality. Faced with such incompetence and hypocrisy, the speaker suggests that it is inevitable that "my generation / never stopped being children" (47). Without any recourse to social justice or recognition from politicians or civil society, "our only possessions were our winged imaginations, / sitting on the brim of the ocean, / waiting for the tide to bring something in" (47). The last two lines bring the poem full circle, the difference being the speaker's recognition that his generation's creativity (their "winged imaginations") is their first and last resource to give themselves a voice – a critical voice that Omar himself makes audible through the writing and performance of his poem, a product of hyphenational poetics that brings Omar and his words across the ocean from Malaysia.

In contrast to the frustration expressed in "My Generation", Omar's critique of Australian society and politics in "The Mansion on the Hill" is couched in more assertive tones. The poem itself is dedicated to the memory of Ollie MC and Andrew McMillan, two Australian activists who were also musicians and writers. The speaker acknowledges at the beginning that power is often located "where patricians mill on chessboard floors / and make decisions beyond all reckoning" (Musa 2014, 36). But what is more important is the existence of

> a parallel world
> where the bush weed grows
> and the panting things are.
> In the lands of fire and dust
> where
> kinship lines are tattooed
> and the roads wander on like they have nothing to do.
> These are places where the people exist
> in all their pettiness and grandeur (36)

In contrast to the "patricians" who walk the sterile regularity of "chessboard floors" in governmental spaces, the "parallel world" where everyday people (including the speaker and his departed activist friends) "exist" is chaotic but alive, a place where things are "grow[ing]" and "panting" in a mixture of "pettiness and grandeur". The "roads" that have been officially paved seem to "wander on" and be less meaningful than "kinship lines" that are "tattooed" on people's skins, suggesting both physical and figurative bonds between the speaker and those around him that surpass social and demographic boundaries designated by state authority. While the poem does mourn Ollie MC and Andrew McMillan ("Bright stars, / unexpectedly gone"), it also affirms and draws inspiration from their activist legacy: "You knew all too well / that the clouded skin of a pool / demands not to be skimmed but pierced" [37]). The poem illustrates Omar's hyphenational poetics, whereby the horizontal dash of the hyphen can connect people and cultures but also, as the blade of a parang, slash and pierce the hypocrisy and empty rhetoric emanating from "the mansion on the hill".

Millefiori

Omar's following collection *Millefiori* contains poems that more consciously interanimate Malaysian, Australian, and world-historical elements and contexts. Millefiori means "a thousand flowers" in Italian, referring to a glass-making technique that depicts a mosaic of "whimsical flowers showing off their beautiful colors" (Glass of Venice n.d.). Omar, possibly playing on the orthographical similarities and the floral and romantic connotations of posy and poesy/poetry, introduces Malaysian elements into "Millefiori I":

> We threw a thousand flowers
> on what could have been.
> [...] *bunga bunga kubur*
> flowers of the grave
> [...]
> *bunga bunga mimpi*
> the flowers of dreams (Musa 2017a, 99)

The thousand flowers of decorative Italian glassware become transformed here through Malay-language phrases into flowers that symbolize both mourning and hopefulness. While the speaker is elegiac about love lost, he nonetheless concludes with a cherished and tender memory: "you are smiling / we are sunlit, // my kiss snagged on the corner of your mouth" (99). This poem, although appearing near the end of the collection, nonetheless sets an emotional tone that connects the speaker's intimate, personal feelings with a sense of the wider world: "Our love felt historic, / like maybe there was some other time / when I was yours & you were mine" (98). This interweaving of personal sentiment and global consciousness, of sadness and loss nonetheless moved by hope and tenderness, informs some of the more politically edged poems in the collection.

In "Paint Me Proud", the speaker is in a museum or gallery displaying "the great procession / of warriors and poets" but sadly realizes that "I do not see myself / or one like me" among these celebrated white men. Because the preceding poem "The Return" is set in London, it is not a stretch to assume that the paintings described here are displayed in a British institution. Whereas in the first half of the poem the speaker frets that in these paintings he would be "the wolf skin / tied on the waist" of these famous white men, "chased, gutted and flayed, / taught humility by the snicker of a blade" (Musa 2017a, 28), his confidence in his own identity and heritage emerges in the second half. The speaker focuses on the irrepressible mixing of colonial history and postcolonial presence with an imperative voice:

> Paint me in new,
> if you must,
> among the lunar white faces.
> Take the brown pigment you used
> for cloak and kilt,
> paint me shirtless,
> paint me brown as a river in a distant latitude,
> paint me in a sarong, so akin to what you wear,
> paint me proud as you are,
> [...]
> illuminated by gold. (29)

The intermixing of Britain and Malaysia comes across through the "brown pigment" of "cloak and kilt" that the speaker wants to represent his skin colour, which recalls the brownness of "a river in a distant latitude" in the tropics instead of the Thames. The speaker's assertive presence and commentary represents what Edward Said (1993) calls "the voyage in" in which those who were formerly colonized by Europe make a "conscious effort to enter into the discourse of Europe and the West, to mix with it, transform it, to make it acknowledge marginalized or suppressed or forgotten histories" (216). Hence the speaker's insistence that he be painted "shirtless" wearing a traditional "sarong" akin to the cloaks and kilts worn by the white men, standing "as proud as" they are with the countenance of an equal instead of a subordinate.

Omar's world-historical consciousness also articulates almost-forgotten connections between indigenous inhabitants of Australia's northern regions and people from Makassar (today part of Indonesia). The poem "Djulirri" is inspired by the discovery of Aboriginal rock art in Australia's Arnhem Land, some of which depicts "Southeast Asian sailing vessels visiting Australia in the mid-1600s", in particular "a yellow painted prau" that lies "underneath a large beeswax snake" (Australian National University 2010). The speaker first pays tribute to the original inhabitants of the land and their lifeworld, with the synaesthetic images attesting to their continued existence and vitality: "Name the chalk-white rush / of voice in the throat // Name the place & shelves of stone, / the spirits & the bone-written earth" (Musa 2017a, 69). Next, the speaker describes the appearance of fishermen from Makassar: "Name the Makassan *praus* / sailing over the rim of the world, / name the *trepang* they search for" (69). The poem culminates with the arrival of Europeans and the beginning of colonization: "Name the tall ship, / the white man at the stern, / the hands on the hips, the pipes on the lips" (69).

Whereas Makassan fishermen, with their focus on gathering *trepang* or sea cucumber, are represented as benign, the arrival of "the white man" with his imperious and imperializing hand-on-hip posture suggests turmoil and upheaval: "Name all that might follow. // Name it 'contact'; / this thing that upturns a world" (Musa 2017a, 69). The speaker anaphorically encapsulates a long history of cross-cultural encounters between different peoples but emphasizes that such encounters are not all equal. By placing quotation marks around "contact", the speaker highlights how this euphemistic word for conquest and colonialism makes light of "all that might follow", namely the enormous devastation of existing human societies and natural environments. The Makassan fishermen sail over the rim of the world but the European colonizers are the ones who upturn it, bringing to mind the original image of a boat that inspired this poem – only now the vessel has turned over or capsized.

Omar's hyphenational poetics that bring together multiple historical and cultural contexts while critiquing their social and racial inequalities expand outward in the penultimate poem of *Millefiori*, "The Ranthem II". As the portmanteau title implies, this spoken-word poem is not only a rant – a personal outpouring of anger and frustration – but also an anthem to agitate and inspire the audience. Here, as in many slam poetry performances, Omar himself becomes the poem's speaker as he begins by recounting a childhood growing up in Australia with a mix of cultural influences and an acknowledgement of his place among the indigenous people and their lands:

> I'd come running home, shrugging off my school bag.
> Curry chicken & white rice, then throwing on some Wu Tang.
> Sitting on the riverbank, staring at the gumtrees,
> new feet tread the most ancient of Country. (Musa 2017a, 93)

This stanza, short but bursting with kinetic, olfactory, auditory, and visual descriptive imagery, paves the way for Omar's awareness that even though "the empire's fallen & the ground is uneven", there is still "the legacy / of being down, treated as a lesser human being. / Invading Europeans took my forefathers' dreams, / labelled them as savage & hung 'em in museums" (93). This is a clear reference to the colonization of Borneo by the Englishman James Brooke in the mid-19th century, which Omar previously critiqued in "Paint Me Proud".

But in this poem there is a key difference: if Omar's forefathers and their dreams have been tragically turned into ethnographic curios and museum artefacts, he will revive those dreams while bearing witness to past and present racial discrimination:

> Omar Musa, anti-Sonia Kruger
> Andrew Bolt
> all other persecutors.
> In a world that is bloody as Fallujah,
> Dreamtime is lucid, music therapeutic (Musa 2017a, 95)

The Australian context is unmistakable: Sonia Kruger and Andrew Bolt are conservative figures – a TV presenter and a journalist respectively – who have publicly called for a ban on Muslim immigration to Australia (Meade 2016). Even though he is not a practising Muslim, because of his name and appearance Omar knows and speaks first-hand about experiences of racism and Islamophobia in Australia, remarking that people often tell him to "go back to your own country" (Toh 2014). But the stanza's scope is not limited to Australia: the name "Fallujah" invokes a larger geopolitical context, referring to the Iraqi city where protesting civilians were massacred by US soldiers in 2003 and which has been the bloody battleground for American, Iraqi, and later Islamic State forces up until 2016.

Confronted by an angry haze of racism and Islamophobia at home and abroad, Omar declares that the dreams he has inherited from his ancestors will give him clarity and lucidity. His next argument is, unsurprisingly, conveyed lucidly: "I can't say it simpler – Black Lives Matter. / But every single day we're seeing black lives battered, / falling in avenues named for black scholars, / the coffers of the coppers are funded by tax dollars" (Musa 2017a, 95). Omar further argues that "even if race is a construct, / certain races now suffer more police misconduct. / Back here, it's just done in a different way, / even though there's fewer guns, black bodies aren't safe" (95). Referring to the Black Lives Matter movement that began in the US in 2013 but has since spread worldwide, Omar minces no words in pointing out the terrible irony of African Americans being "battered" on the streets of US cities through "police misconduct" even as the country pays lip service to the memory of "black scholars" such as Martin Luther King, Jr, after whom many of those streets are named. The rhetorical arc of Omar's verse curves "back here" to Australia where "black bodies aren't safe" as well, as scholars of police violence against Indigenous Australians have documented (Cunneen 2017). In the Australian context, "black" as a demographic or an identifying term often refers to Aboriginal Australians and Torres Straits Islanders, although there is emerging scholarship connecting indigenous Australians with Africans and people of African descent in diaspora (Aboagye 2018). The poem therefore critically connects a relatively recent social movement centred on black lives that originated in the US with the need to recall and resist centuries of British colonialism and its white-supremacist legacy that still marginalizes indigenous lives and discriminates against non-white immigrants in Australia.

Conclusion

Omar concludes "The Ranthem II" on a sombre yet hopeful note: "We know that the world is a horror story / but we also know it's got love notes in the margin" (Musa 2017a, 97). This ending is even more poignant and affirmative in his live performance at the Bankstown Poetry Slam, where after delivering the final line Omar softly adds "and that's us" accompanied by a small gesture with his index fingers to indicate the audience and himself (2017b, 7:10). This is hyphenational poetics at its finest: by writing quatrains that generally follow an AABB rhyme scheme, Omar underscores how each set of paired lines can be double-edged, acting as both parang and hyphen. As parang the poem offers incisive comments on national histories and political hypocrisies that have devastated and disenfranchised various groups of people around the world; as hyphen it bridges Omar's personal background and wider political consciousness, brings together shared legacies of suffering and collective acts of resistance, and beckons the audience to reckon with what they have just heard or read.

Omar Musa, writing in English as a Malaysian hyphen Australian, starts from a liminal place between countries and cultures rather than being ensconced in a particular ethno-racial or national silo. Without romanticizing this liminality, it is possible to read this in-betweenness as generating Omar's interest in the hyphen that constitutes his personal subjectivity, which in turn can lead to a greater awareness of shared histories of oppression and collective resistance, as well as a poetry that consciously engages in transnational, cross-cultural, and genre-traversing borrowings. Omar is reshaping and expanding what Nazry Bahrawi (2021) calls a "Malay literary sphere" that involves tracing "cultural transformations within a single culture" and is not constrained by "the coloniser–colonised binary" of postcolonial criticism (68). In this light, Omar might be understood as an anglophone Malaysian author whose poetic parang cuts a new path through the Malay literary sphere by affirming a hybrid Malay, Suluk, and Kedayan heritage and by linguistically combining English and Malay in his verse. This is a challenge to the official notion of a national literature written purely in Malay by authors who identify as Malay Muslims.

At the same time, thinking hyphenationally, Omar's poems also (to use Jahan Ramazani's words) "dislocate" Malaysia and Australia from themselves by representing each country as "a changed space, nonhierarchically mapped" and bridged with each other (Ramazani 2015, 172, 174). His poems also reveal how European colonialism's legacy still causes persistent discrimination and violence, but they do so beyond a colonizer–colonized binary as they evince a broader world-historical consciousness. This diasporic poet's vision might yet prove instructive for authors in Malaysia. Rather than seeing Malaysian literature in terms of divisions or contests between national and sectional languages and literatures, what connections and critiques, what love notes in the margins, are possible if one adopts a hyphenational instead of a strictly national approach to poetry and fiction?

Acknowledgments

The author would like to thank Sheela Jane Menon and Nazry Bahrawi for their advice and assistance.

Disclosure statement

No potential conflict of interest was reported by the author.

ORCID

Weihsin Gui http://orcid.org/0000-0001-5392-2824

References

Aboagye, Kaiya. 2018. "Australian Blackness, the African Diaspora and Afro/Indigenous Connections in the Global South." *Transition: The Magazine of Africa and the Diaspora* 126: 72–85. doi:10.2979/transition.126.1.11.

Australian National University. 2010. "Australia's Earliest Contact Rock Art Discovered by Australian National University." Phys.Org, July 23. https://phys.org/news/2010-07-australia-earliest-contact-art.html

Aw, Tash. 2013. *Five Star Billionaire*. New York: Spiegel and Grau.

Bahrawi, Nazry. 2021. "Were-tigers in Were-texts: Cultural Translation and Indigeneity in the Malay Archipelago." In *Translational Politics in Southeast Asian Literatures: Contesting Race, Gender, and Sexuality*, edited by Grace V. S. Chin, 66–81. New York: Routledge.

Barlocco, Fausto. 2013. "Consuming Ethnic Identities: 'Materializing' the Nation and the Minority in Sabah." *Sojourn* 28 (3): 465–484. doi:10.1355/sj28-3c.

Boey, Kim Cheng. 2018. "'We are All Exiles': Exile and Place in the Poetry of Ee Tiang Hong, Wong Phui Nam and Shirley Geok-lin Lim." *Asiatic* 12 (2): 23–45.

Braginsky, V. I. 1990. "Hikayat Hang Tuah: Malay Epic and Muslim Mirror: Some Considerations on Its Date, Meaning and Structure." *Journal of the Humanities and Social Sciences of Southeast Asia* 146: 399–412.

Chow, Emily, and Joseph Sipalan. 2019. "Malaysia Backs $1.5 Billion in Aid for State Palm Oil Firm." *Reuters*, April 9. https://www.reuters.com/article/us-malaysia-felda/malaysia-backs-1-5-billion-in-aid-for-state-palm-oil-firm-felda-idUSKCN1RL161

Cunneen, Chris. 2017. "Police Violence: The Case of Indigenous Australians." In *The Wiley Handbook on Violence and Aggression*, edited by Peter Sturmey. Malden: John Wiley and Sons. https://onlinelibrary.wiley.com/doi/book/10.1002/9781119057574

Gabriel, Sharmani Patricia. 2014. "'After the Break': Re-conceptualizing Ethnicity, National Identity and 'Malaysian-Chinese' Identities." *Ethnic and Racial Studies* 37 (7): 1211–1224. doi:10.1080/01419870.2014.859286.

Gabriel, Sharmani Patricia. 2016. "'Local' and 'National' Transformations: Cultural Globalization, Heterogeneity, and Malaysian Literature in English." *Journal of Commonwealth Literature* 51 (1): 145–164. doi:10.1177/0021989414566517.

Glass of Venice. n.d. "Millefiori: A Miracle of Murano Glass." Accessed 9 November 2020. https://www.glassofvenice.com/millefiori.php

Haron, Muhammed. 2002. "The Cape Malays: An Imagined Community in South Africa." *African Research and Documentation* 88: 35–58.

Holden, Philip. 2012. "Global Malaysian Novels: Prospects and Possibilities." *Kajian Malaysia* 30 (1): 47–59.

Leng, Rachel. 2017. "The Circulation of Ghostly Women and Li Yongping's Affective Sinophone Malaysian Identity." *South East Asia Research* 25 (2): 122–138. doi:10.1177/0967828X17703435.

Lim, Shirley Geok-lin. 2015. "English in Malaysia: Identity and the Market Place." *Asiatic* 9 (2): 1–25.

Meade, Amanda. 2016. "TV Host Sonia Kruger Calls for End to Muslim Migration to Australia." *The Guardian*, July 17. https://www.theguardian.com/media/2016/jul/18/tv-host-sonia-kruger-calls-for-end-to-muslim-migration-to-australia

Mohamad, Maznah. 2011. "Like a Shady Tree Swept by the Windstorm: Malays in Dissent." In *Melayu: The Politics, Poetics and Paradoxes of Malayness*, edited by Maznah Mohamad and Syed Muhd Khairudin Aljunied, 34–67. Singapore: NUS Press.

Musa, Omar. 2013. "Interview with Omar Musa [With Lian Low]." *Peril Magazine*, July 16. https://peril.com.au/back-editions/the-amok-of-omar-musa-unfinished/

Musa, Omar. 2014. *Parang*. Melbourne: Penguin Books.

Musa, Omar. 2017a. *Millefiori*. Melbourne: Penguin Books.

Musa, Omar. 2017b. "The Ranthem II - Omar Musa | Bankstown Poetry Slam." Youtube. Video, 7: 14. Bankstown Poetry Slam. Accessed 9 November 2020. https://www.youtube.com/watch?v=XMtFQobSeXg

Musa, Omar. n.d.a "Omar Musa." The Garret: Writers on Writing. Accessed 9 November 2020. https://thegarretpodcast.com/omar-musa/

Musa, Omar. n.d.b "The Hat." The Moth. Audio, 11: 37. Accessed 9 November 2020. https://themoth.org/storytellers/omar-musa

Nordhoff, Sebastian, ed. 2012. *The Genesis of Sri Lanka Malay*. Leiden: Brill.

The Pin. n.d. "Omar Musa: Storyteller." Accessed 9 November 2020. http://www.thepin.org/meet/omar-musa

Quayum, Mohammad A. 2018. "Malaysian Literature and Beyond." *Asiatic* 12 (2): 1–5.

Quintero, Desiree A., and Mohd Anis Md Nor. 2016. "The Curvilinear Ethnoaesthetic in Pangalay Dancing among the Suluk in Sabah, Malaysia." *Wacana Seni Journal of Arts Discourse* 15: 1–25. doi:10.21315/ws2016.15.1.

Ramazani, Jahan. 2015. *A Transnational Poetics*. Chicago: University of Chicago Press.

Ros, Aiza Mohd Mokhtar, and Che Zarrina Sa'ari. 2015. "An Assessment of Attitude and Intention of the Kedayan People in Practicing the Local Culture among Different Levels of Educational Background." *International Journal of Arts and Sciences* 8 (7): 453–463.

Said, Edward. 1993. *Culture and Imperialism*. New York: Knopf.

Toh, Terence. 2014. "'Here Come the Dogs' Poet Omar Musa Now a Voice in Verse." *The Star Malaysia*, November 4. https://www.thestar.com.my/lifestyle/books/news/2014/11/04/here-come-the-dogs-poet-omar-musa-now-a-voice-in-verse

Van Neerven, Ellen. 2019. "Rapper, Poet and Novelist Omar Musa." *The Saturday Paper*, November 2–8. https://www.thesaturdaypaper.com.au/culture/books/2019/11/02/rapper-poet-and-novelist-omar-musa/15726132009018

Yahp, Beth. 2017. *The Red Pearl and Other Stories*. Newtown, Australia: Vagabond Press.

On not writing back: Cosmopolitan paradoxes in new diasporic Malaysian writing today

Jason Eng Hun Lee and Sreedhevi Iyer

ABSTRACT

In this article, two contemporary writers, Jason Eng Hun Lee and Sreedhevi Iyer, combine to reflect on emerging issues in their writing practice as deterritorialized writers with connections to Malaysia. Unlike earlier generations of post-independence writers, neither Lee nor Iyer "writes back" to the former colonial centre nor, despite their designation as "Malaysian writers" by commercial publishers, do they "write back" to their condition as sectional writers in the Malaysian literary canon. Instead, taking on a confessional mode, the two writers examine the paradox of their cosmopolitan sensibilities in an age of deterritorialized national literatures. Iyer reflects on her story collection *Jungle Without Water*, and her use of vernacular Malaysian English to transcend cultural explication, while Lee draws on his poetry collection *Beds in the East* to suggest how a double perspective that pivots between Malaysia and the UK can strategically mediate the colonial/postcolonial gaze.

Introduction: Situating the field of new diasporic Malaysian writing

The aesthetics of contemporary diasporic Malaysian writing in English can be said to have evolved from its colonial roots, adding to a corpus of postcolonial Malaysian writing that has defined the country's development at key moments since its independence. While the pioneering generation of writers like Lloyd Fernando, Lee Kok Liang, Ee Tiang Hong, and Wong Phui Nam laboured to exemplify Malaysia as a cosmopolitan, multiracial polity, succeeding generations from the post-1969 period, like Cecil Rajendra, Salleh Ben Joned, K.S. Maniam, and Kee Thuan Chye, struggled to break into the literary mainstream and were sometimes defined as "internal exiles" due to their status as writers of "sectional" – that is, non-Malay-language – literature. It was during this period, characterized by the 1969 race riots and implementation of the New Economic Policy and National Education Policy, which prioritized Malay over English, that a distinct group of diasporic Malaysian writers first emerged, consisting of prominent émigré poets like Shirley Geok-lin Lim, Hilary Tham, and Ee Tiang Hong.

Later, when these government policies were reassessed due to deteriorating standards in English, there was a literary resurgence from the 1990s which helped nurture a new generation of English-language writers, including Bernice Chauly, Dina Zaman, and Huzir Sulaiman, who could express themselves without being circumscribed by the postcolonial discourse of nation-building and Third World allegorical writing characteristic of earlier generations. This newer generation has since been joined by overseas poets like Omar Musa and Kamalia Hasni, and fiction writers like Rani Manicka, Hsu-Ming Teo, Tash Aw, Tan Twan Eng, Preeta Samarasan, Hanna Alkaf, and Zen Cho, all of whom appear at ease with their position as hybrid subjects in a globalized world, and who have taken full advantage of the dominance of English in the internationalized book market and distribution culture to advance their literary careers.

Surveying the state of the literature after the new millennium, Mohammad Quayum (2003a) projected that

> Malaysian writers in English who have chosen the global language as their medium, and ipso facto have chosen multiple ways of life and a sense of a multiple belonging, are well poised to depict the Malaysian "mosaic" reality for the growing readers of a transnational world. (186)

Over the past two decades, this sentiment has gained more support as newer writers within Malaysia have contributed to a concrete post-independence discourse that "envisions its place in an urbanized and globalized modernity of the 21st century" (Chin 2007, 275). The imaginary cultural terrain negotiated by contemporary Malaysian writers becomes less one of alignment with or against the nation-state polity, and more a hybrid mesh of multiple, conflicting associations where a Malaysian identity features as just one among many. The rise of digital media and the possibility of inhabiting multiple identities has liberated (especially non-Malay) writers from any stifling obligation to a totalizing, homogeneous national culture, which had been articulated through a "Bangsa Malaysia" identity (*bangsa* meaning either or both "race" and "nation"). The rise of local publishers like Maya Press, Fixi, and Gerakbudaya, following in the footsteps of earlier publications by Skoob Books and Silverfish Books, has given local writers a global purchase, allowing them to compete with their international peers to some extent, and to participate more fully in a global consumerist culture, albeit one still organized loosely along commodified genre conventions and regional taste cultures (Jay 2001).

These local developments have coincided with the breakthrough of BAME (Black, Asian and Minority Ethnic) poetry writing in the UK and a greater interest in global minority BIPOC (Black, Indigenous and People of Colour) literatures in the US, Canada, and Australia, allowing writers to excavate a niche within these former imperial, metropolitan centres. These twin movements, that simultaneously raise local literatures up to a global consciousness, and the pivot towards cultures once peripheral to the western imagination, have made it increasingly "more difficult to make a neat division between 'local' and diasporic texts" (Holden 2012, 48).

It is within this context of emergent 21st-century writing from abroad as well as locally that we, Jason Eng Hun Lee, a mixed British and Malaysian Chinese poet living in Hong Kong, and Sreedhevi Iyer, a fiction writer of Indian Malaysian heritage currently living in Australia, situate ourselves. Like many diasporic Malaysian writers operating in the global literary marketplace, we occupy a paradoxical position when expressing our cosmopolitan sensibilities. Despite our Malaysian origins and heritage, and the fact that Malaysia is reflected in our literary works, neither of us is physically embedded within its lived reality, and, as such, our work remains alive to both the anxieties and the opportunities that come with this new identity. We are part of a global phenomenon that sees Malaysia as written and produced as much from outside as within; Malaysia as a cultural imaginary in the eyes of the world floats far above the everyday preoccupations experienced by its citizens or residents, and therefore the possibilities for its representation become endless and multifaceted.

Like our contemporaries operating inside and outside Malaysia, we no longer face the charge of mimicking a foreign tongue – a form of expression that had until recently been regarded as a threat to the paramount status of the indigenous and majority Malay populace (Gill 2002). The push-pull logic of resistance to, and yet reverence for, English during the colonial period has been replaced by a spectrum of linguistic intelligibility ranging from an inner circle of native English speakers to an outer and expanding circle of national as well as foreign language users and learners (Kachru 1986). Given the ready availability of multiple vernacular Asian Englishes, many of which have become recognizable in the global imagination, the Malaysian writer can thus project a polyglossic amalgam of English, Malay, Tamil, Chinese, and other native words and syntactic structures onto a diverse linguistic audience across the world.

However, some differences remain between us as diasporic writers and our locally based peers. While resident Malaysian writers must continually "wrestle with the material reality and complexities of their multicultural milieu on a daily basis", we do not "experience the same socio-political boundaries that define the local conditions of production" (Chin 2007, 263). We cannot represent any totality from the peripheral position of our everyday lived experience, as it is not our task to rise above the "psychological and cultural moorings of [our] respective communities" (Quayum 2003a, 187). As a result, we continually fall between the cracks when it comes to the task of literary nation-building, having moved far beyond Bill Ashcroft, Gareth Griffiths, and Helen Tiffin's paradigmatic assessment in *The Empire Writes Back* (1989), where postcolonial literary traditions went through three developmental stages from works representative of imperial centres of power, to nativist or imitative literatures produced under imperial licence, to works of an independent and distinctively postcolonial flavour (5–6).

Whereas the first few generations of Malaysian writers wrote within the discursive frames of home and nationhood, we neither "write back" to the former colonial centre, nor can we "write back" to the attendant language politics, cultural baggage, and problems of self-censorship that have affected writers of sectional literature in the Malaysian national literary canon. Although national literatures have become deterritorialized, detached from the ground realities of their local geographies, questions of authenticity pervade our postcolonial subjectivity, and, despite deploying our work across local settings and markets, we remain part of a capitalist mode of production that raises our transnational profile but projects our cultural differences in opposition to the British colonial or Malaysian national centre.

It is worth recalling Timothy Brennan's (1997) critique of the cosmopolitan subject as a co-opted agent in an industry that produces its own version of cultural "otherness" and which features "authors writing, often experimentally, about their own carefully nurtured marginalities in a sort of highbrow mimicry of the testimonial" (48). The presumption that the postcolonial work is always autobiographical and conflates author and narrator (Booth 1961; Phelan 2005) demands that we possess a unique individual subject matter. Yet our liminal subject position does not extend so far as to reclaim a space, nor radically overturn any power dynamic. Nor would we wish to be party to this commodification of cultural difference, although we recognize that our reception across these different readerships remains at odds with how we wish to be presented.

Under these slippery conditions, we each seek to negotiate our cosmopolitan subject position, mindful that the weight of cultural explication and expectations of authenticity remain, and that our literary narration must be neither too local, nor too alien, and containing just the right amount of the strange and the familiar, to justify our floating position. As we occupy that problematic position of the cosmopolitan elite (Hannerz 1990), carriers of Malaysian authenticity abroad yet uneasy as sectional, even alienated, figures at "home", we represent a cosmopolitanism not from above or below, but certainly from a relatively privileged margin. Our position differs from the vernacular cosmopolitanism outlined by Homi K. Bhabha (1996) which, though expressed as a "cosmopolitan community envisaged in marginality" (195–196), applies more to the subaltern figure fighting against the prevailing colonial hegemon. While we support Kwame Anthony Appiah's utopian desire to forge a more "rooted" cosmopolitanism with everyone being "attached to a home of his or her own, with its own cultural particularities, but taking pleasure from the presence of other, different, places that are home to other, different people" (2006, 91), we must also acknowledge that our privileged position stems precisely from our detachment from the everyday operative burdens faced by the English-language writer in Malaysia.

While the cosmopolitan experience enriches the "national" by enhancing our awareness of its subjectivities and disjunctions, having a diffuse readership across the globe results in multiple "imagined communities", whose projections of the general national experience remains divergent. While these multiple representations are celebrated through our cosmopolitan subject position, they complicate how we make sense of this fragmentary, at times unintelligible, set of forces that circulate the globe as uneasy markers for what Pierre Bourdieu ([1984] 1986) calls "cultural capital". What role might we, as both connoisseurs and critics of this prevailing trend, play to ensure that our voice remains true to ourselves and our own vision of the world?

Drawing on Bhabha, Appiah, and Brennan, as well as earlier postcolonial theories proposed by Ashcroft and others, this article explores how our deterritorialized cosmopolitanism informs the intention and craft of our own writing, particularly as it is received by multiple audiences across the globe. First, Sreedhevi Iyer writes of transcending cultural explication by employing vernacular Malaysian English ("Manglish") as a specific craft choice to subvert the global/glocal English-language reader. She also reflects on the Rorschach element of her short story collection *Jungle Without Water* (Iyer 2017) and how different geographical audiences have responded to her work. Next, Jason Eng Hun Lee outlines how his poetry collection *Beds in the East* (Lee 2019) strategically mediates the colonial/postcolonial gaze, using a" double perspective" (Said 1994) that pivots as the narrator traverses between Sabah, Malaysia, and the UK. In contrast to Iyer's resistance vernacular, Lee frames a dialogical interaction between a variety of local and cosmopolitan readerships, playing on their reflexive assumptions about the poet's identity as "other". In encountering these shifting cosmopolitan positions in our short stories and poems respectively, we negotiate the complex politics of selfhood and reception in our craft, gesturing towards future possibilities for postcolonial literary agency in the new millennium.

Sreedhevi Iyer: The vernacular as resistance

Having lived across Hong Kong, Malaysia, and Australia, my relationship with Malaysia is less embedded in the sociopolitical realities of the country, and characterized more by fondness and naivety. This is a blessing and a curse, as it brings a heightened awareness of locality that forms the "spherical horizon" of my subject position (Gudykunst and Ting-Toomey 1988) and informs my principles on storytelling. Yet the adage of "show don't tell", where "telling" is frowned upon within the creative writing industry in general, renders cultural explication of my specific subject position undesirable, particularly as it is seen as constituting literature that is distancing (Tymoczko 1999), amplifying the foreign without inviting reader participation. As such, a paradoxical Catch-22 position inhabits my writing. I had to delve into what was Malaysian, without explaining it in the text; this requirement becomes "a self-defeating circumstance, requiring engagement in explication, while simultaneously forbidding it" (Iyer 2019, 46).

In this section, I consider how certain vernacular choices in my work "resist" this paradox, insofar as "decisions in the creative process of postcolonial writers to produce meaning in their work would be couched in language, form and style that bring unique elements to the literary product that are outside the normative requirements of the English language" (Iyer 2019, 46). Malaysian literature in English has taken on a new direction that upgrades the vernacular to the narrative voice instead of just dialogue, which serves to challenge the global/glocal English-language reader. This form of stylistic nativization demonstrates a truthful, realistic aesthetic derived from Malaysian traditions of oral storytelling, instead of fitting a mutated version into a pre-existing Eurocentric aesthetic framework. Peter Barry (1995) finds this strategy emblematic of a traditional "writing back" (14) with the notion that postcolonial writers either "adopt" the colonizer's ideology or aesthetics, or "adapt" them to produce hybridized literature, or eventually become "adept" by remaking or re-creating the form through styles and registers (129). However, like Rebecca Fasselt (2016), I argue that this paradigm is outmoded, and that the choice of first-person plural articulates "multiple centers of consciousness" that disrupt binary notions of oppositional forces between the colonizer and the colonized (167). I believe the selection of specific craft choices that remake language and evince the plurality of language use in Malaysian life does not conform to the "writing back" paradigm but exemplifies a contemporary and cosmopolitan ground reality. Additionally, the deterritorialized writer's vantage point makes them particularly aware of the issue of "unintelligibility" (as discussed below) resulting from their craft choices, as opposed to the impulse to contextualize for a universal audience.

In drafting the short story "The Man with Two Wives", which concerns a man justifying his extramarital affair while grappling with race and class issues that make economic mobility impossible, I researched the aesthetics of storytelling in Southeast Asia. I found that long-standing storytelling traditions came from ancient oral epics like the *Ramayana* and the *Mahabharatha* (Benson and Connolly 1994) and that the creative writing aesthetic specific to this region, therefore, is not "show and tell" but literally "telling" (Poddar 2016; Benjamin [1936] 1973). An early precedent can be found in Raja Rao's *Kanthapura* ([1938] 1974), a novel deliberately based on oral narratives. Rao claimed in his preface that "[w]e cannot write like the English. We should not. We cannot write only as Indians. We have grown to look at the large world as part of us" (viii). While many local writers produce a plethora of narratives for a local readership without worrying about cultural explication, innovation comes from taking literary risks, and this, I posit, is the new direction for global Malaysian literature in English.

This led me to the second-person dramatic monologue as a device for "telling" my tale, in a manner similar to Albert Camus's (2006) *The Fall* and especially Mohsin Hamid's (2007) *The Reluctant Fundamentalist*, where the Pakistani narrator discourses while the reader is placed in the position of listener, alongside the suspicious American who functions as the addressee. I wanted to bring the vernacular into the narrative voice itself, foregrounding Manglish at the front and centre to locate the characters' specific voices through a mix of linguistic codes and dialects. They could not be written in Standard English, since someone like my protagonist would not speak in that register. Whereas previous narratives by Preeta Samarasan and Fixi anthology writers foreground Manglish in the narrative voice as opposed to featuring it as dialogue, Dhaya's Manglish in "A Rightful Share" (Samarasan 2009) differs from Kalyani's in "Birch Memorial" (Samarasan 2008). The Manglish of a Chinese Malaysian differs from that of an Indian Malaysian or a Malay person from Penang, Kelantan, or Sabah. I make the protagonist in "The Man with Two Wives" speak the Manglish of a working-class Indian Malaysian, with Tamil inflections, such as "machan" along with the ubiquitous "lah", as well as the occasional absence of verbs, to better situate his class, language, and cultural background.

Unlike my vernacular Manglish-using predecessors, I seek to innovate my technique by embracing unintelligibility (Chien 2004) in my writing for a global readership, transforming it from a tool of confusion to one of creative aesthetics. The postcolonial subject has traditionally encountered the colonial other in literature, from childhood adoration of Enid Blyton books to an adult love of Shakespeare and Jane Austen, where much that is unintelligible in these works – from "lashings of ginger beer" to "get thee to a nunnery" – is a taken-for-granted element. The Dominican American author Junot Diaz speaks of this unintelligibility as

> an absolute bedrock of language [...] there was always going to be a part of language that I wouldn't understand [...]. And there was going to be a part of my speech act that someone wasn't going to understand. There was never this myth of perfect communication. (Diaz quoted in Chien 2004, 201)

Diaz's own language in *Drown* (Diaz 1996) and *The Brief Wondrous Journey of Oscar Wao* (Diaz 2007) acts as a strategic deployment of unintelligibility, geared towards multiple readerships through multiple linguistic registers including Spanish, Spanglish, nerd-speak, and profanity. Noting that "there was going to be unintelligibility for each group", Diaz fosters creative play by having "these different registers going on and to force communities", stating that he "thought it was real nice to put all these people together in one room and to see if they could speak to each other" (Diaz quoted in Chien 2004, 203). Here, Diaz is not producing narratives in dialogue with a dominant white centre so much as showing marginal communities conversing with one another. Diaz is not interested in a dialogical relationship with the dominant linguistic ideologies of this environment; he is interested in overturning it. As Chien extrapolates: "Diaz engages in the art of assertive non-translation, placing Spanish words side by side with English words without calling attention to them, without contextualising them or grammatically indicating that Spanish is other" (2004, 209).

The Malaysian writer today is far more comfortable with the use of Manglish, although the deterritorialized Malaysian writer is more aware of its disruptive nature and conscious of the creative risks involved in presenting this unintelligibility to the global reader. My story "The Man With Two Wives" foregrounds a multitude of idiosyncratic language patterns regularly used in contemporary Malaysia, including the suffixes "lah", "ah", "eh", the Malay grammatical repetition of a single word to emphasize its sentiment ("romantic-romantic", "clip-clip"), the Cantonese use of "wei", the street-slang "feller" for the very British "fellow", anachronistic colonial English phrases such as "a certain kind of regard", unitalicized non-English words in sentences such as "I opened a masala shop", and non-standard syntax such as "because no place for me". The language patterns also include words from other community languages in Malaysia – such as "naataan" (a Tamil slur labelling the Malay community – oddly meaning "native") and "Anney" (a Tamil word for "big brother" widely used within multiple communities in the country) and "makcik" or "pakcik", Malay words for "aunt" and "uncle" – that the narrator utilizes alongside English.

Used together, the transliterated phrases in Malay, Cantonese, and Tamil, along with anachronistic expressions from colonial English, create a highly distinctive register that is true to the story's character but communicates what Diaz terms a certain "unintelligibility" for multiple readers:

> What, you think I suddenly romantic-romantic, after one smile? Like that means, you know, how many girls would have made me pokai by now. No lah, Lata not like that. When I first spoke to her, soon enough I realise, she is different, very intelligent. For one, real speaking. When she speak English ah, like Mat Salleh only. Not like me. The sentences all proper-proper, arranged nicely, as if put together by somebody else. (Iyer 2017, 69–70)

As with Diaz, my non-English words and expressions are not translated, highlighted, or contextualized – nothing indicates that the use of Malay or Tamil grammar is extraordinary, abnormal, or simply other. Like the use of Manglish in the real world, the language here is all-inclusive, normalized, standard in its reflection of reality. The narrative voice in "The Man with Two Wives" renounces a self-consciousness derived from any preset linguistic standards. Any reader, from anywhere, is invited to participate, but there is no implied reader of English-language works or external linguistic aesthetic framework that I am catering to outside the verisimilitude of its environment.

International responses to *Jungle Without Water*: A Rorschach test?

Another cosmopolitan paradox can be found in how different regional readerships responded to the stories in my collection *Jungle Without Water*, which produced a varied, subjective set of responses akin to that resulting from a Rorschach test – a psychological test designed to observe and measure varying interpretive mindsets (Harrower-Erickson 1945) – which I use analogously to explore how and why audiences respond differently to the same set of stories.

First released in the UK, *Jungle Without Water* combines realist narratives set in Malaysia and Australia with surrealist fables on the connecting theme of movement and travel. While I was in Hong Kong, the edition's reviews highlighted different sections of the book yet unanimously praised "Green Grass", a short story narrated in the first-person plural (Rogers 2017; Ho 2017). The collection became better known after it obtained a Southeast Asian edition release and was shortlisted for the Penang Monthly Book Award. After this, the industry discourse around the collection centred around particular stories, with Malaysian university professors and teachers from international schools wanting to teach and prescribe assignments on "The Man with Two Wives" and "IC", while Malaysian reviews also cited these and "Jungle Without Water" as favourites (De Faoite 2019). One reason for this could perhaps be the language and setting – both "IC" and "The Man with Two Wives" feature Indian characters struggling with stunted socio-economic mobility who speak in a highly particularized English exclusive to the Indian Malaysian milieu.

While the UK edition reviews highlighted "Kadaram" and "Green Grass", which both feature Indian characters and incorporate themes of identity and belonging, neither story was mentioned in Malaysian reviews. "Kadaram", which details a Malaysian Indian's family journey to the heart of South India seeking ancestral connections, and "The Lovely Village", which is not specifically set anywhere, had little impact in Malaysia, even though they touch on the realities of migration, something Malaysia struggles with at the present time. Instead, Malaysian reviewers and readers preferred stories on contemporary urban realities and pervading dominant ideologies within the nation state. Narratives that specifically encapsulated or defined elements of the nation state, such as its historical umbilical cords with neighbouring nations, or its firm boundaries imposed on those without such nationhood, were perhaps too distant to resonate, or too damning for reckoning (De Faoite 2019).

After I moved to Melbourne in early 2018, an Australian edition was released with the story order rearranged, and Australian national reviews favoured different stories, such as the fables and surrealist narratives "The Lovely Village" and "The Last Day of the Divine Coconut" (Da Silva 2019; Goldsworthy 2018; Allington 2019). While "IC" and "The Man with Two Wives" were mentioned, they were not seen as deeply affecting in comparison to the surrealist tales; readers in Malaysia responded more to "realist" narratives, while an Australian readership, perhaps unable to draw upon any pre-existing Malaysian context, responded more to satirical fables.

Where multiple stories speak to different readerships, my writing becomes a flashpoint for myriad interpretations – a similar effect to the Rorschach test, where the collection becomes the inkblot. Similarly, I myself appear as a conflicted subject – a humourist, realist writer, migrant, expat, Malaysian, Australian, all and none of the above – a set of classifications which can be interpreted as symptomatic of readers' own projections and subjective backgrounds, rather than the reality of the literary work itself. Though certain stories share a common postcolonial past and have the same latent postcolonial hang-overs embedded in them, they do not provoke a uniform response across the region. Instead, they shift according to the localized cultural elements within the nation-state borders that accompany the publishing journey of the book.

Consequently, this experience clarifies my own positioning as a cosmopolitan author: I do not consider writing back to any centre, or writing forward, nor do I see the validity of writing with a specific reader demographic in mind, as clearly the reader's subjectivity helps frame their own discourse around the narrative. Despite not attributing myself to any one rooted geographical centre or culture, I nevertheless adhere to Appiah's (2006, 151) urging in *Cosmopolitanism* that one finds the universal in the particular, as I seek to reconcile those clashing values of universal concerns and legitimate differences.

A cosmopolitan writer in that sense would be comfortable with a decentralized understanding of their work in global literary discourse, with varying responses of their work highlighting differences in understanding between localized cultural elements. Similarly, a cosmopolitan writer continues to produce texts that draw such myriad responses, where the focus remains on craft choices and allowing the energy of the narrative to determine its reception. Perhaps this might eventually become a writing "out", as opposed to a writing "back".

Jason Eng Hun Lee on double perspective in *Beds in the East*

If Sreedhevi Iyer's writing resists engaging with specific Eurocentric sensibilities at the level of cultural explication, then my aesthetic likewise refuses to be relegated to any single reading demographic. As a transnational mixed-race poet with Malaysian origins, I follow earlier luminaries like Shirley Geok-lin Lim in practising a "poetics of liberation" (Tay 2005, 289) that hovers above exclusionary nation-state politics, though my poetics functions differently from Lim's (and from Ee Tiang Hong's), who contended with a more prevalent nation-centred world view. Whilst Lim (1994) defined herself via a "cosmopolitanism that disavows local identities" (xii), her work remains grounded within as well as against local and nationally discursive spaces, allowing her to be framed as a neo-cosmopolitan globalectic writer (Gunew 2014). This paradoxical situation is not lost on Lim, who comments on the way her "work is deterritorialized, an ironic prior property for a writer to whom 'home' has been such a first-order question and thematic" (quoted in Quayum 2003b, 88), and whose formidable transnational appeal is often defined within the contours of Singaporean, Hong Kong, and Asian American poetry (Quayum 2019).

Like Lim, I position myself at the intersection between voluntary exile and transnational affiliation, though I cannot claim a Malaysian subjectivity to the same extent, as my poetic awakening occurred after I left Malaysia as a child. In some ways, my work parallels that of older contemporaries like Tash Aw and Tan Twan Eng, both of whom have written global Malaysian novels containing Eurasian protagonists who represent an imaginary of the colonial past that eschews the current-day politics of Malaysia, and whose works invite readers to narrativize that past (Holden 2012, 57). I am aware, however, that lyrical poetry does not depict the national imaginary in quite the same way. The past in my work is not viewed from an elevated perspective or situated within a larger milieu of competing historical trajectories but rather reveals my own positionality. My poetic commentary on cultural displacement and western multiculturalism is more aligned with Malaysian Australian Omar Musa's (2013) *Parang*, for example, than with works by locally based compatriots Malachi Edwin Vethamani or Melizarani T. Selva. This explains why I return so persistently to the earlier poetics of Lim, Ee, and other older-generation poets – partly due to their ready availability and presence, but also because their aesthetic aligns most closely to my displaced, hyphenated subject position.

In my poetry collection *Beds in the East* (Lee 2019), I combine nostalgia for an upbringing in multicultural East Malaysia with depiction of a period of adolescence and adulthood in the UK. Portraying a double exoticism of both east and west, I complicate then deny orientalist and occidentalist tropes to continually challenge my readers' perspectives. Like Iyer, I consider how my reception devolves into particular national or cultural concerns, and whether reviews across the UK and Asia might relegate my work to specifically nativist or free-flowing transcultural representations. Unlike Iyer, though, I am keen to funnel certain expectations of readership in my presentation of the poetic self. In doing so, I consider how I might resist that validating process that legitimizes my inclusion in the world literary marketplace yet commodifies me as an object for consumption rather than allowing me to become a subject in communication, and whether I might be guilty of hawking my own cultural otherness to an assumed metropolitan centre, with its problematic (and now wildly outdated) notion of a homogenous western readership.

This fear of reinforcing the status quo stems from a concern that my production of otherness might reinforce what Graham Huggan (2001) has termed "the postcolonial exotic", whereby "the strange and the familiar, as well as the relation between them, may be receded to serve different, even contradictory, political needs and ends" (13). According to Huggan, many postcolonial authors used a "strategic exoticism" to play on familiar binaries of self/other, east/west that were in vogue during the 1990s – they "recognised their own complicity with exoticist aesthetics while choosing to manipulate the conventions of the exotic to their own political ends" (32). However, given the shifting politics of alterity nowadays, such attempts to bring "otherness" into the narrative no longer resonates with a transnational readership, as their own cosmopolitan experience makes them sceptical, if not sometimes hostile, to the identity politics and virtue-signalling that might come packaged with the writing.

My strategy, then, is to reflect that colonial/postcolonial gaze before disrupting it in the subsequent narrative. First, I borrow the title *Beds in the East* from Anthony Burgess's final novel in *The Malayan Trilogy* (Burgess [1956-69] 2000), which covers the period of the Communist Emergency and subsequent independence of Malaya in 1957, as an obvious reminder of the western imperial literary canon. A second strategy comes from my own collection's cover design, which features lush foliage decorating the margins and imitates the primitivist turn in European artwork that accompanied many colonial paintings of Borneo. I borrow further from Shakespeare and Burgess in my opening epigraphs, again, less in imitation and more as a playful foregrounding and later rejection of the colonial gaze. First, I take Shakespeare's classical depiction of the orient in *Antony and Cleopatra* and then immediately counter it with the opening lines of Burgess's *Time for a Tiger* – "They wouldn't know the bloody East if they saw it" ([1956-69] 2000, 5). In turning the cliché upon itself, I hoped to challenge the reader to reflexively weigh up whatever preconceptions they might have of the subject material.

Fortunately, the "strangeness" of my transcultural experience was reflected in critical reviews across the UK and Malaysia. For example, Usha Kishore (2020) read the collection as a " 'self-made myth' with its narrative of contemporary oriental and occidental spaces" (n.p.), while Leonard Jeyam (2020) responded positively to the pastoral, almost Edenic portrayals of the first section, highlighting the paradisal innocence of my childhood exploits as "the recalling of a life once lived, which today resides in memory" while noting how in the second half "the reader becomes more and more aware that childhood innocence must in the end face great dilution in the form of adult experience" (220).

As my childhood mise-en-scène occurs in Sabah, East Malaysia, with its vibrant, multiracial cast, I included representations of Kadazan-dusun and other indigenous fables in "The Longhouse" and "Kinabatangan" to further localize my experience of living in a state already at the periphery of the Malaysian national imagination. This attempt at indigenous self-fashioning might have led readers to accuse me of valorizing others for my own self-serving exotic appeal, echoing Huggan's claim that the unstable and oscillating polemic between self and other remains evident today where " 'Otherness' is writ large [...] but largely in terms of the (sometimes hidden) self that validates it" (2020, 819).

Yet I refuse to self-orientalize my persona as it unfolds itself over the chronology – my maturing poetic consciousness instead attempts to illuminate rather than obfuscate the reader. I do this by exploring the tensions and slippages between the self, nation, and wider diaspora, though the nation as geographical container and political imaginary still looms large in poems that implicitly reference Malay nationalism ("The Keris Speaks") or explicit Malaysian nationalism ("School Parade"). In "School Parade" for example, I narrate my mixed allegiances and passive indoctrination in the following stanza:

> Throughout August we learned of *Merdeka*,
> how the British were fought and overthrown
> by all our patriotic forefathers –
> I too yelled death to the invaders then
> bit my tongue for fear of home reprisals. (Lee 2019, 26)

Here, the discourse of *merdeka* (meaning freedom, or independence) is couched in the metaphor of an all-inclusive Malaysian family containing "all our patriotic forefathers" but fails to console the childhood persona, who chooses to reconcile with his dual British Malaysian identity by later rebelling against the pomp of the National Day celebrations. Similarly, the poem "Sons of the Soil" (a transliteration of the term *bumiputera*) describes the lack of native *bumiputera* status conferred on the palm oil plantation workers essentially living off the land and recreates a neocolonial frame by critiquing the government's affirmative action policies through the rhetorical end question: "what deeds or earth-born titles have they received, / these bumiputera friends of mine?" (Lee 2019, 36).

By contrast, the poetic self in the second half of the collection encounters a corresponding British and English nationalism, foregrounded by the revocation of my Malaysian passport in "45 Belgrave Square" and the multiple tests of allegiance in a packed football pub setting in "Three Lions Pub". The latter poem opens with my teenage persona being confronted by a football hooligan, and dramatizes a series of exchanges that weigh the legitimacy of my subject position against a polyphony of other voices:

> *Psst. His mum's English. Through and through. He's got*
> *the crown on his passport. He ain't Chinese.*
> *He's Malaysian. All look the same to me.*
> *I don't care what he looks like, what matters*
> *is where his loyalties lie.* Heads nodded.
> Tebbit's law had just ruled in my favour! (Lee 2019, 63; original italics)

By rhetorically foregrounding these conflicting perspectives, I force a dialogic interaction through my constant destabilizing of Englishness (or Malaysianness or Chineseness), inviting the reader to deconstruct these overlapping spheres of national, ethnic, and cultural identification by recognizing them as constitutive of an "othering" perspective.

Much of the conceit of the collection lies in this biracial double perspective which, construed through issues of deracination and mongrelization in poems like "Chameleon" and "Mutant", represents a constant pulling away from stable identity markers. One poem, "White Woman", seemingly exoticizes the figure of my mother from my childlike perspective, setting up an occidentalist frame at the beginning where my persona "whispered round corners / behind her back, *Orang Putih*", but which later falls apart when her real identity is revealed to the reader: "I froze as she cupped my face with soft palms. / Reluctant, staring up at mother's face" (Lee 2019, 20). These poems are intended to help the reader arrive at their own decentred narrative world view by perceiving otherness as a received condition, rather than as a marketing strategy. Through my role as a transnational émigré and "half-baked Englishman" (65), I try to excavate those contact zones, contextualizing them in specifically local circumstances through the confessional self.

Ultimately, I arrive at that sense of liberation only after memorializing my own travails growing up, and by seeing things "both in terms of what has been left behind and what is actually here and now" (Said 1994, 60). In the final poem, "Arrivals", I attempt to find roots/routes whilst remaining aware of the complex self-negotiating that comes with every new arrival, knowing that when "my routes have fallen all around me, / I must go back to the very beginning [...] where my past folds out and spreads before me / as one complete life" (Lee 2019, 86). Borrowing from K.S. Maniam's (1997) essay "The New Diaspora", I encompass a desire to create multiple attachments and find "the clay-taste / the deep-rootedness" (1997, 183) in that sense of belonging without having to fully buy into the national project or restricting myself to specific cultural enclaves. Hopefully, the reader will come to empathize with my situation by imagining their own vicarious cosmopolitan position under these myriad circumstances – and, in doing so, rendering the unknown or unintelligible as tangible and familiar.

Conclusion

As contemporary diasporic Malaysian writers, we reflect on the evolution of our own aesthetic in conjunction with the operational realities of the global literary marketplace. We have become more comfortable with the fraught and the fragmented, co-opting it into our practice, craft, and ethos. Rather than experiencing "otherness" at home, a condition much lamented in the works of many post-independence non-Malay writers, we might perhaps be said to be comfortable finding home within that "otherness", as we mediate the global literary marketplace and posit our stories to a multitude of disjunctive readerships and cultural settings. That is not to say that we uncritically frame our stories and poems as belated postcolonial works for the 21st century, however; instead, we are writing within a global heterotopic space that envelops different and occasionally divergent interpretive communities (Fish 1980). Sreedhevi Iyer has articulated the discursive consequence of the industry journey of her story collection and her creative decision to using Manglish while Jason Eng Hun Lee has set out his desire for a reflexive cosmopolitan practice amongst readers.

These strategies arise from the material realities of a decentred literary universe where culture, language, and identity continue to circulate beyond and through the national polity. Collectively then, our process necessarily becomes a form of resistance to the notion of writing back. While mindful of our postcolonial subjectivity, it is our respective positioning as cosmopolitan writers detached from nation-state realities that directly informs our artistic practice. This disembeddedness affords us sufficient distance and courage – Salman Rushdie's "stepping out of the frame" (1999, 43), as it were – to make creative decisions of (un)intelligibility, vernacularization, strangeness, and resistance to contemporary literary aesthetics.

Disclosure statement

No potential conflict of interest was reported by the authors.

ORCID

Jason Eng Hun Lee http://orcid.org/0000-0002-9341-3968
Sreedhevi Iyer http://orcid.org/0000-0001-6233-5525

References

Allington, Patrick. 2019. "Triptych." *The Mekong Review*, April. https://mekongreview.com/triptych/

Appiah, Kwame Anthony. 2006. *Cosmopolitanism: Ethics in a World of Strangers*. New York: Norton.

Ashcroft, Bill, Gareth Griffiths, and Helen Tiffin. 1989. *The Empire Writes Back: Theory and Practice in Post-colonial Literatures*. London: Routledge.

Barry, Peter. 1995. *Beginning Theory: An Introduction to Literary and Cultural Theory*. Manchester and New York: Manchester University Press.

Benjamin, Walter. [1936] 1973. "The Storyteller." In *Illuminations*, by Walter Benjamin, 83–109. London: Fontana.

Benson, Eugene, and L.W. Connolly. 1994. *Encyclopedia of Post-colonial Literatures in English*. Vol. 1. London: Routledge.

Bhabha, Homi K. 1996. "Unsatisfied: Notes on Vernacular Cosmopolitanism." In *Text and Nation: Cross-Disciplinary Essays on Cultural and National Identities*, edited by L. Garcia-Moreno and P.C. Pfeiffer, 191–207. Columbia, SC: Camden House.

Booth, Wayne C. 1961. *The Rhetoric of Fiction*. Chicago: University of Chicago Press.

Bourdieu, Pierre. [1984] 1986. "The Forms of Capital." In *Handbook of Theory and Research for the Sociology of Education*, edited by J. Richardson, 241–258. New York: Greenwood Press.

Brennan, Timothy J. 1997. *At Home in the World: Cosmopolitanism Now*. Cambridge, MA: Harvard University Press.

Burgess, Anthony. [1956-69] 2000. *The Malayan Trilogy*. London: Vintage.

Camus, Albert. 2006. *The Fall*. London: Penguin Classics.

Chien, Evelyn Nien-Ming. 2004. *Weird English*. Cambridge, MA: Harvard University Press.

Chin, Grace V. S. 2007. "New Generation Writings in English: Discursive Conditions and Literary Revival in Malaysia, 1996–2005." In *English in Southeast Asia: Varieties, Literacies and Literatures*, edited by David Prescott, 260–289. Newcastle upon Tyne: Cambridge Scholars Publishing.

Da Silva, Matthew. 2019. "Review of Jungle without Water and Other Stories, by Sreedhevi Iyer." *Mascara Literary Review*, June. http://mascarareview.com/matthew-da-silva-reviews-jungle-without-water-by-sreedhevi-iyer/

De Faoite, Marc. 2019. "Review of Jungle without Water and Other Stories, by Sreedhevi Iyer." *The Culture Review Magazine*, February 28. https://theculturereviewmag.com/2019/02/28/marc-de-faoite-reviews-jungle-without-water-and-other-stories-by-sreedhevi-iyer/

Diaz, Junot. 1996. *Drown*. New York: Riverhead Books.

Diaz, Junot. 2007. *The Brief Wondrous Life of Oscar Wao*. New York: Riverhead Books.

Fasselt, Rebecca. 2016. "(Post)colonial We-Narratives and the 'Writing Back' Paradigm: Joseph Conrad's the Nigger of the 'Narcissus' and Ngũgĩ Wa Thiong'o's A Grain of Wheat." *Poetics Today* 37 (1): 155–179. doi:10.1215/03335372-3452655.

Fish, Stanley. 1980. "Interpreting the Variorum." In *Is There A Text in This Class?*, edited by Stanley Fish, 147–173. Cambridge, MA: Harvard University Press.

Gill, Saran Kaur. 2002. "Language Policy and English Language Standards in Malaysia: Nationalism versus Pragmatism." *Journal of Asian Pacific Communication* 12 (1): 95–115. doi:10.1075/japc.12.1.07gil.

Goldsworthy, Kerryn. 2018. "Jungle without Water Review: Sreedhevi Iyer's Stories of Cultural Cross-currents." *The Sydney Morning Herald*, November 15. https://www.smh.com.au/entertainment/books/jungle-without-water-review-sreedhevi-iyers-stories-of-cultural-crosscurrents-20181109-h17pbo.html

Gudykunst, William B., and Stella Ting-Toomey. 1988. *Culture and Interpersonal Communication*. London: Sage Publications.

Gunew, Sneja. 2014. "'A Multilingual Life': The Cosmopolitan and Globalectic Dimensions of Shirley Geok-lin Lim's Writings." *Asiatic: IIUM Journal of English Language and Literature* 8 (1): 12–24.

Hamid, Mohsin. 2007. *The Reluctant Fundamentalist*. London: Hamish Hamilton.

Hannerz, Ulf. 1990. "Cosmopolitans and Locals in World Culture." *Theory, Culture and Society* 7 (2–3): 237–251. doi:10.1177/026327690007002014.

Harrower-Erickson, Molly. 1945. *Large Scale Rorschach Techniques: A Manual for the Group Rorschach and Multiple Choice Test*. Springfield, IL: Charles C Thomas.

Ho, Melanie. 2017. "Sharing A Space." *China Daily*, June 16. http://www.chinadaily.com.cn/hkedition/2017-06/16/content_29765969.html

Holden, Philip. 2012. "Global Malaysian Novels: Prospects and Possibilities." *Kajian Malaysia: Journal of Malaysian Studies* 30 (1): 47–59.

Huggan, Graham. 2001. *The Postcolonial Exotic: Marketing the Margins*. London: Routledge.

Huggan, Graham. 2020. "Re-evaluating the Postcolonial Exotic." *Interventions* 22 (7): 808–824. doi:10.1080/1369801X.2020.1753552.

Iyer, Sreedhevi. 2017. *Jungle without Water and Other Stories*. London: Jetstone.

Iyer, Sreedhevi. 2019. "Translation as Style and Technique in the Hybrid Englishes of Raja Rao's Kanthapura and Eileen Chang's Lust, Caution." *SARE: Southeast Asian Review of English* 56 (1): 45–66. doi:10.22452/SARE.vol56no1.5.

Jay, Paul. 2001. "Beyond Discipline? Globalization and the Future of English." *PMLA* 116 (1): 32–47.

Jeyam, Leonard. 2020. "Jason Eng Hun Lee, Beds in the East." *Asiatic: IIUM Journal of English Language and Literature* 13 (2): 218–221.

Kachru, Braj. 1986. "The Power and Politics of English." *World Englishes* 5 (2–3): 121–140. doi:10.1111/j.1467-971X.1986.tb00720.x.

Kishore, Usha. 2020. "Jason Eng Hun Lee's Beds in the East." *The Lake* (UK), February. http://www.thelakepoetry.co.uk/reviews/feb20/

Lee, Jason Eng Hun. 2019. *Beds in the East*. London: Eyewear Publishing.

Lim, Shirley Geok-lin. 1994. *Writing S.E./ Asia in English: Against the Grain, Focus on Asian English-language Literature*. London: Skoob Books.

Maniam, K.S. 1997. "The New Diaspora." In *Globalization and Regional Communities: Geoeconomic, Sociocultural and Security Implications for Australia*, edited by Donald H. McMillen, 18–23. Toowoomba: University of Southern Queensland Press.

Musa, Omar. 2013. *Parang*. Dickson: Blast! Publishing.

Phelan, James. 2005. *Living to Tell about It: A Rhetoric and Ethics of Character Narration*. Ithaca, NY: Cornell University Press.

Poddar, Namrata. 2016. "Is 'Show Don't Tell' a Universal Truth or a Colonial Relic?" *Literary Hub*, September 20. https://lithub.com/is-show-dont-tell-a-universal-truth-or-a-colonial-relic/

Quayum, Mohammad A. 2003a. "Malaysian Literature in English: An Evolving Tradition." *Kunapipi* 25 (2): 178–195.

Quayum, Mohammad A. 2003b. "Shirley Geok-lin Lim: An Interview." *MELUS: Multi-Ethnic Literature of the United States* 28 (4): 83–100. doi:10.2307/3595301.

Quayum, Mohammad A. 2019. "To Honor the Poet: A Festschrift for Shirley Geok-lin Lim." *Journal of Transnational American Studies* 10 (2): 10–20. doi:10.5070/T8102045750.

Rao, Raja. [1938] 1974. *Kanthapura*. 2nd ed. New Delhi: Oxford University Press.

Rogers, Kate. 2017. "Sreedhevi Iyer, Jungle without Water and Other Stories." *Asiatic: IIUM Journal of English Language and Literature* 11 (1): 336–339.

Rushdie, Salman. 1999. *The Ground Beneath Her Feet*. London: Vintage.

Said, Edward. 1994. *Representations of the Intellectual*. London: Vintage.

Samarasan, Preeta. 2008. "Birch Memorial." *A Public Space*, 6. https://apublicspace.org/magazine/detail/birch-memorial

Samarasan, Preeta. 2009. "A Rightful Share." *Guernica*, November 9. https://www.guernicamag.com/a_rightful_share/

Tay, Eddie. 2005. "Hegemony, National Allegory, Exile: The Poetry of Shirley Lim." *Textual Practice* 19 (3): 289–308. doi:10.1080/09502360500196250.

Tymoczko, Maria. 1999. "Post-Colonial Writing and Literary Translation." In *Post-colonial Translation: Theory and Practice*, edited by Susan Bassnett and Harish Trivedi, 19–40. London: Routledge.

The ruins of referentiality: Allegorical realism and traumatic fragments in *Scorpion Orchid* and *The Search*

Augustine Chay

ABSTRACT

This article uses Antony bin Thomas's *The Search* (1978) a relatively unknown novel, to reappraise its well-studied contemporary, Lloyd Fernando's *Scorpion Orchid* (1976). By drawing from Walter Benjamin's literary theory of allegory, the article reads both texts' socio-aesthetic of allegorical realism as a response to the mass trauma and nationalized cultural trauma of May 13, 1969. To emplot a tentatively optimistic trajectory towards interethnic reconciliation, each text recontextualizes traumatic memories of the watershed Chinese–Malay conflict of 1969, its sequelae, parallel antecedents, and other discursive events of the 1970s. Benjamin's theorization of the ruin as an emblem for allegory is used to rethink each text's reliance on rape as a vernacular metaphor for collective trauma and as a gendered modality of social coping. While acknowledging the conventionality of each novel's emplotment of interethnic reconciliation, the article reconsiders the referentiality of two of Fernando's most enigmatic characters: the transcultural prostitute Sally/Salmah and the messianic Tok Said.

The Search – written by T.J. Anthony and published under the (ethnically ambiguous) pseudonym Antony bin Thomas (1978) – begins with the following scene: a man walks into a police station soon after the watershed Chinese–Malay sectarian conflict of May 13, 1969. He is looking for his son, who had departed for Kuala Lumpur on the morning of May 13 and disappeared without a trace. The novel's characters are immediately marked by their respective ethnic identities: "Sergeant Bakar barked out at the Indian [...] Sergeant Bakar shouted out to a young Chinese corporal" (bin Thomas 1978, 1–2). The man and his missing son's ethnic identities, however, prove to be exceptionally indeterminate. He is Indian in appearance, but his legal name is K.U. Tan (he goes by Kutan). He claims to be "a Eurasian or something", "Indian in a way", "a British subject", and "a citizen of the United Kingdom and Colonies" (6). When asked to identify his son's race, Kutan initially states "Human race" (1). He then reveals that his son's name is Bujemo Tan and that Bujemo is a portmanteau for "Buddha, Jesus, Mohamed" (5). Sergeant Bakar eventually allows Kutan to look through the large pile of identity cards on his desk, and the mortuary where "half a dozen naked corpses lay inside like sardines" (10). Kutan experiences an initial reaction of shock and revulsion as he takes in this sight and its attendant stimuli (the intolerable smell, the eye-watering effect of the disinfectant). He nevertheless makes a quick recovery from a violent "urge to vomit" (10) and finds a measure of comfort and solace in the observation that death has seemingly dissolved the distinctions of race and gender: "No, I can't even make out whether they are Malays or Indians or Chinese. They all look alike to me [...] I can't even say whether they are male or female" (10–11).

As Walter Benjamin ([1928] 1977) argued in *The Origin of German Tragic Drama*, the allegorical mode is inextricably characterized by ambiguity and a multiplicity of meaning. It reveals a "crossing of the borders of a different mode" (177) as it shifts from representation to rhetoric. The initial promise of *The Search*, with its direct references to the immediate aftermath of May 13 – literature as witness, literature as documentation, literature as counter-memory – is thus seemingly betrayed by the paradoxical deracination of bodies that had been marked for murder based on phenotypical appearance. Though disfiguring physical violence and/or advanced decomposition *did* render many victims of May 13 (grotesquely) unidentifiable by visual perception alone, the scene ultimately foregrounds the novel's pedagogical imperative: "When they are dead, they all look alike. When they are alive, they don't. That is why they fight outside" (10–11). This shift from representation to rhetoric also compromises the consistency of the novel's psychological realism. If all the bodies in the mortuary are indeed indistinguishable from one another, how can Kutan be certain that Bujemo's corpse is not among them?

This line of criticism – allegory as artifice, allegory as convention, allegory as obfuscator, allegory as inauthentically didactic – is, of course, hardly new. In his defence and rehabilitation of the allegorical mode, however, Benjamin ([1928] 1977) argues that "allegory, like many other old forms of expression, has not simply lost its meaning by 'becoming antiquated'" (161). In a similar vein, Cowan (1981) makes the useful observation – one that predates Jameson's (1986) controversial conflation of "Third World literature" with national allegory – that "From the perspective of world literature, allegory seems to have fled Europe for cultures where an older religious tradition remains in uneasy coexistence with a modern discourse just becoming dominant" (122).[1] This postulation foregrounds the transhistorical parallels between postcolonial Malaysia, where secular modernity coexists uneasily with competing strands of Malay-Muslim ethno-religious nationalism, and the historical context of the German *Trauerspiel* (translated as "mourning play" or "baroque drama") which formed the basis for Benjamin's theories of allegory: the transition from Christian eschatology (during the overtly religious medieval era) to a secularized conception of history (during the Renaissance) in the cultural capitals of Western Europe. The multidimensional implications that Benjamin attributes to the concept of literary allegory – philosophical, religious, aesthetic, political, and historical – are of transhistorical and cross-cultural relevance to the immediate post-riot years, when a new vision of a modern postcolonial nation state was built on the charred ruins of Kuala Lumpur and the uneven legacies of British colonial capitalism.

While Benjamin turns the image and the materiality of the ruin into an emblem for the destructive character of allegory, its emblematic potential can be extended to include the nature of memory in general and traumatic memory in particular:

> In the ruin history has physically merged into the setting. And in this guise history does not assume the form of the process of an eternal life so much as that of irresistible decay.

> Allegory thereby declares itself to be beyond beauty. Allegories are, in the realm of thoughts, what ruins are in the realm of things. ([1928] 1977, 177–178)

Exposed to the danger of complete obliteration by a combination of factors – indifference and neglect, intentional vandalism, impersonal erosion – the ruin nevertheless retains (for a time) its ability to engender an affective emotional impact. It embodies the stubborn persistence of fragments and remnants of the past in the present – and the vulnerability of that concretized continuity to defacement, distortion, and dilapidation. In the realm of thoughts and textuality, Benjamin ([1928] 1977) argues that "what has survived is the *extraordinary detail of the allegorical references*: an object of knowledge which has settled in the consciously constructed ruins" (182; emphasis added). The "extraordinary details" contained within *The Search*'s opening chapter become apparent when compared to a rare, recently surfaced public account of the post-traumatic realities that some of the relatives of May 13 victims endured in their desperate attempts to ascertain if a missing loved one was alive or dead:

> [D]uring the riot, despite the curfew and being pregnant, I visited so many different places . . . my sister-in-law accompanied me, we went from one police station to another, and from police stations to different hospitals . . . KL [Kuala Lumpur] hospital, UM [University of Malaya] Hospital, Assunta Hospital . . . we all went, we wanted to find my husband [...] people know we were looking for our family member, they brought us around the wards, [back then] we didn't know he died already, we were hoping to find him alive . . . but we also looked into every single drawer [in the mortuary], still couldn't find my husband. (Tan Siew Choo, quoted in Por 2017, 49)

The Search evidently draws direct inspiration from some of the sites of memory that are part of the survivor generation's post-riot "itinerary" – police stations, hospitals, mortuaries, the stadiums that served as temporary refugee centres – while consciously constructing a telos of interethnic reconciliation. These historic spatial details are inseparable from the setting, even though the *real* identities of the fictionalized victims (Bujemo and the ethnicity of the bodies in the morgue), the bereaved (Kutan), and the perpetrators are conscientiously decontextualized in the service of an overarching allegorical schema. Unlike Mrs Tan, who remembers how the photograph of her dead husband – bloodstained and lying in a ditch – "was ugly, so ugly" (Por 2017, 49), Kutan's final reaction to the sight of May 13 victims in the morgue is notably aestheticized: "The sleeping and the dead were but as pictures to him. No sound. No fury. All over" (11). Kutan's fictional trajectory from visceral disgust to aestheticized acceptance exemplifies how post-1969 modalities of social coping generally perpetuated a forgetful remembrance towards the experiences of *actual* victims and survivors of May 13. The government's decision to bury victims of May 13 who were identified as non-Muslims within the grounds of the Sungai Buloh leprosarium was ostensibly made to prevent the act of burial or the graveyard from inciting further interethnic conflict. However, it ultimately "made it difficult for victims' families to locate their loved ones and suppressed the potential for public memorialization of the riot" (Por 2017, 48).

Revisiting *Scorpion Orchid* and the post-1969 status quo

Despite its obscurity and questionable aesthetic merits,[2] *The Search* (bin Thomas 1978) can be compared to its much better-known contemporary – Lloyd Fernando's (1976)

Scorpion Orchid – on the grounds of its unmistakable similarities. Both novels feature a schematic and allegorical recontextualization of the mass trauma and nationalized cultural trauma of May 13 as violence against hypersymbolic characters (the multi-religious Bujemo and the transcultural prostitute Sally/Salmah) that appear and disappear within a seemingly panoramic social landscape where ethnic tensions are omnipresent. As Andrew Ng Hock Soon (2009) argues, *Scorpion Orchid*'s setting in the tumult of 1950s Singapore "serves as an allusion to a still too recent socio-political incident which must remain unspoken due to the volatile nature of the situation at hand" (117). *Scorpion Orchid* recontextualizes traumatic affect within another time and place, with characters that are proto-Malaysian rather than Malaysian. Fernando's decision to transpose the racial anxieties of post-1969 Malaysia to 1950s Singapore also allowed him to draw from autobiographical memories. He lived in Singapore during the Japanese Occupation and throughout the 1950s, before relocating to Kuala Lumpur in 1960 (Newton 2008). This arguably explains why it is 1950s Singapore – rather than other Chinese–Malay conflicts prior to May 13 – that serves as a parallel setting.

As Jeffrey Alexander (2012) argues, a cultural trauma does not necessarily involve the wounding of individual bodies and psyches on a massive scale; it "occurs when members of a collectivity feel they have been subjected to a horrendous event that leaves indelible marks upon group consciousness, marking their memories forever and changing their identity in fundamental and irreversible ways" (15). I use the phrase "*nationalized* cultural trauma" to describe a general tendency (in literary and journalistic discourse alike) to generalize and recontextualize May 13 as a threat to a specific vision of national identity (inclusive, multicultural, pluralistic) – rather than a mass trauma (or a racialized cultural trauma) that disproportionately affected the Chinese residents of Kuala Lumpur. Written and published not long before the concept of psychic trauma became ubiquitous in popular, academic, and psychiatric discourse, *Scorpion Orchid* and *The Search* both rely on rape as a multivalent metaphor for nationalized cultural trauma in a "post-traumatic" time, place and discursive space – instead of attempting to represent the violence, destruction, and immediate aftermath of May 13 in a more direct manner.

This form of post-traumatic allegorical realism can be understood as part of a broader consensus – within official and counter-official narratives alike – "that all discussion and narratives about the May 13 riot must [paradoxically] serve the collective purpose of nation-building" (Por 2017, 39). Though May 13 ostensibly "proved how little the concept of 'nation' had been accepted by its citizens" (Hooker 2000, xvi), the destabilizing force of the event – mass murder and arson in Kuala Lumpur; the nationwide emergency; the suspension of parliament for 21 months; the transition from consociational democracy to electoral authoritarianism – ultimately cemented its status as Malaysia's "birth trauma". The colonial legacy of racialized economic inequality between the Malays and non-Malays (particularly the Chinese) was diagnosed as the ultimate cause of May 13, necessitating the urgent construction of a new Malay-centric post-1969 national order that "would ensure the future peace, security and unity of [Malaysia] and that the May 13 tragedy would not recur" (National Operations Council 1969, vi). Furthermore, there were numerous post-May 13 legislations that criminalized publications (and speech acts) that spread "rumours" or racially provocative sentiments. These restrictions were rationalized by the prescribed "lesson" of May 13: "This Nation cannot afford to perpetuate a system that permits anybody to say or do things which would set one race against another" (v). Offenders faced a prison sentence and even the loss of citizenship. The controversial Constitution (Amendment) Act 1971 – the "sensitive matters amendment" – prohibited the issues of indigenous rights, stratified citizenship, the national status of Islam and the Malay language, and the New Economic Policy's affirmative action policies from being discussed openly, even in Parliament.

Given this overwhelming historical-structural context, it is not surprising that the post-1969 novel's mode of allegorical realism ultimately straddles the imperatives of realist representation and generic schemas that emplot the recuperation of "racial harmony" and "national unity". After all, "[a]llegory could not exist if truth were accessible" (Cowan 1981, 114). It is worth noting that while the post-1969 national order institutionalized the political, cultural, and economic imperatives of Malay ethno-nationalism in an unprecedented manner, the ethno-nationalist Malay-language novels of the 1970s often featured unambiguous warnings of the Malay race and homeland being under threat *without* referring to the precise nature of the threat or expressing direct hostility towards non-Malays, "perhaps because of censorship concerns, perhaps because it was so obvious to readers of the texts" (Hooker 2000, 357). Despite their generalizing and nationalizing registers, however, each novel's allegorical recontextualizations of traumatic memory reflects its author's spatial proximity to the epicentre of May 13: the capital city of Kuala Lumpur. In other words, both authors ostensibly draw inspiration from first-hand observations of the racialized mass trauma (rather than rumour, official pronouncements, and censored reportage alone). In this sense, both authors approximate the positionality of the bystander "who feels impelled to bear an impossible witness to the extreme from a place of relative safety" (Rothberg 2000, 13).

As Norman Saadi Nikro (2014) argues, postcolonial trauma critics should not insist on historicization and contextualization in a manner that overlooks how "post-traumatic" literary texts "implicate and respond to terrains of social disintegration and modalities of social coping, often blurring any neat distinction between normality and abnormality" (2). Drawing from Benjamin's multifaceted defence of allegory and the literary archive of historical references within *The Search*, I present a reconstructive reading of *Scorpion Orchid* – one that carefully traces how fragments of traumatic memory have been recontextualized into the schematic artifice of allegorical realism. My objective here is not to reiterate familiar critiques of allegory, but to explicate how it functions as a modality of social coping and forgetful remembrance in the specific context of post-1969 Malaysia. I read against the grain of each novel's (ultimately conventional) construction of May 13 as a nationalized cultural trauma (a threat to the ideal of a multicultural and multireligious Malaysia) to recuperate the historicity of the allegorical references that inspired two of Fernando's most enigmatic characters: Sally/Salmah and Tok Said.

The hypersymbolic victim: Sally/Salmah and rape as a vernacular metaphor for cultural trauma

Though many critics (and Fernando himself) have highlighted *Scorpion Orchid*'s pioneering status as "one of the first Malaysian novels seriously and imaginatively to address race as *the* major social issue challenging Malaysia/Singapore" (Diamond 2002, 128; original emphasis), an early newspaper review suggests that – in its initial reception –

the novel's affective force may have been more striking and noteworthy than its convoluted allusions to the extratextual sociopolitical climate of the 1970s:

> Of all the characters, Sally, to me, seems to be the most real. She is assaulted and raped by a gang in a lane during the riots [...] The author's description of that savage happening is vivid, and proves that an expert in language finds it unnecessary to go deep into intimate physical detail in order to paint a terrible scene of brutality and horror [...]
>
> I feel I would like to have known more about Sally (or Salmah). Indeed, I would liked to have known more about most of the characters in this novel, more about them as human beings and less about them as talkative characters in a shadow play. (Josey 1976)

Savage, vivid, terrible, brutal, horrific: this proliferation of affect-laden qualifiers gesture towards an intuitive sensibility of how the spectacularly traumatized female body can be read as an evocative metaphor for (nationalized) cultural trauma. As previously noted, Benjamin's analysis of the *Trauerspiel* reveals that it retains an implicit eschatological structure (a primary attribute of medieval Christian literature), creating an inherent contradiction between medieval religiosity and Renaissance secularization. A similarly Christian framework underlies the allegorical realism of *Scorpion Orchid* and *The Search*. The loss of "racial harmony" is coded as a fallen event; each novel's (relatively sparse) plot points with a quasi-mystical certainty towards a redemptive future where ethnic polarization finally gives way to "forgiveness" and reconciliation between "the races".

In *The Search*, however, it is not the return of the hypersymbolic son alone that fulfils this telos. Kutan only manages to find Bujemo (in 1976, seven years after May 13) after "forgiving" Vasu, the man who raped his aunt and caretaker – a Catholic nun in India – decades ago. His aunt became pregnant with Vasu's child, but died two months later when she fell down the stairs in the convent. Kutan accidentally finds Vasu – who has converted to Islam and adopted a new identity as Syed Maideen – at his bookstore in 1975. After initially insisting on (belated) justice and retribution, Kutan decides to accept Syed Maideen's "hand of friendship" (bin Thomas 1978, 66). The latter promises to ask his son Syed Omar (the Assistant Superintendent of Police) to help locate Bujemo. In the final chapter, Kutan visits Syed Omar's home on Hari Raya. There, he discovers that his estranged daughter, Latifa a.k.a. Lee La, is Syed Maideen's daughter-in-law (and that she has converted to Islam). During this unexpected reunion, Latifa reveals that she knows where Bujemo is.

In *Scorpion Orchid*, the xenophobic violence that Peter D'Almeida (the Eurasian member of the Malay-Chinese-Indian-Eurasian quartet) experiences is not the traumatic climax of the novel. Fernando deliberately recontextualizes the anti-British motivations of the 1950 Maria Hertogh riots in Singapore in the novel; Peter is beaten up by 20 (racially indistinct) "figures" in Chinatown for being perceived as "a complete stranger [...] a creature made in the likeness of someone they did not know, whom they feared because he was so wholly foreign to them" (Fernando [1976] 1992, 69). Chapter 7 ends with a vivid scene that appears to recontextualize the murder of Royal Air Force Corporal Peter Hugh Bell (who was attacked and set on fire on Victoria Street) as the "rightful" murder of an unnamed Eurasian man "who wanted to be European" (74). The traumatized male bodies of *Scorpion Orchid*, however, are not encoded with the same pivotal status as the rape of Sally/Salmah.

Indeed, if the recontextualization of the violence of the Maria Hertogh riots as schematic violence against Eurasian and European identity makes the process by which "the events of history shrivel up and become absorbed in the setting" (Benjamin [1928] 1977, 179) become relatively transparent, the transcultural character Sally/Salmah has remained far more enigmatic. Sally is initially identified as a Chinese prostitute who makes "no race distinctions" (Fernando [1976] 1992, 123) when accepting clients. Effortlessly bilingual in Malay and Cantonese, she is described as "the pole around which [the quartet] had all been magnetised unawares" (112); their transethnic solidarities and youthful idealism shatter after she endures a devastating gang rape during the novel's referentially chimerical riot.[3] The police investigation that ensues reveals that her real name is Salmah binte Yub. The detectives declare her to be "a real multiracial girl" who potentially experienced "a multiracial rape" (123). However, the specificity of Sally/Salmah's identity suggests that she, unlike Bujemo, is not merely the personification of an endangered ideal. Her unexpected fluency in Malay and Cantonese is not attributed to established traditions of Malay–Chinese hybridity such as the Peranakan community or the once common phenomenon of Malay families informally adopting unwanted Chinese daughters.

Elleke Boehmer (2005) argues that women in postcolonial contexts – whether in political or literary discourse – are often idealized as personifications of national virtues (e.g. "earth mother" types) or made abject by symbolic vehicles "in the imagining of failed, flawed or disjointed community" (26). Working along the abject vein of this general either/or proposition, Ng (2008) argues that *Scorpion Orchid*'s imposition of "metaphors of unity and boundary-transgression upon Sally's body, only to have her brutally violated, suggests a rhetorical misogyny at work" (179) – even if she is not the prototypical "pure woman" who embodies racial and religious ideals. On the other hand, Zainor Izat Zainal (2010) interprets Salmah from an ethnographic perspective – rather than as a literary trope – and argues that her decision to achieve financial independence by becoming a prostitute can be seen as a form of feminist defiance against the prescriptions of *adat* (Malay customary law) and Islam. Whether read metaphorically or literally, Sally/Salmah straddles the distinction between allegory and realism, the imaginary and the real. As Hamish Dalley (2014) argues, "when fictional characters are presented as invented exemplars typifying historical phenomena, the symbolic interpretation of the past their experiences signify is constantly troubled by their status as *singular* entities that overflow exemplarity" (40, my emphasis). The difficulty of arriving at a conclusive interpretation of Sally/Salmah is compounded by the trans/historical character of *Scorpion Orchid*, with its interwoven affective and referential registers of 1950s Singapore and post-1969 Malaysia. This inherent referential heterogeneity means that the rape of Sally/Salmah signifies "a trauma that takes place and is repeated in multiple epochs and, in this sense, exceeds its historicity" (Van Styvendale 2008, 204).

Though the duality of Sally/Salmah evidently resembles the spectacularly contested identity of Maria/Nadra – the Dutch Catholic teenager who converted to Islam under highly atypical circumstances – she can also be linked to a sequela of the anti-colonial revolt that Maria/Nadra unintentionally catalysed:

> Another source of unanticipated trouble emerged out of a ploy by four Malay prostitutes. These prostitutes were known to have serviced several men who were working at the

> Salvation Army Home. On one fateful evening, the prostitutes were heard shouting over a wall at the Home, appealing to a Malay passerby for help. They claimed to have been coerced into attending Christian religious services. The Special Branch reacted swiftly. [...] The British hastened to seek the assistance of members of the Muslim Advisory Board, who clarified to the Muslim public that the rumours of the forceful conversion of the four prostitutes were untrue. All police and military units on the island were placed on high alert so as to act swiftly in response to any form of disorder or outbreak of riots at any moment. (Aljunied 2009, 42)

The claim of forceful conversion by four prostitutes fulfilled Jeffrey Alexander's criteria for a cultural trauma in Singapore in 1950: "a claim to some fundamental injury, an exclamation of the terrifying profanation of some sacred value, a narrative about a horribly destructive social process" (2012, 16). For the Muslim community, the affective power of this discursive event did not lie in the fact that Malay prostitutes were serving Christian/non-Malay men (i.e. it did not trigger collective anxieties about racial and sexual purity), but that Muslim women were being coerced into apostasy: an intolerable insult to Islam. Fernando thus decontextualizes the specifically *religious* character of the Maria Hertogh riot and its aftermath, but retains the trans/historical phenomenon of a woman's body wielding the power to represent and embody a collective ideal in a visceral manner.

Syed Muhd Khairudin Aljunied (2009) observes that women and children were typically left unharmed during the Maria Hertogh riots. When British serviceman John W. Davies was killed, for example, he was travelling on a bus with his wife and eight-year-old daughter – both were left unscathed (1). This selectiveness in victim choice exemplifies what Horowitz (2000) describes as the "bizarre paradox of rationality in rioting" (124). With May 13, however, the target group was not so narrowly defined. Chinese women and children and Indian men, women and children were not spared (von Vorys 1975). From the perspective of history (as opposed to biographical memory), the post-World War Chinese–Malay conflict of 1945 is the clearer antecedent to May 13. Horowitz (2000) observes that interethnic violence was "preceded by not only by stories of outrages perpetrated by Chinese men against Malay women, but also by reports that the British were planning to give Malaya over to the Chinese guerilla force that had fought the Japanese" (82). Likewise, Karl von Vorys (1975) notes that one of the most provocative rumours that circulated in the Malay community just before the May 13 attacks began was "the assertion that Malay women and children had been killed by the Chinese while the men were on their way to Kuala Lumpur" (329). During the early days of the emergency, the most lurid rumour recorded involved "four Chinese nurses from Assunta Hospital in Petaling Jaya being assaulted, mutilated, then murdered by their military escorts" (von Vorys 1975, 369). Though the "killing and mutilation of men is much more common than is the murder or rape of women" (Horowitz 2000, 73) during the deadly ethnic riot, rumours of *female* victimization and violation may have been a compelling incentive for participation in (and rationalization of) mass interethnic violence.

Sally/Salmah's body thus becomes a site of forgetful remembrance and the symbolic recontextualization of racialized mass trauma to a deracinated and nationalized cultural trauma. When Sally/Salmah regains her consciousness, she thanks a moustached Indian man named Arokiam (who was beaten up for interfering with the gang rape, rather than his ethnicity) (Fernando [1976] 1992, 121). The Chinese and Malay members of the quartet (Guan Kheng and Sabran) each offer emotional support and communal solidarity after her ordeal, but she pointedly rejects both men. The schematic implication is that "Indians" were innocent bystanders, but victimhood is shared by the "Malays" and "Chinese" – and not claimed exclusively by either community. Sally/Salmah is uninterested in helping the police identify the men who raped her, leaving them unable to "tell how the races were involved in the rape" (124). Fully estranged from the quartet and unwilling to assist the police with identifying and prosecuting her assailants, she embodies the novel's framing of May 13 as an ultimately "unknowable" trauma (unidentifiable perpetrators; an ethnically ambiguous victim who refuses to politicize her pain) – but one with unmistakable implications for everyone: "the disturbances were no more, even Salmah herself was no more, and only the dark mystery of what happened to her and to them oppressed their flesh" (127).

The phantasmatic perpetrator: Tok Said and the return of Mat Kilau

While the spatial and temporal relocation of May 13 to 1950s Singapore has made it difficult to ascertain *Scorpion Orchid*'s "real time and place of enunciation" (Nikro 2014, 2–3), *The Search* provides a literary archive of post-1969 memories that helps to illuminate the often-forgotten contingencies of the aftermath. Though the phrase suggests a familiar emphasis on temporal and spatial contextualization, Nikro (2014) argues for an inquiry into how a literary text anticipates the intellectual, social, political, and aesthetic sensibilities that will inform the way it is read, reviewed, translated, and/or commented on.

As with *Scorpion Orchid, The Search* is riddled with familiar anxieties and insecurities about the status of non-Malay identities and cultures in post-1969 Malaysia. Since Kutan works at a Chinese vernacular school, however, the contradictions and hypocrisies of ethnocentrism are dramatized from the vantage point of reactionary Malaysian Chinese politics. For example, Kutan observes that the principal, Herbert Khoo, publicly extols the virtues of single-minded devotion to Mandarin for the "common ignorant Chinese man's son" (bin Thomas 1978, 17) while enrolling his own son in an Australian university and gleefully looking forward to the prospect of a German daughter-in-law. When the idea of staging Ramayana at a school event is presented, he vetoes it: "it is pure waste of time looking for unChinese thoughts and unChinese ideas to corrupt our Chinese children" (52). Despite Kutan's remarkably hybrid identity – he is married to a Chinese woman and speaks Mandarin, English, Malay, and Tamil – he is evidently powerless to change the prevailing climate of Chinese ethnocentrism. This is presumably left to the new Punjabi headmaster who has been appointed by the Ministry of Education to replace Mr Khoo. All his hopes for a post-racial future are embodied in Bujemo, who is finally found at the end of the novel. Having been rendered insane by "the killing and the burning of May 13th" (108), however, it is up to Kutan's baby grandson – a half-Siamese child who does not look like any particular race – to miraculously transcend the divisions of "religion, caste, race and nationality" (109). As with *Scorpion Orchid*, it is evident that *The Search* anticipates a local anglophone readership that hopes to preserve – and potentially elevate – a supra-ethnic political agenda.

Nestled within the novel's overarching schema, however, are revealing references to several post-1969 events. These include the reappearance of the colonial-era warrior Mat Kilau in December 1969 (bin Thomas 1978, 21), the high-profile boxing match between Muhammad Ali and Joe Bugner in Stadium Merdeka on July 1, 1975 (63), the Japanese Red Army's involvement in the Kuala Lumpur Hostage Crisis of August 1975 (68), the bombing of the National Monument by communist guerrillas on August 26, 1975 (73), and the unexpected death of Malaysia's second Prime Minister Tun Abdul Razak Hussein (from leukaemia) on January 14, 1976 (91). Antony bin Thomas and Fernando would have also been aware of Selangor Chief Minister Datuk Harun's dramatic removal from political life. As Michael Leifer (1976) observes:

> Datuk Harun is widely regarded in Malaysia as having played a notorious role in fomenting Malay agitation just prior to the outbreak of communal violence in May 1969. [...] When it became known that Datuk Harun had been arraigned on charges of corruption, the Chinese of Kuala Lumpur were reported to have trembled at the prospect of young Malays from local *kampongs* going on the rampage to protest at this action against their patron and father-figure. (158)

Datuk Harun's arrest was thus a hyper-visible affair: "On November 24, 1975, in an atmosphere of great tension with armed troops stationed in the largely deserted streets of the city, Harun was arrested and charged with sixteen counts of corruption" (Crouch 1996, 100). *The Search*'s direct references to the high-profile terrorist attacks of 1975 explicitly evoke the (now generally forgotten) fears about the dangers from "gangsters, thieves, robbers, pickpockets, extortionists, communists" (bin Thomas 1978, 59) in 1970s Kuala Lumpur, while the fear that violence and chaos may also be caused by a "power hungry, upstart, stupid, wicked politician" (3) is only an offhand possibility. These textual possibilities of interethnic symbolic reconciliation thus emerge in the Malaysian public sphere as the bodies of two major politicians – each associated with May 13 in a different manner – announce their respective departures.

Meanwhile, the explicit reference to Mat Kilau – "this is history or myth?" (bin Thomas 1978, 24) – unveils the obscure referent behind the enigmatic character of Tok Said in *Scorpion Orchid*. While his name and characterization imply the identity of a charismatic Malay-Muslim figure with occult powers (recalling the magico-mystical practices of the Sufi mystic, the *bomoh* and the *pawang*), the novel emphasizes his irreducibility to a singular identity, location, or message. He is described by the various characters who claim to have met him as "an old Indian man" (Fernando [1976] 1992, 31); "Malay" (32); "an agent planted by the communists to cause panic" (61); as having gone mad after being seduced by a Chinese prostitute (62); a non-entity (76); a "toothless hulk [...] who could have been Malay or Chinese or Indian or Eurasian" (77); and "a psychological campaign" (141). Readers learn that the Anthropological Society commissioned a research team to "establish his identity and clarify exactly what, if anything, he was predicting, and on what basis" (76). Due to the lack of hard evidence, they conclude that he does not exist. The government, however, rejects their report. Ng (2008) argues that Tok Said is simultaneously an agent of anarchy and a messianic embodiment of "a transcendent mode of hospitality that is advocated by Derrida and Levinas" (172). He is thus a paradoxical assemblage of all sociological forces that threatened the stability and authority of (post)colonial governmentality (ethno-religious "primordialism" and extremism, deep-rooted superstition and magical thinking, destabilizing rumours, communist politicking) – and an ahistorical symbol for transethnic and pan-religious spiritual unity.

Upon closer scrutiny, however, Tok Said can be seen as a de-martialized recontextualization of Mat Kilau: a charismatic Malay warrior who opposed British rule in the early colonial period. Once labelled as "rebels", "traitors", and "troublemakers", Mat Kilau and his contemporaries were belatedly canonized and commemorated as anti-imperialists, freedom fighters, and patriots par excellence. Tok Said's name may have been inspired by Tok Janggut (a key figure in the 1915 Kelantan rebellion) and Dol Said (leader of the 1831–32 Naning Revolt); "tok" is a Malay kinship marker that is assigned to a grandfather or to a (typically older) person with an important status. Years before these historical actors were reclaimed by the Malaysian autonomous history movement (Cheah 2006, 19–32), a very old man appeared at the Pulau Tawar mosque in Jerantut, Pahang, on December 26, 1969 (Black 2014, xviii). He declared himself to be Mat Kilau: a prominent warrior who opposed the encroaching British presence in Pahang from 1891 to 1895. Front-page newspaper headlines ensued, creating nationwide intrigue and controversy. The Pahang state government commissioned an investigation on January 8, 1970. After several months, it confirmed that he was the man who had been reported (by British colonial officers) to have died in 1896.

As noted in an article in *The Star* on January 29, 2007, (Shahani and Ishak 2007, n.p.), Mat Kilau claimed that he had attended the proclamation of the Malayan Declaration of Independence in Kuala Lumpur, but kept his identity a secret for decades because he had been branded a traitor to the Sultan of Pahang for his role in the revolt. A few days after the official confirmation, he died on August 16, 1970 – allegedly at the record-breaking age of 123 years old. A. J. Stockwell (1998) observes that Tun Abdul Razak, the Deputy Prime Minister at the time, commemorated him as "a warrior against colonialism" (338). He hoped that "the spirit of Mat Kilau will serve not only as an example but also as a challenge to the people in facing future problems in defending the independence and sovereignty of the nation" (as quoted in Stockwell 1998, 338). The historian Khoo Kay Kim (1979) observes that Mat Kilau's reappearance was followed by news reports and rumours about the respective "returns" of Dato Bahaman, Mat Kelantan, Tok Sa'gor, and descendants of the Sultanate of Melaka (which was dissolved in 1511) (248–249). Though professional historians are understandably sceptical of such claims, it is evident that Mat Kilau's reappearance had a powerful affective appeal that influenced popular memory on a national scale – in a manner that transcended the localized folk legends surrounding his contemporaries.

By repurposing the story of Mat Kilau, Fernando retains his magico-religious prowess while substituting his physical singularity with a metaphysical potentiality to transcend ethnic and religious distinctions. Tok Said makes revolutionary prophecies, but the messiah never materializes to lead the charge of revolution himself. Given the highly visible transformation of an ageing Malay warrior's body into an iconic emblem of postcolonial ethno-nationalism, it is not surprising that *Scorpion Orchid* strips that very same body of its martial associations while retaining its unusual charisma and powers of affect. Whether the motivations for his actions during the Semantan War are interpreted as being "anti-British", "feudalistic", "self-interested", "a peasant revolt", or "proto-nationalist", Mat Kilau embodies what Cheah (2012) has described as the "peculiarly unique" Malay method of warfare, which combines "traditional Malay martial arts,

Islamic religious fervor, and faith in supernatural powers" (294–295). This "fanatical force" – often accompanied by the rallying cry and diagnostic sign of "amok" – left an indelible impact on the nation through May 13 and grass-roots retaliation during the communist "reign of terror" (Cheah 2012, 194–239), as it once did, on sporadic occasions, on the frontmen of empire as they pacified Malay-Muslim dissent.

The anglophone Malaysian readers who picked up a copy of *Scorpion Orchid* or *The Search* in the late 1970s presumably did not need an explicit reminder of this "negative other that announces itself in real events, real bodies, and real pain" (Teskey 1996, 25). As Gayl D. Ness (1972) observed, the "charred remains of Chinese houses and shops bore for a long time stark evidence that the riots concentrated on Chinese settlements that ringed the Malay neighborhood in Kuala Lumpur's center" (735–736); the asymmetric nature of the conflict was rhetorically de-emphasized by an official and counter-official desire for racial harmony and national unity. May 13's "direct and personal meaning" to the survivor generation was ultimately overshadowed by the "sharp realisation that the racial problem in this country is a serious one" (National Operations Council 1969, iii) – at a time when the dichotomy between modern rationality and "primordial" ethno-religious tradition was being re-imagined. The overwhelming desire for civil repair and interethnic reconciliation thus manifests itself in unidentifiable perpetrators of violence and hypersymbolic victims, while the ethno-religious motivations for (and magico-religious modalities of) violence are conscientiously decontextualized. Like the allegory of the 17th century, however, this is not "convention of expression, but expression of convention" (Benjamin [1928] 1977, 175). The fragments and remnants of traumatic memory – which recall the mass trauma of deadly ethno-religious riots and fears of collective "amok" – nevertheless retain a semblance of their affective power in the ruins of allegorical realism, giving shape, form and substance to its schemas.

Notes

1. Cowan posits that the oeuvres of Dostoevsky, Hawthorne, Melville, and Faulkner are sites for the persistence of allegory in 19th and 20th century literature.
2. Antony bin Thomas's novels, *The Nightmare of Youth* (1970) and *The Search* (1978), are out of print. T.J. Anthony worked as a lecturer in English at Singapore Polytechnic before becoming the principal of Vanto Academy in Petaling Jaya, Malaysia.
3. Fernando (1991) revealed how he subconsciously integrated memories of the Maria Hertogh riots and the Middle Road Strikes (a.k.a. the Hock Lee bus riots) while writing this scene.

Acknowledgements

This article draws from the author's master's thesis on the post-1969 anglophone Malaysian novel. He would like to thank Tania Roy and Bruce Lockhart for their guidance, and the anonymous *Journal of Postcolonial Writing* reviewers for their comments.

Disclosure statement

No potential conflict of interest was reported by the author(s).

ORCID

Augustine Chay http://orcid.org/0000-0001-8339-7821

References

Alexander, Jeffrey C. 2012. *Trauma: A Social Theory*. Cambridge: Polity Press.

Aljunied, Syed Muhd Khairudin. 2009. *Colonialism, Violence and Muslims in Southeast Asia: The Maria Hertogh Controversy and Its Aftermath*. London: Routledge.

Benjamin, Walter. [1928] 1977. *The Origin of German Tragic Drama*. Translated by John Osborne. London: Verso.

bin Thomas, Antony. 1970. *The Nightmare of Youth*. Kuala Lumpur: Vanto Publications.

bin Thomas, Antony. 1978. *The Search*. Kuala Lumpur: Vanto Publications.

Black, Jeremy. 2014. *Contesting History: Narratives of Public History*. London: Bloomsbury Publishing.

Boehmer, Elleke. 2005. *Stories of Women: Gender and Narrative in the Postcolonial Nation*. Manchester: Manchester University Press.

Cheah, Boon Kheng. 2006. *To' Janggut: Legends, Histories, and Perceptions of the 1915 Rebellion in Kelantan*. Singapore: Singapore University Press.

Cheah, Boon Kheng. 2012. *Red Star over Malaya: Resistance and Social Conflict during and after the Japanese Occupation, 1941–1946*. 4th ed. Singapore: National University of Singapore Press.

Cowan, Bainard. 1981. "Walter Benjamin's Theory of Allegory." *New German Critique* 22 (22): 109–122. doi:10.2307/487866.

Crouch, Harold. 1996. *Government and Society in Malaysia*. Ithaca, NY: Cornell University Press.

Dalley, Hamish. 2014. *The Postcolonial Historical Novel: Realism, Allegory, and the Representation of Contested Pasts*. London: Palgrave Macmillan.

Diamond, Catherine. 2002. "Maturation and Political Upheaval in Lloyd Fernando's 'Scorpion Orchid' and Robert Yeo's 'The Singapore Trilogy'." *Comparative Drama* 36 (1/2): 125–144. doi:10.2307/41154113.

Fernando, Lloyd. [1976] 1992. *Scorpion Orchid*. Singapore: Times.

Fernando, Lloyd. 1991. "Truth in Fiction." In *Perceiving Other Worlds*, edited by Edwin Thumboo, 220–225. Singapore: Times Academic Press.

Hooker, Virginia Matheson. 2000. *Writing a New Society: Social Change through the Novel in Malay*. Honolulu: University of Hawaii Press.

Horowitz, Donald L. 2000. *The Deadly Ethnic Riot*. Berkeley, CA: University of California Press.

Jameson, Fredric. 1986. "Third-World Literature in the Era of Multinational Capitalism." *Social Text* 15 (15): 65–88. doi:10.2307/466493.

Josey, Alex. 1976. "Coming Home, Baby." *New Nation*, August 15. 23. *Newspaper SG*.

Khoo, Kay Kim. 1979. "Recent Malaysian Historiography." *Journal of Southeast Asian Studies* 10 (2): 247–261. doi:10.2307/20070303.

Leifer, Michael. 1976. "Malaysia after Tun Razak." *The Round Table* 66 (262): 153–160. doi:10.1080/00358537608453215.

National Operations Council. 1969. *The May 13 Tragedy: A Report*. Kuala Lumpur: National Operations Council.

Ness, Gayl D. 1972. Review of *May 13: Before and After* by Tunku Abdul Rahman; *Malaysia: Death of a Democracy* by John Slimming; *The May 13 Tragedy: A Report* by The National Operations

Council; and *The May Thirteenth Incident and Democracy in Malaysia* by Goh Cheng Tiek. *The Journal of Asian Studies* 31(3): 734–736. doi:10.2307/2052316.
Newton, Pauline T. 2008. "Lloyd Fernando's Circle: An Interview with Marie Fernando, Wife of Lloyd Fernando." *Asiatic* 2 (2): 101–110.
Ng, Andrew Hock Soon. 2008. "The Vision of Hospitality in Lloyd Fernando's *Scorpion Orchid*." *Journal of Postcolonial Writing* 44 (2): 171–181. doi:10.1080/17449850802001983.
Ng, Andrew Hock Soon. 2009. "Nation and Religion in the Fiction of Lloyd Fernando." In *Sharing Borders: Studies in Contemporary Singaporean-Malaysian Literature I*, edited by Mohammad A. Quayum and Wong Phui Nam, 114–127. Singapore: National Library Board.
Nikro, Norman Saadi. 2014. "Situating Postcolonial Trauma Studies." *Postcolonial Text* 9 (2): 1–21.
Por, Heong Hong. 2017. "Family Narratives and Abandoned Monuments of the May 13 Riot in the Sungai Buloh Leprosarium." *Journal of the Malaysian Branch of the Royal Asiatic Society* 90 (2): 35–54. doi:10.1353/ras.2017.0019.
Rothberg, Michael. 2000. *Traumatic Realism: The Demands of Holocaust Representation.* Minneapolis, MN: University of Minnesota Press.
Shahani, Tuan Sharifah and Mohd Shukri Ishak. 2007. "Mat Kilau: The Malay Warrior." *The Star*, January 29. https://www.thestar.com.my/news/community/2007/01/29/mat-kilau-the-malay-warrior
Stockwell, A. J. 1998. "Conceptions of Community in Colonial Southeast Asia." *Transactions of the Royal Historical Society* 8: 337–355. doi:10.2307/3679301.
Teskey, Gordon. 1996. *Allegory and Violence.* Ithaca, NY: Cornell University Press.
Van Styvendale, Nancy. 2008. "The Trans/Historicity of Trauma in Jeannette Armstrong's Slash and Sherman Alexie's Indian Killer." *Studies in the Novel* 40 (1/2): 203–223. doi:10.2307/29533868.
von Vorys, Karl. 1975. *Democracy without Consensus: Communalism and Political Stability in Malaysia.* Princeton: Princeton University Press.
Zainor Izat Zainal. 2010. "Against Adat and Islam: A Feminist Reading of Malay Women Characters in Lloyd Fernando's *Scorpion Orchid* and *Green Is the Colour*." In *Reading the Malay World*, edited by Rick Hosking, Susan Hosking, Noritah Omar, and Washima Che Dan, 225–235. Adelaide: Wakefield Press.

Diffractive spaces: An analysis of Malaysian cyberpunk

Netty Mattar

ABSTRACT

The impact of new information technologies on Malaysian spatiality today is complicated by the ongoing processes of colonialism, which have violently disrupted old attachments to the land, leading to the imbrication of racial divisions and global capitalism. Malaysian cyberpunk, an emergent literature, "maps" these new spaces of global informational capitalism. While theories of hybridity and syncretism have been used to explain the assimilation and negotiation of culture in Malaysia, this article proposes an alternative approach. It reads the nation's fundamentally polyvalent nature through the concept of diffraction, arguing that reading diffractively allows us to be attentive to how spaces connected to diverse ontologies impede, pass through, or interfere with one another, with differences being upheld rather than reduced. Analysing a selection of Malaysian cyberpunk short stories, this article shows how diffractive entanglements are constitutive of Malaysia's complex spatial identity, offering an alternative spatial imaginary.

Global science fiction

In 2017, the theme of the Cooler Lumper Festival in Kuala Lumpur, Malaysia, was "Notes from the Future". This fifth installation of the festival explored how social, political, and technological transformations are shaping Malaysia's collective future. Participants were also invited to consider how extrapolations of the future express anxieties about the present world. In addition to launching *Cyberpunk: Malaysia* (Cho 2015), Malaysia's first anthology of cyberpunk short stories, the festival featured an art exhibition inspired by the idea of nanotech-powered graffiti, art that is motile and capable of subverting fixed, state narratives, and therefore a tool of political change (Mazlan 2017). The festival theme and interests aptly capture the growing popularity of science fiction (SF) in Malaysia. The premise of the art exhibition expresses emerging concerns about spatiality, which I will explore in this article. Firstly, it conveys concerns about how new technologies of the globalized post-industrial age might unsettle hegemonic narratives, and what the sociopolitical ramifications of this might be. In addition to this, the motif of graffiti on walls symbolizes how art might intervene in the existing sociopolitical spaces and divisions, through layering or erasure, indicating an awareness of how Malaysian spatiality is transforming.

While often regarded as the preserve of the west, SF is a genre that has become increasingly popular all over the world. Istvan Csicsery-Ronay (2012) suggests that this is due to technological and economic globalization, which has enabled the spread of not only the genre and its subsequent hybridization, but also common experiences of "dominant event-flows" (480) that are science-fictional in nature and which affect all of humanity. Global events such as ecological disasters, the invasion of nations by unknown "others", corporate imperialism, and corrupt and clandestine global networks, for example, are global realities that have long been themes in SF (Csicsery-Ronay 2012, 479–480). This has led writers such as Kim Stanley Robinson to assert that "science fiction is the realism of our times" (quoted in Lea 2015, n.p.).

Cyberpunk and the mapping of space

SF is the literature of "cognitive estrangement", whose main formal strategy is the introduction of a strange newness, a *novum* (a new technology or ideology, for example), into an otherwise realistic representation of reality. Estrangement compels us to see our world with new eyes and question the processes and beliefs of the present that might lead us to these alternative realities (Suvin 1988, 48). Fredric Jameson (1991) suggests that SF's relevance is linked to our postmodern disorientation within globalized networks (412). For Jameson, cyberpunk in particular, the subgenre emerging in the 1980s and 1990s, is "the supreme *literary* expression if not of postmodernism, then of late capitalism itself" (419; original emphasis). He adds that cyberpunk is "fully as much an expression of transnational corporate realities as it is of global paranoia itself", pointing to how writers are able to represent the symbolic, simulated, mass-mediated, networked worlds and the dissolution of boundaries separating the real and the virtual, which has characterized spatiality in this postmodern epoch (38). "Spatiality" refers to the meaning of space brought about by intersecting social relations (Massey 1994, 265) and is a term that I will use interchangeably with "space". The focus of cyberpunk on the spaces of global information and communication, Jameson proposes, means that it has less to do with the extrapolation of "individual destiny onto collective history", which might be seen in naturalist fictions, than with "the mediation of space itself" (2005, 313). Cyberpunk is able to "map" the "unrepresentable totality" of global informational capitalism, a reality that "transcend[s] our phenomenological mapping systems and our cognitive abilities to think them" (229–230, 234). Cyberpunk is characterized by a fixation upon the impact of new technologies of global capitalism on everyday life. William Gibson's (1984) novel *Neuromancer*, in particular, provided the vocabulary for this new reality, with characters who use prostheses to "jack in[to]" the virtual networks of "cyberspace", thus escaping the confines of corporeality. These transhumanist dreams of technological immortality are played out against the dystopian backdrop of corporate authority and corruption. Fighting against control, the cyberpunk anti-hero, often a lone hacker or rebel, moves through data networks, disrupting and destroying corporate power. In these ways, cyberpunk raises old concerns related to space and power now actualized in the hidden structures of digital paraspaces.

The ubiquity of cyberpunk in the Global South today (see McFarlane, Schmeink, and Murphy 2020) suggests that the genre has become a global language for representing and thinking about these alternative geographies. However, this leads to certain questions about the global circulation of literary and cultural forms. Does the spread of cyberpunk mean, for example, that the presumably pre-existing (Anglo European) core culture will inevitably dominate and influence peripheral cultures? Such a view would indicate, as some theories assert, an unequal relation between core and periphery, in which the core cultures dominate and the peripheries are at a disadvantage (Wallerstein 2004; Moretti 1998). Following this, critics argue that SF from core cultures, with their inherent philosophical assumptions, will inevitably submerge alternative ontologies (Milner 2014; Milner and Burgmann 2017). This process can lead to the hybridization of SF, catalysed by the desire of the non-west to engage with western popular culture, and resulting in the mixing and fusing together of diverse cultural symbols into cohesive products. While these intermixtures may be "new" cultural products, they entail the "violent deterritorialization" of indigenous and traditional cultures, weakening ties to specific histories and ancestries as these cultures are incorporated into global economic systems. The dominant culture of hybridity requires the "volatilization of diversity within it" such that cultures are seen as impermanent and strategically mutable, in order to encourage the commodification of symbolic products and the strengthening of economic power (Csicsery-Ronay 2012, 479–480). This loss of cultural difference leads to a kind of homogenization recast as the universalization of cosmopolitan culture. These accounts of global culture seem to overemphasize the homogenizing effects of globalization, focusing on Self/Other dialectics in which differences are assimilated and eventually erased. Yet, in Malaysia, difference and polyvalent diversity are fundamental and persistent aspects of the everyday and the familiar. Diversity was present in the pre-colonial era when Others (travellers and traders, for example) were "accepted" and became "part and parcel of the public culture of the indigenous people" (Embong 2002, 38–40). This toleration of difference, while not without tension or conflict, continued under colonialism with the inflow of Chinese and Indian migrants, and also characterizes the era of post-independence migration. Theories that emphasize the loss of cultural difference thus cannot sufficiently explain the multiplicity of Malaysia's sociocultural landscape.

Multiplicity, contradiction, difference: Malaysian spatiality

This multiplicity can be seen in the contested spaces of present-day Malaysia. Malaysia's landscape is a discordant mix of modern and historic, residential and industrial, rural and commercial. In addition to this, there is socio-ethnic stratification in religious, economic, and educational spaces (Selvaratnam 1988). This spatial plurality is, at least to some extent, a reflection and result of the colonial reordering of space (Hirschman 1986; Embong 1996). Prior to colonial intervention, spatial belonging in the Malay peninsula was based on spiritual connections to the land. Indigenous Malays nurtured not only a personal relationship with the land, but also an interdependence with nature that deepened one's relationship with God. They were taught the idea of *berbakti pada tanah* ("to serve the land") and trusted that the land would, in return, provide food and shelter (Ani, Mohamed, and Rahman 2012, 64–65, 75). The indigenous Malays were *bumiputera* – literally, "sons of the soil". Colonial intervention violently disrupted this spatial identity and cultural knowledge. Establishing themselves in Malaya in the late 18th century, the British redistributed the land, appropriating unoccupied areas in order to secure British interests through the control of the supply of raw materials. Laws were introduced to encourage external investment in the land and to bring Malay farms under government or private control. Land was therefore transformed into a commodity, a process which alienated the indigenous communities (Kratoska 1975, 135). The British Empire thus established itself through the dispossession of the original peoples, claiming the right of ownership, a privileged status bolstered by accounts that presented colonialism as a civilizing mission gifting the native people with democracy and the free market (Baxstrom 2008, 60, 88). At the same time, low-cost foreign labour from China and India was brought in to expand the rubber and tin-mining industries, leading to tensions between the different ethnic groups, aggravated by economic competition. (see Khoo 1975, 1981). The British had considered these workers to be merely temporary immigrants, fostering the idea that they had no real attachment to the land. These workers themselves did not intend to stay, but hoped to make money before returning to their "home" countries. However, growing numbers from these communities were born in Malaya and did not leave (Roff 1995, 110–111). The assumption that immigrants had only a tenuous attachment to Malaya deepened divisions, replacing the pre-colonial spirit of accommodation. This was reinforced by physical segregation. The British assigned the different ethnic groups their own neighbourhoods, and their own rigid place in the economy, thus discouraging interaction between them (Hirschman 1986, 353).

The colonial structures of opportunities and restrictions in Malaya thus created a hierarchical space, where old attachments to land were violently disrupted and new polarizing racial attachments enforced. In post-independence Malaysia, these racialized policies have continued to regulate and authorize policymaking (Koh 2018, 90). At the same time, older spiritual connections have re-emerged along with the resurgence of Islam as a result of both religious reform and the anti-colonial movement (Baxstrom 2008, 72). The ongoing processes of colonial modernity in post-independence Malaysia and the secularization of space within this context have led to tensions which were only compounded by the radical changes occurring in the context of globalization. Globalization has led to the government encouraging the development and use of information technology in the communications and multimedia industry, and labour flows, with the aim of integrating the nation into the global economy. However, this has brought about Malaysia's increasing vulnerability to changes in the international economy, which has in turn led to political crisis, and the imbrication of racial divisions and global capitalism (Welsh 1999, 266–267). If cyberpunk is about the impact of such changes on our understanding of spatiality, then Malaysian cyberpunk can tell us how the new spaces of globalization are appropriated under current capitalist conditions, and the extent to which exploitation, dispossession, and racialization have intensified.

Reading Malaysian cyberpunk: Diffractive encounters

The above observations suggest that postcolonial theory might offer a useful way of reading Malaysian cyberpunk. While very little has been written about Malaysian SF in English,[1] many studies of Malaysian literature in English have applied postcolonial theory, emphasizing the concepts of hybridity, syncretism, and mimicry (see, for example, Tay 2011; Quayum and Wicks 2001). However, postcolonial theory has been criticized as being complicit in the imperialist structures it aims to critique. Its critics have argued that postcolonial theory is aligned to neocolonial trajectories of global capitalism (see Dirlik 1994; Ahmad 1995). Simon During (1998) argues that notions of hybridity and mimicry imply the integration of the colonized into colonizing cultures, and the reduction of difference, which is more "reconciliatory than a critical, anticolonialist category" (31). At the same time, it has been noted that key postcolonial theorists such as Homi Bhabha and Gayatri Spivak are deeply influenced by French poststructuralism, which suggests the re-inscription of Eurocentric ideals and the potential reinforcement of the colonial gaze (see Mignolo 1998).

Indeed, theories of syncretism and hybridity do not seem to fully account for what I have suggested is Malaysia's fundamentally polyvalent nature. Syncretism draws attention to how different cultures merge into a new synthesized whole. Similarly, conceptions of hybridity diminish perceived tensions between different cultures by putting forward new amalgamated identities that join both worlds (the ideology of *mestizaje*, for example). In Homi Bhabha's (1994) account, hybridity is an in-between space of negotiation, characterized by an ongoing process of homogenization ("affiliative" engagement) and heterogenization ("antagonistic" engagement), of being the same and yet not exactly the same (2). This ambivalence renders any claims of cultural purity untenable. The hybrid merging of cultures, of moving beyond dichotomies, becomes a space of opportunity, facilitating cultural transformation. In these accounts of hybridity, difference is reduced, even if momentarily, and new unified identities can emerge. Several critics have highlighted how accounts of hybridity often involve the assimilation, mitigation, and neutralization of differences (see Chow 1993; Werbner 1997; Van der Veer 1997; García-Canclini 1989). Such accounts of hybridity, therefore, may deny the legitimacy of particular, local oppositions between the different ethnic practices, between the religious and the secular, the traditional and the modern, for example; oppositions and dichotomies that may in fact be constitutive of a particular culture. Malaysia, I argue, is characterized by multiple traditional and ideological spheres that are not necessarily hybrid domains of negotiation. Rather, Malaysia is *also* a space of polycultural diversity where contradictory systems function alongside each other, maintaining distinct borders and differentiated identities. It is a place where differences are often unresolved. We thus need expanded conceptual frameworks that acknowledge this diversity without erasing differences.

I would like to go beyond notions of hybridity and syncretism and read Malaysian cyberpunk writing as diffractive encounters between different cultures and ontologies. Diffraction is a concept that was established initially in the field of physics to describe what happens when waves encounter obstacles (barriers, openings, or other waves) on their path. When this happens, waves bend, overlap, and move obliquely around the obstacles, interfering and extending into one another. Diffraction patterns thus can be seen as "patterns of difference that make a difference" and are "the fundamental constituents that make up the world" (Barad 2007, 72). New Materialist thinkers such as Donna Haraway (1997) and Karan Barad (2007), who explore the inter-constitutive relations between matter and meaning, have adopted diffraction, often figuratively,[2] as a means to talk about overcoming entrenched Self/Other dualisms inherited from the Enlightenment. The western binary system of thought imagines the Other as opposite to the Self, a lack or an absence of Self. It reinforces the idea that what is Self cannot be Other. This is a "colonizing logic" (Barad 2018, 5) that is static and hierarchical, where the Self preserves and stabilizes itself by dominating and eradicating the Other. Difference is used as "a tool of segregation, to exert power on the basis of racial and sexual essences", an "apartheid type of difference" (Minh-ha 1988, n.p.). Here, the Other is inevitably dominated while desiring equality. However, this is not the only way to understand difference. Thinking diffractively enables us to see non-dualistic patterns of difference. It considers what happens when dissimilar or conflicting elements interfere with one other, attending to the effect (not eradication or suppression) of their differences. Hierarchies are transformed into networks of entanglements. Difference pervades everything it encounters, reconfiguring identities, with difference itself being reconfigured, while distinctions between elements are maintained. The idea of diffraction allows feminist theorists to think outside phallogocentric structures that reproduce sameness, and to consider how differences are generated (Haraway 1997, 273). It also provides a means of reading different texts and ontologies "through one other" to generate unexpected ideas (Barad 2007, 30). Applying the idea of diffraction to literary analysis allows us to be more attentive to how different cultural entities and ontologies impede one another, pass through or interfere with one another, while observing how differences are upheld and strengthened. In this way, we can think beyond hegemony whether it be of globalization or nationalism, and past the binary logics of western ontologies that assimilate and eradicate difference.

In the following section, I apply the concept of diffraction to selected cyberpunk short stories, all of which are taken from the anthology *Cyberpunk: Malaysia* (Cho 2015), and chosen for their exploration of spatiality in this postcolonial globalized era. I read these texts as diffractive encounters where the cultures of global informational capitalism enter upon the unique, polyvalent spaces of Malaysia. As I will show, these new spaces of global flows are less utopian spaces of possibility than encounters of/with difference: spaces connected to local ontologies are entangled with colonial attachments, which collide and interfere with the new postcolonial and postmodern spaces of a globalized digital age. These texts convey how these diffractive entanglements are neither resolved nor reversed, but are instead constitutive of Malaysia's complex spatial identity, offering an alternative spatial imaginary outside western binary frames of understanding.

Inharmoniousness: Non-hybrid spaces

Tariq Kamal's (2015) "Unusual Suspects" presents readers with a data-saturated, post-industrial topography that characterizes cyberpunk. This future Malaysia is an urban wasteland. Climate change has caused the districts of Klang and Kuala Selangor to "sin[k]", and after "the evacuations [...] the petitions for corporate sovereignty, the reconstruction, the demographic upheaval, bubble and crash, only Kolumpo remains". We are told that in the "[f]our thousand plus square kilometers of urban sprawl" there are "40 million plus souls, one third of that existing in the margins, invisible" (255). This landscape of disaster is overlaid with a cybernetic paraspace, an expansive "superconsciousness" (261), the "timeless ecstasy" of "Deep Data" (256), which, in typical cyberpunk fashion, neutralizes the catastrophe by offering a new frontier of limitless possibilities through the transcendence of the human body.

Kolumpo is a city ruled by multinational corporations, the new global power. The foundation of this corporate imperialism, Kamal highlights, is colonialism, which was the original version of global multinational capitalism (Walvin 1986). The references to the "glittery heights [...] of Fairmontshire and Effingham Place" (Kamal 2015, 255), for example, are reminiscent of the superimposition of colonial structures upon Malaysian identities, and the erasure of original linguistic significance and cartographical-historical value. This connection is further amplified by objects within these corporate spaces: rooms are decorated with "real vintage" signs that say "WHITES ONLY" (262) and call attention to the racist legacy of colonialism that continues in the post-industrial age. Garett Bryn, a "Mat Salleh" (a colloquial expression meaning Caucasian) has been brought in to clean up the mess left by a major systems crash at Dalvik-Tellus (DT), an information technology corporation. This crash has cost billions of dollars and, more alarmingly, has put "equity holders" who had been "plugged in" (260) to the system into a catatonic state. His patronizing attitude towards local employees highlights global capitalism's role in the reproduction of racism. The fact that DT has been using climate-change refugee orphans for mind "upload" experiments that would secure profits from the "transhumanist gold rush" (262) further amplifies the persistence of the hierarchical system that normalizes labour exploitation and the commodification of "other" bodies so crucial to the evolution of capitalism during the colonial period (see Macedo and Gounari 2015). These postcolonial spaces in the story continue to be understood as an "ever-replenishing pool of human resources and cheap labor" (Kamal 2015, 272). Additionally, we learn that these human subjects are "dark brown" and Muslim (Garett scoffs at a young woman's "underscarf", considering it "DT's concession to political correctness" [259]), further emphasizing the racialization of global capitalism.

For the first part of the story, we view Kolumpo through the eyes of Garett. Significantly, the narrative here closely resembles *Neuromancer* (Gibson 1984). Its overt references to Gibson's text – characters "jack in" to the "consensual hallucination" (Kamal 2015, 265) of cyberspace – establish this space as a utopian future of neo-liberal freedom, tied to the subject's disembodied mobility through virtual infoscapes. This aesthetic, however, is starkly contrasted to the language used in the final part of the narrative. Garett's search for a surviving research subject leads him into the Arkology Rakyat (Arcology of the Public). Here, space is starkly material. The "ecstasy" of disembodiment is replaced by imagery of unrelenting corporeality: Garret enters the "silent guts" of the Arkology, a "cancerous nightmare" of buildings (272), and feels "buried in civilization" stifled by the humidity and the mud (273). Here, Garett is "needled by a feeling he could not put into words" (273). Time seems to pass differently and the "buzz of the infosphere", his "constant companion", is "reduced to the merest whispers now" (273–274). The Arkology "is a land which creates its own laws" (273), has a different temporal and emotional logic from that of Garett's world, and is ultimately incomprehensible to him. In his "ludicrous" Hawaiian shirt, Garett is transformed into a tourist, a stranger, "isolated" (273), and keenly aware that he does not belong.

There is a clear difference between the digitized, disembodied corporate spaces of global capitalism and the earthly, corporeal space of the Rakyat. The difference between these spaces does not open up a space of negotiation where "mimicry" (Bhabha 1994, 122–123), for example, might challenge hegemonic purity. Instead, the distinction between the two spaces is reinforced. The characterization of Garett is abruptly halted in the final section, which interrupts the flow of the tale, and emphasizes the insurmountable gap between the ontologies of the two spaces. In contrast to western paradigms, the text offsets potential foreign threat not through assimilation but by maintaining its difference and insisting that its expression be limited to a designated area.

This division is magnified by Kamal's use of the Malay language in the final part of the narrative, which indicates a shift to the perspective of the subaltern. Irfan, the only research subject to be successfully merged with the system, has crashed the system from within. He speaks to his sister, the only living survivor, from the digital afterlife:

> You cabut lari, they chase you, you slip [...] masuk guang. Too dark to see. Tragis. Mayat takder. And then, kasi lead, a nice wild goose chase around the world. Thanks to your lanun work with the security keys, I ikut sama, one step ahead, until [...] apa-apa je lah. See how. Amacam? (Kamal 2015, 276)

The vernacular language is troublingly inaccessible to non-native readers and the story acquires a strange dissonance. This is amplified by the tone of this passage, which, for a high-stakes chase scene, is incongruously casual, mild, and affectionate. The language makes clear that Irfan has not reinvented the system that has oppressed him and his family; there is no third space of redefinition or sovereignty. Instead, as an upload, he can only slip past, elude. Even though Irfan is able to move with some agency, he is "already dead" (277). His incorporation does not signify a bridging of spaces but instead a discontinuity in self and belonging. The story ends on this note of separation as he tells his sister that he will never see her again. We can see here that Irfan's difference is diffracted. He is reconstituted within, but still differentiated from, the system he is entangled in. The linguistic and spatial disjunction signifies the incommensurability of these two spaces. The gap between local public topographies and the spaces of global informational capitalism remains unresolved, and we are left with a sense of splitting. This splitting does not, I argue, imply the undoing of either space but is rather a refusal to treat Malaysian spatiality as one-dimensional, or to concede to the assimilation of difference inherent to western binarism. Kamal's depiction of a postcolonial globalized Malaysia offers instead an image of alternation between the two finite spaces of meaning, each with its own logic, their difference upheld.

Diffraction and divided identities

There is a similar pattern of distinctive but contiguous spaces in "Codes" by Anna Tan. Tan imagines a future in which new digital technologies are used as tools for government surveillance and control. This story extrapolates from the reification of race-based identities in postcolonial Malaysia and the integration of Islam into governance and public life. After independence, the colonial divisions between the ethnic groups remained, and the government advanced a "national culture" based on indigenous Malay culture which was blended with an Islamic "govermentalism" (see Nonini 1997). "Malayness" became identified with *bahasa, agama, raja* (literally, "language, religion, royalty"), and was defined in opposition to "Chinese" and "Indian". At the same time, the nation was committed to modernized growth. The resulting system of governance was seen as highly bureaucratic, and a form of global corporate masculinity (see Connell 2000). "Codes" explores the effect of the hierarchical orderings of global information networks on local Malay Muslim female subjectivity.

Protagonist Nadia, a Malay Muslim youth, has to manage her identity in the real world as well as in the paraspaces of new information technology, accessible via brain implants. These paraspaces are highly masculinized, as suggested by the artificial intelligence (AI) programme, "Corporal Abdullah", that monitors these spaces. The AI is a "highly sophisticated" programme that analyses data for "criminal usage and anomalies" (Tan 2015, 58). The AI is aggressive, "watch[ing]" and "track[ing]" users, particularly female users, who break the rules (48). Capable of sabotaging those that ignore it, the AI represents the instrumental masculinity of cyberspace, a masculinity that is typically associated with a Eurocentric image of man (see Parsons and Bales 1956, for example). This type of masculinity is contrasted with a different kind of masculinity we see in the AI's supervisor, Inspector Zakri. Inspector Zakri, who is also Nadia's father, is the figure of Malay patriarchy, and markedly passive in comparison. He is unconcerned when the AI reports anomalies to him and indifferent to the affairs of others. His passivity seems to be at odds with the western view of masculinity but conforms to a view prevalent in Southeast Asia. This view considers the "exert[ion of] force, explicit commands, or [...] direct activity"; in other words, the exertion of "power" in the western sense, a spiritual deficiency and weakness, which lessens prestige (Karim 1995, 17). The differences in these masculinities results in a clash between the AI and the Inspector, but not to the extent that one dominates the other or that they merge. Instead, their divergence causes a rupture. This rupture opens up a space for the Malaysian female to more fully participate in this infosphere. Because her father dismisses the AI's concerns, Nadia is able to hack into the "big and scary [...] Internet" (Tan 2015, 44).

Nadia's entry into cyberspace is not quite the utopian image of democratization that we might expect. Instead, we are presented with a picture of a diffractive encounter between local female spaces and the spaces of western modernity. Female spatiality in Malaysia is based upon the values of the society and religion. In Malaysia, as with most Asian cultures, women are expected to be responsible for the home and children (Hofstede and Bond 1988). Malay women, in particular, are expected to maintain shy and gentle behaviour (Abdullah, Noor, and Wok 2008). In line with this, Nadia affects a "timid" and confused demeanour in the real world and ensures that she looks "innocent" and "trustworthy" (Tan 2015, 57) by wearing a *baju kurung* (traditional modest dress). Because the AI clamps down on any behaviour in cyberspace that does not fit these algorithms, Nadia is forced to divide herself into multiple online identities. Her "official" identity space is filled with what is expected of a Malay Muslim girl, such as "talking-head sermons from the local Ustaz [religious teacher]" and other materials on "how to be the perfect Muslimah" (45). Malay female subjectivity passes through technology, which intervenes and translates femininity into a narrowly defined religious piousness. This subverts the narrative of free choice that underpins canonical cyberspace narratives. To freely access the vast possibilities of cyberspace, Nadia must hide her true ethnicity and pretend to be what she is not. As "Nadia Tan", Nadia can experience some of the freedoms afforded to Chinese female adults. She learns "how to have good sex (all with illustrations and videos!)", and pop-up tutorials teach her how to make "koay teow fried with pig lard" (45), a dish forbidden to her as a Muslim. While racial passing might suggest liberation from reified ethnic identities, we realize that “freedom” here is, paradoxically, highly racialized. Race and racial differences still matter both in virtual space and in real space. In the real world, Nadia must still perform the role of pious Malay girl, and she participates in racial violence herself, sabotaging her Chinese friend in the end to save herself from being tracked down (59–60).

What is significant is that Nadia traverses several subject positions in these spaces. Her Self does not disappear as a result of encounters with what is not-Self. Instead, she is entangled with each space, partially reconfigured in each context, in an endless process of inclusion and exclusion. Her difference entails various relations that can be either oppressive or liberating. Tan questions the assumption that cyberspace can subvert hegemonic norms by offering a space of freedom from gender and ethnicity. She reveals that these local hierarchies do not fade away in cyberspace but are diffracted, transformed into diverse relations, where parts exist in tension with other parts in a network of multiple entanglements.

Uncanny landscapes

The rupture between different spaces can sometimes result in radical strangeness. The uncanny strangeness of Adiwijaya Iskandar’s (2015) “The Twins” is an example of what happens when the spaces between different cultures are filled with the effects of their dissonance. The uncanny is a specific feeling that arises when something that used to be familiar becomes strange, evoking fear (Masschelein 2011, 3). Freud, quoting Schelling, further explains that the “unheimlich is that what ought to have remained hidden, but has nonetheless come to light” (Freud 1958, 123–124), relating the idea to the return of that which has been repressed. In “The Twins” we see how globalized technological spaces interact with older conceptions of space, resulting in an uncanny landscape. This landscape is at once familiar and strange, a combination which unsettles the reader, forcing them to reflect on how the past connects to the future.

The setting of the story is a jungle, which is the heart of Malaysian identity, the ancestral lands of the indigenous tribes, and the source of their livelihood, spiritual belief, and belonging (Aiken and Leigh 2011). The story opens upon a terrifying scene of a young boy, Crmiel, watching a creature with a “black tongue” and “gaping mouth” (Iskandar 2015, 183) consume the body of his sister. The boy recognizes the creature as a *penunggu*, an evil spirit of Malay folklore that haunts areas where death takes place. Spirits are an expected and accepted part of the traditional Malay world. However, expectations of old Malay folk horror are subverted when we later learn that the *penunggu* is a “droi[d] possessed with the spirits of familiars” (184). In an effort to ward off the creature, the boy whispers a verse of the Qur’an, a “magical word” that wards off unwanted spirits. Unnervingly, the *penunggu* mimics the boy, speaking the verse in a “tinny voice” (184). As Crmiel stands stunned, the creature tells him “Do not. Be. Kufoor [disbeliever]. Do not. Inkar [be disobedient]. Repeat” (184). The boy notes that its voice is “strange”, “crackling”, and “digital” but also almost “lilting and sweet” (185). At once comforting and horrifying, the unexpected mechanization of the spirit world here upsets the logic of Malay spatiality and unsettles the reader. Other elements progressively heighten this discomfort. We learn that Crmiel is a child of nature who mourns “every fallen tree” (188), yet he is also genetically enhanced and able to absorb energy from the trees. The "Bibiks" (aunties) who cared for him and his sister, teaching them how to pray and be "kind to each other" (190), are droids, inhuman. The old man that Crmiel meets in the jungle is a farmer, but one whose "best work" is "harvest[ing] Children" such as Crmiel, selling them off to the "Administration" for genetic research (192). Comforting figures of Malay cultural heritage have been turned into strange figures through the rationalization of old Malaysian spatiality. They are not hybrids but uncanny monsters that are at once threatening and impure.

The uncanny landscape is constituted by diffractive interferences resulting from the disparate components. The science-fictional digitized space is not subordinate to the "original" jungle landscape. Nor is the convergence of different spaces within the story based on a hierarchical link between an "original" and the "copy". Instead, both spaces must be read *through* each other, which creates new meanings that would not have been there otherwise. This uncanny landscape provokes a critical reflection on history. The era of late capitalism is an era of simulacra (Baudrillard 1994; Jameson 1991),[3] characterized by the ubiquity of mechanical and digital representations, artificial copies that are devoid of referents, a phenomenon that disconnects us from the past. The past becomes, according to Fredric Jameson (1991), displaced by nostalgic and ahistorical imitation, symptomatic "of the waning [...] of our lived possibility of experiencing history in some active way" (21). SF, in this story, becomes a way of emphasizing how the past is directly connected to the future, and not simply a point of reference for the present. By overlaying the ecological consciousness of Malaysia's indigenous tradition upon a socially disconnected world of digital capitalism, and by accentuating the dissonance between the two spaces, Iskandar forces us to see how the destruction of the past is in fact the erosion of the social processes that connect our contemporary experience to the past. Our discomfort, largely, has to do with the absence of human intimacy and empathy that is rooted in spirituality: the droids have more love, compassion, and piety than the exploitative adults of the future. The uncanny landscape thus stages an absence, implying that something that should be there is not. I believe that this constitutes an appeal to readers to actively reattach themselves to the past, through compassion and spirituality, which distinguishes the story from mere nostalgia.

Conclusion

As an emergent literature in Malaysia, SF challenges familiar paradigms and offers alternative ways of experiencing reality. I have argued that Malaysian cyberpunk engages with the multiple identities located within Malaysia in this increasingly complex global era, where foreign influence has become more pervasive and embedded within new technologies, interacting with Malaysia's multiple local identities. The complexities of these interactions lead to questions about the sufficiency of dominant western paradigms based on binary structures that, historically, neutralize otherness through assimilation and erasure. Notions such as syncretism and hybridity, while accounting for the blending of traditions and spaces in Malaysia, do not fully account for the polyvalent multiplicity that is also characteristic of the nation.

As literary study goes beyond models of hybridity (see Patell 1999, for example), we need to look at alternative ways of reading difference. I have suggested that reading Malaysian cyberpunk through the concept of diffraction allows for a difference-focused reading that is open to completely different world views. This approach allows us to explore Malaysian spatiality in a way that preserves local identities, attends to its contradictory and dynamic nature, and moves away from the idea that space is passive or stable. More importantly, this approach is a search for connection with alterity, that is not simply an appreciation of its instrumental value for global capitalism, an attitude that has characterized much of the transformations brought about by globalization. It is a way of connecting with alterity that is constructive and advocates coexistence, and this perhaps constitutes true globalization.

Notes

1. Isa and Shuri (2017), for example, read Malaysian SF written in Malay as an expression of ethical concerns about biotechnological advancements and the impact on Islamic values. Analysing Malaysian SF written in English, Elias and Louth (2018) suggest that selected cyberpunk stories convey anxieties about labour, the racial ordering of domestic work, and the subsequent abuse of the "other". These engagements with SF are primarily ethical rather than literary, reading SF as an unproblematic reflection of future reality, not taking into account the formal aspects of genre.
2. Apart from metaphor, diffraction is also regarded as methodology that attends to the material engagement with information and the "relations of difference and how they matter" (Barad 2007, 71).
3. Jean Baudrillard (1994) suggests that "[s]imulation is no longer that of a territory, a referential being, or a substance. It is the generation by models of a real without origin or reality: a hyperreal. [...] It is no longer a question of imitation, nor duplication, nor even parody. It is a question of substituting the signs of the real for the real" (1–2). Fredric Jameson (1991) suggests that the "peculiar function [of simulacra] lies in what Sartre would have called the *derealization* of the whole surrounding world of everyday reality" (34).

Disclosure statement

No potential conflict of interest was reported by the author.

ORCID

Netty Mattar http://orcid.org/0000-0002-0506-5431

References

Abdullah, Kalthom, Noraini M. Noor, and Saodah Wok. 2008. "The Perceptions of Women's Roles and Progress: A Study of Malay Women." *Social Indicators Research* 89 (3): 439–455. doi:10.1007/s11205-008-9242-7.

Ahmad, Aijaz. 1995. “The Politics of Literary Postcolonialism.” *Race and Class* 36 (3): 3–19. doi:10.1177/030639689503600301.

Aiken, S. Robert, and Colin Leigh. 2011. “Seeking Redress in the Courts: Indigenous Land Rights and Judicial Decisions in Malaysia.” *Modern Asian Studies* 45 (4): 826–875. doi:10.1017/S0026749X10000272.

Ani, Anisa, Noorizan Mohamed, and Nordin Abdul Rahman. 2012. “Socio-Cultural Influences in the Composition of Traditional Malay House Compounds in Rural Melaka.” *Alam Cipta* 5 (1): 63–78.

Barad, Karen Michelle. 2007. *Meeting the Universe Halfway: Quantum Physics and the Entanglement of Matter and Meaning.* Durham, NC: Duke University Press.

Barad, Karen. 2018. “Diffracting Diffraction: Cutting Together-Apart.” In *Diffracted Worlds: Diffractive Readings: Onto-Epistemologies and the Critical Humanities*, edited by Birgit Mara Kaiser and Kathrin Thiele, 4–23. New York: Routledge.

Baudrillard, Jean. 1994. *Simulacra and Simulation.* Ann Arbor, MI: University of Michigan Press.

Baxstrom, Richard. 2008. *Houses in Motion: The Experience of Place and the Problem of Belief in Urban Malaysia.* Stanford, CA: Stanford University Press.

Bhabha, Homi K. 1994. *The Location of Culture.* London: Routledge.

Cho, Zen, ed. 2015. *Cyberpunk: Malaysia.* Malaysia: Fixi Novo.

Chow, Rey. 1993. *Writing Diaspora: Tactics of Intervention in Contemporary Cultural Studies.* Indianapolis, IN: Indiana University Press.

Connell, Raewyn. 2000. *The Men and the Boys.* Los Angeles, CA: University of California Press.

Csicsery-Ronay, Istvan, Jr. 2012. “What Do We Mean When We Say ‘Global Science Fiction’? Reflections on a New Nexus.” *Science Fiction Studies* 39 (3): 478–493. doi:10.5621/sciefictstud.39.3.0478.

Dirlik, Arif. 1994. “The Postcolonial Aura: Third World Criticism in the Age of Global Capitalism.” *Critical Inquiry* 20 (2): 328–356. doi:10.1086/448714.

During, Simon. 1998. “Postcolonialism and Globalisation: A Dialectical Relation after All?” *Postcolonial Studies* 1 (1): 31–47. doi:10.1080/13688799890228.

Elias, Juanita, and Jonathon Louth. 2018. “Producing Migrant Domestic Work: Exploring the Everyday Political Economy of Malaysia’s ‘Maid Shortage’.” In *Feminist Global Political Economies of the Everyday*, edited by Juanita Elias and Adrienne Roberts, 44–59. New York: Routledge.

Embong, Abdul Rahman. 1996, December. “Social Transformation, the State and the Middle Classes in Post-Independence Malaysia.” *Southeast Asian Studies* 34 (3): 524–547.

Embong, Abdul Rahman. 2002. “Malaysia as a Multicultural Society.” *Macalester International* 12 (1): 37–58.

Freud, Sigmund. 1958. “The ‘Uncanny’.” In *On Creativity and the Unconscious: Papers on the Psychology of Art, Literature, Love, Religion*, edited by Alix Strachey, 122–161. New York: Harper and Row.

García-Canclini, N. 1989. *Culturas Híbridas: Estratgegias Para Entrar Y Salir De La Modernidad* [Hybrid Cultures: Strategies for Entering and Leaving Modernity]. Mexico City: Grijalbo.

Gibson, William. 1984. *Neuromancer.* New York: Penguin.

Haraway, Donna. 1997. *Modest Witness@Second Millenium.FemaleMan Meets OncoMouseTM: Feminism and Technoscience.* New York: Routledge.

Hirschman, Charles. 1986. “The Making of Race in Colonial Malaya: Political Economy and Racial Ideology.” *Sociological Forum* 1 (2): 328–362. doi:10.1007/BF01115742.

Hofstede, Geert, and Michael Harris Bond. 1988. “The Confucius Connection: From Cultural Roots to Economic Growth.” *Organizational Dynamics* 16 (4): 5–21. doi:10.1016/0090-2616(88)90009-5.

Isa, Noor Munirah, and Muhammad Fakhruddin Hj Safian Shuri. 2017. “Ethical Concerns about Human Genetic Enhancement in the Malay Science Fiction Novels.” *Science and Engineering Ethics* 24 (1): 109–127. doi:10.1007/s11948-017-9887-1.

Iskandar, Adiwijaya. 2015. “The Twins.” In *Cyberpunk: Malaysia*, edited by Zen Cho, 181–204. Malaysia: Fixi Novo.

Jameson, Fredric. 1991. *Postmodernism Or, the Cultural Logic of Late Capitalism*. Durham, NC: Duke University Press.

Jameson, Fredric. 2005. *Archaeologies of the Future: The Desire Called Utopia and Other Science Fictions*. London: Verso.

Kamal, Tariq. 2015. "Unusual Suspects." In *Cyberpunk: Malaysia*, edited by Zen Cho, 253–278. Malaysia: Fixi Novo.

Karim, Wazir Jahan. 1995. *"Male" and "Female" in Developing Southeast Asia*. Providence, RI: Berg Publishers.

Khoo, Kay Kim. 1975. *The Western Malay States, 1850–1873: The Effects of Commercial Development on Malay Politics*. Kuala Lumpur: Oxford University Press.

Khoo, Kay Kim. 1981. "Sino-Malay Relations in Peninsular Malaysia before 1942." *Journal of Southeast Asia Studies* 12 (March): 93–107. doi:10.1017/S0022463400005002.

Koh, Sin Yee. 2018. *Race, Education, and Citizenship: Mobile Malaysians, British Colonial Legacies, and a Culture of Migration*. New York: Palgrave Macmillan.

Kratoska, Paul H. 1975. "Peasants, Yeomen and Rice Farmers. Cultural Categories in British Malaya." PhD diss., University of Chicago.

Lea, Richard. 2015. "Science Fiction: The Realism of the 21st Century." *The Guardian*, August 7. www.theguardian.com/books/2015/aug/07/science-fiction-realism-kim-stanley-robinson-alistair-reynolds-ann-leckie-interview

Macedo, Donaldo, and Panayota Gounari. 2015. *Globalization of Racism*. New York: Taylor and Francis.

Masschelein, Anneleen. 2011. *The Unconcept*. New York: State University of New York Press.

Massey, Doreen. 1994. *Space, Place and Gender*. Oxford: Polity Press.

Mazlan, Melissa. 2017. "Interview: Hardesh Singh of the Cooler Lumpur Festival." *Time Out Kuala Lumpur*, August 15. www.timeout.com/kuala-lumpur/things-to-do/interview-hardesh-singh-of-the-cooler-lumpur-festival

McFarlane, Anna, Lars Schmeink, and Graham Murphy, eds. 2020. *The Routledge Companion to Cyberpunk Culture*. New York: CRC Press.

Mignolo, Walter D. 1998. "Globalization, Civilization Processes, and the Relocation of Languages and Cultures." In *The Cultures of Globalization*, edited by Fredric Jameson and Masao Miyoshi, 32–58. Durham, NC: Duke University Press.

Milner, Andrew. 2014. "World Systems and World Science Fiction." *Paradoxa* 26: 1–16.

Milner, Andrew, and J. Burgmann. 2017. "Climate Fiction: A World-Systems Approach." *Cultural Sociology* 12 (1): 22–36. doi:10.1177/1749975517725670.

Minh-ha, Trinh T. 1988. "Not You/Like You: Post-Colonial Women and the Interlocking Question of Identity and Difference." *Inscriptions* 3 (4). https://culturalstudies.ucsc.edu/inscriptions/volume-34/trinh-t-minh-ha/.

Moretti, Franco. 1998. *Atlas of the European Novel 1800–1900*. London: Verso.

Nonini, Donald. M. 1997. "Shifting Identities, Positioned Imaginaries: Transnational Traversals and Reversals by Malaysian Chinese." In *Ungrounded Empires: The Cultural Politics of Modern Chinese Transnationalism*, edited by Aihwa Ong and Donald M. Nonini, 203–227. New York: Routledge.

Parsons, Talcott, and Robert F. Bales. 1956. *Family Socialization and Interaction Process*. London: Routledge and Kegan Paul.

Patell, Cyrus. 1999. "Comparative American Studies: Hybridity and Beyond." *American Literary History* 11 (1): 166–186. doi:10.1093/alh/11.1.166.

Quayum, Mohammad A., and Peter C. Wicks. 2001. *Malaysian Literature in English: A Critical Reader*. Petaling Jaya, Malaysia: Pearson Education Malaysia.

Roff, William R. 1995. *The Origins of Malay Nationalism*. London: Oxford University Press.

Selvaratnam, Viswanathan. 1988. "Ethnicity, Inequality, and Higher Education in Malaysia." *Comparative Education Review* 32 (2): 173–196. doi:10.1086/446755.

Suvin, Darko. 1988. *Positions and Presuppositions in Science Fiction*. Basingstoke: Palgrave Macmillan.

Tan, Anna. 2015. "Codes." In *Cyberpunk: Malaysia*, edited by Zen Cho, 39–60. Malaysia: Fixi Novo.

Tay, Eddie. 2011. *Colony, Nation, and Globalisation: Not at Home in Singaporean and Malaysian Literature*. Hong Kong: Hong Kong University Press.

Van der Veer, Peter. 1997. "The Enigma of Arrival: Hybridity and Authenticity in the Global Space." In *Debating Cultural Hybridity: Multi-cultural Identities and the Politics of Anti-racism*, edited by Pnina Werbner and Tariq Moddod, 90–105. London: Zed Books.

Wallerstein, Immanuel. 2004. *World-Systems Analysis: An Introduction*. Durham, NC: Duke University Press.

Walvin, James. 1986. *England, Slaves and Freedom, 1776–1838*. Jackson, MS: University Press of Mississippi.

Welsh, Bridget. 1999. "Malaysia and Globalization: Contradictory Currents." *Asian Perspective* 23 (4): 261–286. doi:10.1353/apr.1999.0009.

Werbner, Pnina. 1997. "Introduction: The Dialectics of Cultural Hybridity." In *Debating Cultural Hybridity: Multi-cultural Identities and the Politics of Anti-racism*, edited by Pnina Werbner and Tariq Moddod, 1–26. London: Zed Books.

Satire and community in the time of COVID-19: An analysis of Ernest Ng's *Covidball Z*

Susan Philip

ABSTRACT
This article examines how a sense of community is evinced among readers of the satirical Malaysian webcomic *Covidball Z*, in which the author Ernest Ng uses satire to give voice to common responses and experiences around which his readers can gather for moments of levity, as a group, united in their ridicule of their leaders and themselves. Ng's comic opens up a space of sharing where netizens can see their worries and fears represented, while also allowing them, through Facebook, to take part in wider discussions. The analysis of the comic and of the comments by Ng's readers argues that building or supporting community is a significant part of satire as a form of commentary. Ng's political satire is calibrated to allow himself and his readers to respond to and critique the Malaysian situation, while shielding themselves from prosecution, within a community enabled by the network society.

Introduction

Politics, the pandemic, and *Covidball Z*

This article examines how a sense of community is evinced among readers of the satirical Malaysian webcomic *Covidball Z*, created by Ernest Ng. I will show how the author uses political satire not so much to stir outrage or strong criticism, as to give voice to common responses and experiences around which his readers are able to gather for moments of levity, as a group, a network society, united in their ridicule of their leaders and themselves. The author expresses criticism, but also uses a number of techniques to evade the country's response to political challenge and critique, which is frequently stringent and punitive.

Ernest Ng began his career as a webcomic writer and artist with his series entitled *Bro, Don't Like That La, Bro*, which was shared via Facebook. These were short comic strips which chronicled some common Malaysian foibles. *Covidball Z* is his first foray into longer-format comics which tell a continuing story. Currently his "Bro, Don't Like That La, Bro" Facebook page (Ng 2010–2021), which carries the *Covidball Z* series, has over 300,000 followers – up from 180,000 at the end of 2019 (Tan 2020). As a result of their popularity, his *Covidball Z* comics have been published in book form (three volumes so far), and Ng continues to create online content with the same cast of characters.

Ng began the comic to articulate his feelings about the political machinations which rocked Malaysia in early 2020 and resulted in the government elected in 2018 essentially being replaced by members of a different faction within it. Following on very quickly from these events in February 2020 was the March 2020 COVID-19-induced lockdown. Ng ties the two events together, saying: "I started drawing about the political crisis that happened in February but then the pandemic happened and my story just continued from there onwards" (Ahmad 2020). Ng's comics articulate the generalized worry, bewilderment, and dissatisfaction of the population at large in a simple, hilarious, and relatable way. The mixture of content and medium made it an ideal way of forming community at a time when physical, face-to-face communion was strictly curtailed. Ng's comic allowed the opening up of a space of sharing where netizens could see their worries and fears quite accurately represented, while also allowing them the ability, through the "comments" space in Facebook, to take part in wider discussions and critiques of political leaders. The "share" button also enabled the growth of this virtual community.

I will approach my analysis of the comic, as well as of the comments by Ng's readers, by arguing that building or supporting community is a significant part of satire as a form of commentary and critique. My examination of Ng's approach to satire will highlight how he negotiates with restrictive laws in order to articulate political critique that is shared with and echoed by his readers.

Satire and community

Satire is humour of a distinctly and unarguably critical kind, centring around elements such as aggression, judgement, and attack (Caron 2020, 2; Simpson 2003, 3, 52). However, satire cannot be purely about aggression or attack. In attacking, there needs also to be a desire for or urge towards (positive) change and growth (Caron 2020, 5; McClennen and Maisel 2014, 10). As Pollard 2018) states, satire "is always acutely conscious of the difference between what things are and what they ought to be" (20) and urges readers to embrace what "ought to be". But, as John T. Gilmore (2018) points out, it also "depends on norms which are shared between satirists and their expected audiences" (278). This comment implies that there is already a community of sorts, made up of individuals who share the satirist's ideas. In addition, it can be said that listening to the satirist and consuming their material helps to actually bring together otherwise disparate individuals as a group. Sophia A. McClennen and Remy M. Maisel (McClennen and Maisel 2014), for example, declare that "[s]atirists bring their audiences together by creating a shared community that 'gets' the joke and cares about the reality behind the joke" (18). George Test also suggests that "like other religious and social rituals", satire can "serve solidary functions for both individuals and communities" (quoted in Yang and Jiang 2015, 226). Thus, apart from speaking to like-minded people, satire can actually *gather* these people in a shared space (conceptual or virtual).

The element of humour in political satire is also significant in the context of creating community: as Paul Simpson (2003) points out, "[h]umour may also act as 'a fine-grained social sandpaper', because comedy makes frankness less threatening and conveys criticism less contentiously" (3–4). Given that Malaysia is a society in which criticism of leaders can result in prosecution,[1] the possibility of using humour to deflect any harshness towards its targets, while still managing to articulate some criticism, is certainly important.

To what extent does Ng's webcomic series adhere to these ideas of satire and community building? There is no doubt that it attacks its targets. Malaysian political figures come in for critique; their foibles, mistakes, and general mishandling of the pandemic are highlighted and mocked through caricature and satirical retellings of world events. But he uses comedy to make "frankness less threatening" and to convey "criticism less contentiously" (Simpson 2003, 3–4), while still making a critical point. Maria Brock (2018), writing in the context of the Soviet Union, notes that "jokes or *anekdoty* thereby operated as a kind of 'hidden transcript' (Scott 1990), a type of resistance that granted subjects a sense of not having been co-opted entirely by the regime" (285). In a similar way, Ng's work targets politicians as a way of saying "we see what's going on, and we don't like it", without being overtly challenging or provocative. In that sense, Ng can be seen as adhering more closely to the ideals of Horatian satire – a form which is critical and didactic, without being harsh or cruel in its mockery; it avoids the kind of contempt for its subject shown, for example, by Juvenalian satire. However, Ng's decision to be more Horatian in his approach is governed, I would suggest, by a desire to skirt punitive responses from the state.

Again, we can compare this with Brock's analysis of political humour in the Soviet Union: "the parodic deconstructions of *stiob* enable the audience to experience transgressive enjoyment without any need for a more active response" (2018, 288). The ability to respond "passively" is significant within the Malaysian context, since "active" responses can be punished. But it is vital to remember that, as James E. Caron (2020) states, "along with play, a serious or earnest aspect to satire always exists in that it involves itself with social and political issues of the moment" (5). However dissipated the critique may seem, satirical content ensures that social and political issues are highlighted for its audience.

The satirical material and its medium invite the formation of loose ties amongst readers, creating a space, part of a network society, where strangers are able to express their responses to Malaysian politics and the pandemic. The interactivity allowed by online platforms such as Facebook further enhances the formation of a community otherwise separated by time, distance, and pandemic-induced isolation. Ng's comic takes part in the "real virtuality" of the network society, as theorized by Manuel Castells (2010): "on-line communities are fast developing not as a virtual world, but as a real virtuality integrated with other forms of interaction in an increasingly hybridized everyday life" (xxix). Given the strictures of the COVID-19 world, "real virtuality" has embedded itself ever deeper into our experience, and has become essential to how we experience community. Ng's satirical work takes part in this experience of community as real virtuality, by evoking recognition of people and situations, and creating laughter around them, in a medium which allows people to participate despite obstacles such as time, place, and lockdowns. However, Ng also has to pick his way around the remaining obstacle of Malaysia's draconian response to satire.

Satire in Malaysia has long been treated by the state as an antisocial form which aims purely at criticizing things and tearing them down, to the detriment of the general population. Former Deputy Prime Minister Ahmad Zahid Hamidi, for example, cautioned:

> If something that is good is caricatured or cartoonised with a cynical language or in the form of satire, that knowledge is something new that will affect the people. We don't have to be intellectuals who feel good when other people are in trouble. (quoted in Kumar 2017)

He acknowledges that satire "will affect the people" – that is, the community – but paints a picture of the satirist as a mean-spirited intellectual who can only "feel good when other people are in trouble". The satirist, in this view, is an isolated, out-of-touch figure, not a part of the community. Ahmad Zahid emphasizes this idea by stating that while satire and cynicism might be "permitted in the ethics of other cultures [...] in the Malaysian culture it shouldn't be so" (quoted in Kumar 2017). Again, the implication is that the satirist is an outsider, part of "other cultures", but alienated from "the Malaysian culture".

To say that satire is "not part" of Malaysian culture is disingenuous. There are numerous indigenous Malay forms of satire; the folk figure of Pak Lebai critiques those who would take advantage of Lebai's naivety or foolishness. Another folkloric figure, the mousedeer Sang Kancil, critiques ideas of strength and power, and highlights the foolishness of the powerful by showing how the tiny animal routinely trounces much larger, predatory ones through his quick wit. Ann Lever (2019) has pointed out the existence of the clown or trickster figure Semar, as well as Pak Dogol and Wak Long (in Kelantanese culture), in Malay folklore. Ronald Provencher (1990) notes that performances such as *boria* and *wayang kulit* contain social critique mixed with humour (7). He also points out that from the 1970s onwards, local satirical humour magazines, inspired by *Mad* magazine, continued and heightened this satirical trend. Magazines such as *Gila-Gila* and *Gelihati* in 1978, followed in 1984 by *Batu-Api, Humour, Komedi*, and *Toyol*, touched critically on issues such as politics, religious practice, and social behaviour. Noritah Omar (2006) discusses the *Hadiah Sako II*, a national literary prize named after satirical novelist Ishak Haji Muhammad, whose pen name is Pak Sako. She states that the "Malay works selected for this award are mainly satires" (108). As she suggests, "the award itself may be read as recognition of the importance of satire as a genre in Malay literature" (108). This is further underlined by the work of novelist Shahnon Ahmad, who wrote several novels which, rather than providing moralistic or didactic social critique, took the form of uncompromisingly scathing political satire aimed at the country's leaders; among these novels are *Shit* (1998), *Maha Maha* (1999), and *Muntah* (2000). Clearly, satire is well entrenched as a form in Malaysian literature generally, with influences coming from both indigenous and western styles of the genre.

Comics and manga in Malaysia

The content and style of comic magazines such as *Gila-Gila* point to the influence of western-based works such as *Mad*. Other American comic series – *Archie* and the Riverdale universe, as well as comics by DC and Marvel – have also been popular. Comics from China (such as *Old Master Q*) and India (the *Amar Chitra Katha* series) were also consumed, though these tended to be limited to readership from particular ethnic groups. From the 1980s, Japanese manga became increasingly popular, via pirated Chinese translations that came through Taiwan (W.-M. Ng 2000, 45–46); the Japanese influence was further strengthened by the prevalence of Japanese anime on television in Malaysia. It has influenced the development of Malaysian manga which follows the visual style of Japanese manga, but increasingly is recognizably rooted in everyday Malaysian life.

Rachel Chan (2018) quotes Iwabuchi's characterization of Japanese manga as "culturally odourless", meaning that these comics avoid specifically Japanese cultural references in order to ensure that they can appeal to broader international markets (207). Many

Malaysian manga artists, however, use "stylistic elements of manga [...] to signify identifications of ethnicity, gender and social class that is recognisable to the Malaysian reader" (Chan 2018, 205). While remaining largely true to the "culturally odourless" aesthetics of Japanese manga, they nonetheless infuse a sense of Malaysianness; for example, through visual and linguistic clues. Gan Sheuo Hui (Gan 2011), discussing the work of Malaysian manga artist Kaoru, notes that "it shows an active form of selecting and transforming different cultural elements, or more precisely, demonstrates an alternative form of 'local identity' without an apparent 'local style' " (164). Gan suggests that, rather than accepting imposed identities, Kaoru is able to express an "alternative" local identity, despite the absence of obvious markers of "local style". As Chan notes, "[t]his suggests that manga may be seen as a platform for the dramaturgy of 'everyday-defined' realities" (2018, 205), as opposed to the strictures put in place by the state.

Added to this is the fact that the visual style of manga allows the artist to create "imaginary narrative settings that have apparently little to do with the reality of Malaysia", thus providing "a comfortable platform to entertain diverse audiences" (Gan 2011, 172). The human figures in manga are impossible to tie to a particular ethnic group – they are not recognizably Asian, yet they are too closely connected with Japanese culture to be considered Caucasian; this gives them a kind of neutral aspect which allows them to speak across Malaysia's tightly regulated borders of ethnicity and culture. Manga in Malaysia has developed rapidly from being an imported art form that is consumed, to one that has been borrowed and adapted for local consumption, and for expression of local ideas and identities. This is the framework within which Ng works.

Covidball Z

Ernest Ng began his comic as a way to work through his personal response to the events of early 2020, as he explains in a roughly drawn sketch at the end of volume 1. As he draws the virus, he tells himself: "Simply design, lah! Nobody will care anyway!" (2020, 111). He then wakes up to "25 K+ shares" and says: "Well, this was unexpected." Clearly, even without deliberate intent on his part, his work spoke to and gathered an online community. Part of this is due to the visuality of the webcomic form. Mark Berninger, Jochen Ecke, and Gideon Haberkorn (2010) point to the mass appeal of comics, stating that comics are "uniquely suited to describe the multiple fragments of human experience" (3). Mark Long and Chris Lamb (2017), citing Linus Abraham, note "the power of editorial cartoons to affect public opinion and to ignite public anger" (210). Ng's simple visual style, with its references back to anime and manga, ensures that it is accessible to a very wide audience; this accessibility is increased by the fact that his work is shared online, on a free, open site, which is not associated with a particular publication, as an editorial cartoon would be. His webcomics have the potential to be influential to the readers, without the overlay of political intervention from the owners or editors of more mainstream media.

Nonetheless, Ng is careful in how he approaches satire. First, he makes sure that he does not put himself in a position to be prosecuted for purveying false news:

> In order to ensure that he won't mistakenly cover fake news, the illustrator will verify reports with some journalist friends to confirm or debunk news that goes through. "I'll make sure at least I am not covering fake news", he said. (Tan 2020)[2]

Ng is aware of the threat posed by the possibility of censorship or other forms of punishment, but obviously cannot create a comic dealing with current events without some level of critique entering his work. He admits "that he tries not to think too much into that as to not stifle his creativity" but is "also aware that he should keep it balanced and neutral to avoid being too controversial" (Ahmad 2020). The possible fallout from being "controversial" can be seen in what has happened to political cartoonist Zunar, who has faced prosecution multiple times because of his scathing portrayals of leading political figures (see Abdul Latif and Elgarrai 2021, 147). Street artist Fahmi Reza has faced similar persecution for his caricatures of then Prime Minister Najib as well as subsequent leaders as sinister clowns.

Part of the reason that artists such as Zunar and Fahmi face punitive action is because of the hard, biting style of their cartoons. Their caricatures of leaders emphasize their worst qualities – for example, Zunar portrayed Najib's wife Rosmah as being extremely short and stocky, sporting huge hair and a huge ring. Both the hair and the ring spoke directly to issues of corruption and greed. Fahmi's clown pictures, with their sharply arched eyebrows and the smirks on their faces, also highlight negative traits rather than suggesting the good humour that might otherwise be associated with clowns. Ng, as I will show, takes a different, more circumspect, approach to his critiques of political leaders.

Ng's webcomic series focuses primarily on the global war against the COVID-19 virus, which is portrayed as a villainous humanoid bent on world destruction. Here, the influence of the anime series *Dragon Ball Z* is apparent; the virus is the alien Saiyan warrior which has come to conquer earth. Along the way, Ng pokes fun at (primarily Malaysian) political events and figures. His strip is clearly satirical – it lampoons some of the more ridiculous actions or statements by political figures as well as ordinary people, and chronicles the response of the Malaysian public to these actions and statements. His choice of *Dragon Ball Z* is significant in relation to the satirical element as well. Bounthavy Suvilay (2018) notes that the *Dragon Ball* manga are influenced by Jackie Chan's parodic martial arts films, and have a generally "humorous emphasis": "This burlesque orientation undermines all serious discourse regarding exemplary manhood" (253). This suggests that the heroes in *Dragon Ball* are presented as comedic and fallible; in *Covidball Z*, then, it follows that the "heroes" also do not adhere to patterns of "exemplary manhood".

Ng uses caricature to satirize the leaders and their responses to the spread of the pandemic. However, he is also careful in how he puts forward his criticism of Malaysia's top leadership. While his portrayals of lower-level leaders such as ministers are often extremely comical, his portrayal of the former and current prime ministers is more circumspect. They are shown to make the wrong decisions, or the politically expedient decisions, but they are not shown to be laughable or ridiculous in the same way as the lower-status leaders. Grant Julin (2018) has noted that "[p]olitical satire's less benevolent edge is its cut – a method that wounds by weakening its target through linguistic and artistic barbs" (150). Ng, however, does not use these cutting barbs. Rather, he maintains a somewhat "benevolent" Horatian edge. Even when he mocks his characters, they are portrayed as being merely somewhat hapless; Ng's work does not aim to have the sharply critical, more Juvenalian, bite that marks the work of Zunar and Fahmi Reza.

For example, Ng portrays the world's leaders (including then Prime Minister Tun Dr Mahathir and current Prime Minister Muhyiddin Yassin) as superhumans. Tun and Muhyiddin (referred to in the comic as "Muhidin") are shirtless, muscular heroes. Tun can fly, and Muhidin is "here to save the country from a continued crisis" (Ng 2020, 22). The trope of politician as superhero is common among political cartoonists (Abdul Latif and Elgarrai 2021, 150). Indeed, Zunar has used the iconography of both superheroes and supervillains in his cartoons – for example, portraying Najib as a Darth Vader-like figure (Abdul Latif and Elgarrai 2021, 154). Ng, however, avoids this kind of pointed commentary by not tying the leaders to specific and recognizable heroes or villains from popular culture. Rather, he draws them so that they are still recognizably themselves – just with more muscular bodies and some superpowers.

While Ng tells Jason Leong in a podcast that he chose to portray the leaders in this way because he just likes drawing buff bodies, it remains that these heroic portrayals serve to mitigate the cut of the satire somewhat. When they first confront the virus, Tun is shown using his power of flight to literally fly away from the issue, telling Muhidin: "I'm out. He's your problem now" (Ng 2020, 26). Ng also undercuts Muhidin's superhuman status by having him first defy the virus (challenging it to "Bring it"), but then immediately saying: "But can we fight on Monday? I wanna go play golf" (26–27).[3] While the critique is apparent, it is softened by Ng's drawing style, which not only never edges over into the realm of the cruel barbs of some political satire,[4] it actually confers some small degree of heroism (see Figure 1).

Figure 1. (Reproduced with permission from Ernest Ng).

It is when he critiques the more minor characters such as Cabinet ministers that Ng uses overt mockery, but, again, without the sharp edge. In drawing these episodes, Ng does not soften the satire by giving the characters heroic physiques, but his caricatures do avoid grotesque exaggeration, while highlighting the ridiculous. One iconic panel came about as a result of then Health Minister Dr Adham Baba advising people, during a televised interview on Malaysia's state-run television network, that if they drank warm water, it would flush the virus down the throat and into the stomach, where stomach acids would kill it. He was widely lambasted for this statement, and Ng promptly included it in his series.

The first panel, which takes up half the page, shows the Health Minister adopting a fighting stance, holding a glass of water as if it is a weapon. He declares heroically that he has found a way to defeat the virus. He then shouts "Air suam no jutsu" (Ng 2020, 33), like an anime fighter.[5] The background of the panel is bright and dynamic, creating a sense of movement and action. Thus, in this panel, Ng presents the Health Minister as a warrior with a special technique to defeat the virus.

Ng then immediately undercuts this portrayal in the next three panels, which together take up the same amount of space as the first panel. The background of these three panels is a dull greyish brown, completely lacking the dynamism of the earlier panel. The "heroic warrior" of the first panel now appears tiny and ineffective in relation to the tall, frowning, muscled COVID-19 virus. He is shown flinging the contents of his "weapon" (the glass of water) at the virus. It makes a small "splash" (represented here by the use of a small font, in contrast to the large font and bold type of "air suam no jutsu"), which has no effect whatsoever on the virus – a point underlined by the fact that in the next two panels, the Health Minister maintains his "throwing" stance while the virus just stands there, unmoving and unaffected (see Figure 2).

Ng's caricatures reduce these characters to single issues, usually of the most trivial kind. These are precisely the issues which the general public are likely to pick up on and respond to, as an online community.Indeed, Ng says that ideas come to him when he "receives news or people start sharing something [or . . .] it starts trending" (quoted in Gasper 2020). A trending topic indicates that something is being shared within the online community – Ng's work is inspired by what is already in the community, and he then expands or solidifies that community through his own viralized work. We can relate this point to Manuel Castells's (2010) contention that online communication "does not substitute for other means of communication; it reinforces pre-existing social patterns" (393). Ng's comic has not created a brand-new community; rather, it has given a platform to a community which did not previously have one – a platform from which to share opinions and to form online relationships.

Grant Julin (2018) asserts that satire must provide "a balanced representation of the multiplicity of voices implicated in the piece" (159). Its readers, then, cannot be exempt from being satirized or critiqued. In line with this idea, a proportion of the comics is given over to the actions and reactions of the general public. Although the political figures are drawn as individuals, the general public is shown as an undifferentiated group of roughly drawn, fleshed-out, grey stick figures; they have mouths, but eyes are only added to depict some sort of extreme emotion. By creating figures that are completely non-specific in terms of ethnicity, Ng uses the potential of manga to provide "a space which is relatively free of the ethnic tensions of everyday life" (Gan 2011, 174). The Malaysian public in these comics is united by the issues they have to face, not by

Figure 2. (Reproduced with permission from Ernest Ng).

ethnicity. This unity is further underscored by their shared language – Malaysian English mixed with Malay. This is accurately reflective of how many Malaysians actually speak; and again, the focus is on what is shared, rather than on what might divide them.

By introducing the general public as characters, Ng not only represents a multiplicity of voices as suggested by Julin, but also concretizes the inclusive, communal potential of his webcomic – society at large is shown to be central to, rather than distanced from, the events depicted in the comics. The public in this comic series play a very important role by articulating, as a group, actual public responses to the pronouncements and policies of the leaders.

For example, in March 2020 the Prime Minister announced a financial aid package, but instead of focusing on numbers and statistics, he spoke about how it would help someone called "Makcik Kiah",[6] an imagined character who was meant to represent the average Malaysian affected by the lockdowns. This tactic was, apparently, popular with Malaysians, many of whom expressed approval on Twitter ("'Makcik Kiah' Is Famous Now But Who Is She?" 2020). Ng includes the Makcik Kiah concept in his comic as an actual person, in an initially touching series of panels. As the infection rate increases, the virus taunts Muhidin, who starts to doubt himself, but Makcik Kiah turns up to reassure him that people know he is doing his best. This gives Muhidin the confidence he needs to challenge the virus, which is reflected visually by the tough look on his face, his defiantly pointing finger, and the focus on his muscles.

However, Ng reduces this potentially touching, uplifting moment to something silly. Instead of rousing to Muhidin's rallying cry, the gathered crowd starts asking "Who is Makcik Kiah?", seemingly puzzled as to whether or not she is a real person (Ng 2020, 52–53). No one in the crowd is paying attention to Muhidin's heroic challenge, as they focus instead on the gimmick – which is similar to the actual public response. By thus visually representing this response, Ng gives his readers a concrete community to relate to within the comic, while also critiquing them for focusing on trivialities. However, his visual representation of the public mitigates his criticism by making them appear unthreatening and oddly appealing. As one Facebook commenter notes, "I like how all gray figures are short short one, shorter than important key figures XD so cute." Since the public are presented as essentially likeable, it is easier for Ng's readers to identify with them. They are a visual representation of the sort of general community which has formed online in response to the actions and faux pas of the leadership.

This community is able to interact quite effectively, both with each other and with Ng, via the Facebook comments section. Ng says "that the most fun was when people tried to guess the characters in his series. 'It sparks a conversation in the comment section. People guess the references and when they're right, I like the comment' " (Gasper 2020). The comments reflect how Ng's portrayals resonated with his audience. For example, there is an acknowledgement of how accurately Ng has rendered the situation through the comic: "Best summary of the current situation"; "We could certainly use your skills to make our History lesson and books in our schools enjoyable for our children"; "finally i [sic] understand the whole story ... thanks to the anime ... no need to read here and there ... the anime has it all". The comments indicate that Ng's outlook, as presented in the comics, is widely shared by the public (an idea reinforced by the literal sharing of the post).

The sense of common or shared experience is emphasized by the way in which commenters react to specific characters within the comics. As soon as a politician or other leader hits the headlines for doing or saying something foolish, many commenters actually turn to Ng's comics to see how he will portray that person or incident. His portrayals are important for what they offer the public – a chance to ridicule these people and thus reduce them in significance; they are also able to engage in dialogue with other commenters, which underlines the fact that this is a shared experience, and that they are part of a community.

These dialogues can be seen in comments about Rina Harun (the Minister for Women, Family and Community Development) and Dr Noraini Ahmad (the Minister for Higher Education). Both were lambasted for their tone-deafness, and attracted a great deal of ridicule: Rina, because her Ministry put out a poster advising women to (among other things) avoid fights at home by giggling coyly and speaking using a "Doraemon"[7] voice; and Dr Noraini for suggesting that university students beat lockdown-induced boredom by taking part in a TikTok competition that her Ministry was going to organize.[8]

When the caricature of Rina Harun appeared in Part 3, comments indicated a level of expectation that she would be featured: "Doraemon finally is out now"; "Waiting for menteri Doraemon to meet her fate"[9]; "Where doremon". One comment encapsulates the idea of a community of shared ideas and concerns by saying "We all knew this will appear", indicating priorities and expectations held in common by both Ng and his readers.

In Part 3, a reader tells Ng "Don't forget tiktok plz", referring to Dr Noraini, and she duly appears in Part 4, encouraging a frustrated and disconsolate group of citizens to "Jom Tik Tok"[10]; she is rudely told off and then left, ignored and forgotten, when the citizens realize that movement restrictions might be eased. Visually, she is consigned to a corner of the panel, tiny in comparison to the other figures, tearfully asking "why?"

Although Ng states that he is not actually taking his writing cues from this online community (Leong 2020), he is, as noted earlier, influenced by trending topics, so he and his readers are partaking of a community, by engaging in a virtual dialogue centred around current affairs.

It is not only through criticism that Ng brings his readers together, but also through shared optimism, or admiration for certain public figures, such as the Malaysian Director-General of Health (DG). In this series, General Hisham, modelled after Dr Noor Hisham Abdullah, Malaysia's DG of Health, is the only character presented as being unequivocally heroic. Tasked with making daily reports about the pandemic after the Health Minister's warm-water faux pas, the DG quickly earned the respect of the general public for his calm demeanour and clear, no-nonsense presentations. Multiple headlines present him as a national hero.[11] Visually, General Hisham is unlike the "superhuman" leaders. He is dressed in normal clothes, but with a dramatic overcoat.[12] He is also armed with a sword.[13] When he decides to take a hand in battling the virus, Ng captions the panel: "A hero finally makes his move!" There is no ironic critique here; the General is drawn as a lone figure heading out into the light, resolute, with his weapon by his side (vol. 1, 62–63).

Unlike those of Muhidin, General Hisham's rousing speeches are not undercut by irony, or the frivolous responses of the public. His statement that the virus is "not fighting the strength of one man" but "all of Malaysia" is reinforced by a sudden glimpse of a blue and white friendship band on the General's wrist. The band references a gift made for Noor Hisham by a young schoolgirl. Ng depicts a (fictional) scene where the happy little girl hands the bracelet to a kneeling General Hisham, who says: "Everyone is playing their part ... because the future is worth fighting for" (Ng 2020, 102). Hisham's statements about the virus having to fight "all of Malaysia", and "Everyone [...] playing their part" help to foster a sense, among the readers, of a community united around a clear purpose.[14] Again, the comments show that a sense of community built on shared feelings does exist. In Part 4, the arrival of the Frontliners as reinforcements for General Hisham sparked an outpouring of positive emotion: "its touched my heart ... how they really fighting for us"; "Don't know why, but 3/10 made me choke up. These guys are truly our heroes!"; "This scene really touch my heart, shoulder, knees and toes, knees and toes"; "I teared up at this ... Well done bro."

Conclusion: A community of sharing

The online interactivity of these comics allows Ng and his readers "to share their outrage and create a community of dissent" (McClennen and Maisel 2014, 5). However, Ng does not push the idea of dissent very far. Rather, the comic creates more of a community of sharing and expression. Particularly during the lockdowns necessitated by the pandemic, and the isolation and pessimism which resulted, the comments function allowed a space of sharing and communication which could in some measure combat, or at least slightly mitigate, the isolation. Readers experience a kind of comfort which Jonathan Coe suggests is an essential quality of satire: "It creates a welcoming space in which like-minded people can gather together and share in comfortable hilarity" (quoted in Brock 2018, 288).

However, in Malaysia, satire and satirists are always under the watchful eye of the government. Not every individual has the courage or visibility of Zunar or Fahmi Reza. It is here, perhaps, that Ernest Ng's gentler, less biting form of satire comes into play. It enables a level of emotional release among its community and unites them in mocking and lampooning their leaders – but does not (yet) open them to the threat of the Sedition Act.

Notes

1. In recent years, Malaysian cartoonist Zunar and graphic designer/street artist Fahmi Reza have both faced punitive legal action for their satirical work. Their work is discussed in more detail later in this article.
2. This strategy is quite frequently deployed in Malaysia: comedian Douglas Lim, for example, posted a video on May 26, 2021 in response to the appallingly fumbled response of the chairman of Prasarana Malaysia Berhad (a corporate body charged with running transport infrastructure, including the Light Rapid Transit or LRT system) to an LRT train crash which injured 213 people, some very severely. While Lim lampoons the chairman, he does so through a very thin veil of allegory; also, much like Ng, he does not go beyond what actually happened. His video is essentially a slightly exaggerated version of the actual events. That it resonated deeply with his audience is evident from the fact that it amassed one million views within one day (https://www.facebook.com/thedouglaslim/posts/330438091773452). Again, as with Ng's comics, Lim's video serves to gather a community around shared outrage, without any further incitement to action. The goal seems to be creating awareness of and commenting on the reprehensible behaviour of the chairman.
3. This references the fact that the Prime Minister did actually go golfing that weekend, despite the increasingly worrying COVID-19 situation.
4. Again, we can draw a distinction between Ng's artwork and that produced by Zunar and Fahmi Reza.
5. *Air suam* means "warm water", while the phrase *no jutsu* is frequently used by characters in manga such as *Naruto. Jutsu* means something like "technique", so to shout it out during a fight is a way of saying what fighting technique the hero is going to use.
6. *Makcik* means "aunty", and is a polite term used to refer to an older woman, while "Kiah" is a shortened name. By using the term *makcik*, together with the diminutive of a longer name, the Prime Minister sought to appeal to something cosy, familiar, and unthreatening.
7. A Japanese anime character, very popular in Malaysia.
8. Rina was castigated for glossing over the fact that many women were actually in greater danger of abuse from family members during lockdown because of constant enforced proximity, while Dr Noraini received backlash for not seeming to be aware of the multiple serious mental and logistical issues faced by university students stuck either at home or on campus as universities struggled to find ways to cope with the situation.
9. *Menteri* means "Minister".
10. This translates roughly as "Come on, let's Tik Tok."
11. *Sinar Harian* calls him "Manusia paling popular di Malaysia" (The most popular man in Malaysia), while *The Star* calls him "Dr Noor Hisham – the Man of the Hour" (https://www.sinarharian.com.my/article/77386/PROFIL-DI-SEBALIK-BERITA/Manusia-paling-popular-di-Malaysia; https://www.thestar.com.my/news/nation/2020/04/18/dr-noor-hisham—the-man-of-the-hour).
12. Multiple comments focused on trying to identify the manga inspiration behind the coat. There is, in fact, another community being built in these comments – fans of anime and manga, who are able to identify the multiple intertextual references Ng makes. Ng himself says: "I also realised that many people are very into Japanese manga and they tend to get all the (cheeky) references I put in the panels . . . I find that very enjoyable" (quoted in Toh 2020, n.p.).

13. This sword is drawn to look like the sword in the Dettol logo – a reader noticed the reference and commented on it, with the author responding that he was happy someone had picked up on it.
14. Noor Hisham sent the girl a letter thanking her for the bracelet. In the letter, he tells her that "I am not doing it alone" – echoing the notion that the whole country must fight. The exchange between the two touched the hearts of the public (see Sivanandam 2020).

Disclosure statement

No potential conflict of interest was reported by the author(s).

ORCID

Susan Philip http://orcid.org/0000-0002-2325-1916

References

Abdul Latif, Roslina, and Sojoud Elgarrai. 2021. "The Power of Political Cartoons: A Case Study of Zunar's 'Twit-twit Cincin'." *Jurnal Komunikasi: Malaysian Journal of Communication* 37 (1): 146–180.

Ahmad, Fatin. 2020. "Meet Ernest Ng: The Cartoonist Who Turned Malaysia's Covid-19 Battle into our Favourite Comic Series." *World of Buzz*, October 15. Accessed 15 March 2021. https://worldofbuzz.com/meet-ernest-ng-the-cartoonist-who-turned-malaysias-covid-19-battle-into-our-favourite-comic-series/

Berninger, Mark, Jochen Ecke, and Gideon Haberkorn, eds. 2010. *Comics as a Nexus of Cultures*. Jefferson, NC: McFarland and Company.

Brock, Maria. 2018. "Political Satire and Its Disruptive Potential: Irony and Cynicism in Russia and the US." *The International Communication Gazette* 77 (3): 248–266.

Caron, James E. 2020. "Satire and the Problem of Comic Laughter." *Comedy Studies* 11 (2): 171–182. doi:10.1080/2040610X.2020.1729485.

Castells, Manuel. 2010. *The Rise of the Network Society*. 2nd ed. Oxford: Wiley-Blackwell.

Chan, Rachel S.K. 2018. "Breaking Windows: Malaysian Manga as Dramaturgy of Everyday-Refined Realities." *JATI–Journal of Southeast Asian Studies* 23 (2): 205–229. doi:10.22452/jati.vol23no2.10.

Gan, Sheuo Hui. 2011. "Manga in Malaysia: An Approach to Its Current Hybridity through the Career of the Shōjo Mangaka Kaoru." *International Journal of Comic Art* 13 (2): 164–178.

Gasper, Desiree. 2020. "Malaysian Comic Artist Ernest Ng Turns the COVID-19 Battle into a Hit Comic Series." *Rojak Daily*, May 4. https://rojakdaily.com/lifestyle/article/9375/m-sian-comic-artist-ernest-ng-turns-the-covid-19-battle-into-a-hit-comic-series

Gilmore, John T. 2018. *Satire*. London: Routledge.

Julin, Grant. 2018. “Satire in A Multi-cultural World: A Bakhtinian Analysis.” *Comedy Studies* 9 (2): 150–170. doi:10.1080/2040610X.2018.1494357.

Kumar, Kamles. 2017. “DPM: Political Satire Misunderstood in Malaysia.” *Malay Mail*, April 14. http://malaymail.com/news/malaysia/2017/04/14/dpm-political-satire-misunderstood-in-malaysia/1356165

Leong, Jason host. 2020. *Plagiarism and Piracy in the Comic Artist’s World.* Getting Heaty with Jason Leong (podcast). https://vurbl.com/listen/getting-heaty-with-jason-leong-ep-2-plagiarism-and-piracy-in-the-comic-artists-world-51kuS4Gry8S/

Lever, Ann Elizabeth. 2019. “Outbreaks of Satire: A Political Epidemiology of Dissent in Theatre, Television and Social Media Memes (Malaysia and Indonesia, 1989–2018).” PhD diss., National University of Singapore. https://scholarbank.nus.edu.sg/handle/10635/162431

Long, Mark, and Chris Lamb. 2017. “Editorial Comics: From ‘Boss’ Tweed to ‘Dubya’ Bush.” In *The Routledge Companion to Comics*, edited by Bramlett Frank, Roy T. Cook, and Aaron Meskin, 209–226. New York: Routledge.

“‘Makcik Kiah’ Is Famous Now But Who Is She?” 2020. *New Straits Times*, March 27. https://www.nst.com.my/news/nation/2020/03/578738/makcik-kiah-famous-now-who-she

McClennen, Sophia A., and Remy M. Maisel. 2014. *Is Satire Saving Our Nation? Mockery and American Politics.* New York: Palgrave Macmillan.

Ng, Ernest. 2010–2021. “Bro, Don’t Like That La, Bro.” Webcomic. Facebook. https://www.facebook.com/dontlikethatbro

Ng, Ernest. 2020. *If Malaysia Was Anime: Covidball Z, Volume 1.* Malaysia: Nadi Studios.

Ng, Wai-Ming. 2000. “A Comparative Study of Japanese Comics in Southeast Asia and East Asia.” *International Journal of Comic Art* 2 (1): 45–56

Omar, Noritah. 2006. “Colonialism and Malay Masculinity: Malay Satire as Observed in the Novel *Kawin-Kawin.*” *Sari* 24: 107–120.

Pollard, Arthur. 2018. *Satire.* London: Methuen.

Provencher, Ronald. 1990. “Covering Malay Humour Magazines: Satire and Parody of Malaysian Political Dilemmas.” *Crossroads: An Interdisciplinary Journal of Southeast Asian Studies* 5 (2): 1–25.

Scott, James C. 1990. *Domination and the Arts of Resistance: Hidden Transcripts.* New Haven, CT: Yale University Press.

Simpson, Paul. 2003. *On the Discourse of Satire: Towards a Stylistic Model of Satirical Humour.* Amsterdam: John Benjamins.

Sivanandam, Hemananthani. 2020. “Health DG Warms Hearts with Response to Nine-Year-Old.” *The Star*, April 18. https://www.thestar.com.my/news/nation/2020/04/18/health-dg-warms-hearts-with-response-to-nine-year-old

Suvilay, Bounthavy. 2018. “*Dragon Ball*: Body Control and Epic Excess in Manga and Anime.” *Loisir Et Société/Society and Leisure* 41 (2): 250–267. doi:10.1080/07053436.2018.1482670.

Tan, Jocelyn. 2020. “He Documented Malaysia’s COVID-19 Situation Thru Comics & Sold 1k Copies upon Launching.” Vulcan Post, n.d. Accessed 15 March 2021 https://vulcanpost.com/715938/covidball-z-webcomic-covid-19-malaysia-ernest-ng/

Toh, Terence. 2020. “Pandemic, Anime Style: Ernest Ng’s *Covidball Z* Webcomic Has Been Turned into a Book.” *The Star*, October 11. https://www.thestar.com.my/lifestyle/culture/2020/10/11/pandemic-anime-style-ernest-ngs-039covidball-z039-webcomic-has-been-turned-into-a-book

Yang, Guobin, and Min Jiang. 2015. “The Networked Practice of Online Political Satire in China: Between Ritual and Resistance.” *The International Communication Gazette* 77 (3): 215–231. doi:10.1177/1748048514568757.

Index

Note: Page numbers followed by "n" denote endnotes.

For Product Safety Concerns and Information please contact our EU representative GPSR@taylorandfrancis.com
Taylor & Francis Verlag GmbH, Kaufingerstraße 24, 80331 München, Germany

www.ingramcontent.com/pod-product-compliance
Lightning Source LLC
Chambersburg PA
CBHW081357090726
47908CB00011B/2708

* 9 7 8 1 0 3 2 6 6 9 7 3 1 *